MICHAEL COLLINS' OWN STORY

MICHAEL COLLINS.

MICHAEL COLLINS' OWN STORY *Told to*
HAYDEN TALBOT ::   ::   ::

LONDON: HUTCHINSON & CO.
::   PATERNOSTER ROW   ::

"Multitudinous is their gathering . . . a great host with whom it is not fortunate to contend . . . the battle-trooped host of the O'Coileain."—*The ancient slogan of Collins' ancestors, chieftains of the tribes of Munster 450 years ago.*

To
ESTHER TALBOT

CONTENTS

CHAPTER		PAGE
I.	HOW IT HAPPENED	11
II.	INTRODUCING MICHAEL COLLINS	21
III.	EOIN MACNEILL—ULSTERMAN	29
IV.	COLLINS' OWN STORY OF "EASTER WEEK"	40
V.	ARTHUR GRIFFITH'S LAST STATEMENT	48
VI.	THE AFTERMATH OF "EASTER WEEK"	58
VII.	COLLINS' ESTIMATE OF ERSKINE CHILDERS	67
VIII.	COLLINS' PLAN OF TERRORISING TERRORISTS	73
IX.	OUTWITTING THE BLACK AND TANS	79
X.	UNDER THE TERROR	86
XI.	THE MURDER OF FRANCIS SHEEHY SKEFFINGTON	95
XII.	CHILDERS' OPINION OF AMERICANS	115
XIII.	THE TRUTH ABOUT THE TRUCE	123
XIV.	THE INVITATION TO NEGOTIATE	134
XV.	THE TREATY NEGOTIATIONS	145
XVI.	THE MISGUIDED ONES	153
XVII.	DISHONEST TACTICS	162
XVIII.	THE ULSTER PROBLEM	170
XIX.	THE REBELLION—ITS CAUSE AND COST	181
XX.	THE FUTURE OF IRELAND	191
XXI.	WHAT THE TREATY MEANS—A SYMPOSIUM	202
XXII.	ADDENDUM	249

Michael Collins' Own Story

CHAPTER I

HOW IT HAPPENED

It began belligerently. It grew into a friendship I valued more than any other I ever made. The reference is to my relationship with Michael Collins. I tell it not because these two facts matter to anyone except me, but because they are in themselves proof of the greatness of this Irishman. And, inasmuch as I found him, in nine months of intimate association, the finest character it has ever been my good fortune to know, I mean to adduce such proof as I can as will tend to justify my opinion.

My job as a newspaper correspondent took me to Dublin early in December, 1921. I made the trip from London aboard the train that carried the five plenipotentiaries and the Treaty they had signed the night before. But it was not until several days later that I met Collins.

Of the 110 correspondents representing newspapers in all parts of the world at that first public session of Dail Eireann, none could have been more unconversant with the Irish situation than I was. But that did not prevent my quickly discovering that Collins was far and away the most interesting figure in all that remarkable parliament. An interview with him was patently what newspaper readers most wanted. So I made it my business, during a lull in the proceedings, to follow him into the lobby and introduce myself to him. He made an appointment to see me at ten o'clock that evening at the Gresham Hotel.

A quarter of an hour before time, I arrived at the Gresham and sent my card upstairs. Ten minutes later—boiling with rage, all the more maddening because I realised that the interview would be regarded in newspaper circles as a rare " beat," and at the same time in the depths of my ignorance counting these inexperienced, untried statesmen as distinctly small fry—I sat down at a desk in the lounge and wrote the following note :

"DEAR MR. COLLINS,
 "You invited me to visit you here at ten o'clock this evening. Word is now brought me you are ' too busy ' to see me. Is this the answer you wish me to send to my fifteen million readers in America ?
 "Sincerely,
 "HAYDEN TALBOT."

Further to express my outraged feelings I scorned to put the impudent note in an envelope. I folded the sheet of paper once and addressed it merely, " Michael Collins."

In three minutes by the clock the note was returned to me with the following reply written in one corner :

 "I thought I said 10.30 and will be down at 10.30. Please wait and oblige, "M. C."

It was not only a case of the " soft answer " ; it was evidence sufficiently striking to convince me that here was a big man. Even before I knew more about him than what these few words told me, he had made me ashamed of myself for my arrogance.

He kept me waiting only half as long as I had expected, and as soon as our eyes met it was apparent he intended to go more than half-way to be friendly.

"This is no place to talk," he said hurriedly. "Come upstairs with me."

Now that I look back on it I am sure Collins had quite forgotten who I was. Many times since he has proved possession of a marvellous memory, but with the desperately urgent matters then weighing on his mind it would have been impossible for him to have visualised me from my card. Seeing me was different. And a sense of this, even while my earlier hostility was still uppermost, had place in my consciousness.

He sprang up the stairs two at a time—physically, as well as mentally, Collins was the embodiment of speed—and swiftly showed the way down a corridor that led to the rear portion of the hotel. Later, I was to learn that this whole wing was occupied by the organisation that since has come into official being as the Free State Government. As we passed quickly along I caught sight of one room stripped of its bedroom fittings and literally packed with men for the most part wearing trench coats and caps.

Almost at the end of the passage Collins stopped and pushed open a door, nodding to me to follow. As I stepped over the threshold I saw Arthur Griffith seated at a table busily writing. He glanced at Collins and then immediately resumed his labours. Collins strode across the room and opened the door of the adjoining room, again nodding to me to follow him. So finally we came face to face in the last of ten communicating rooms. I noted that the door opening into the passage was fitted with two heavy bolts.

" Have a drink ? " asked my host, for the first time his eyes showing the glint of a smile.

Almost before he had removed his thumb from the push-button, a youngster in the inevitable trench coat and cap opened the door of the adjoining room, took Collins' order and disappeared. In ten seconds he was back again with a tall glass containing my wish.

" Sorry," apologised Collins, " but I am not drinking myself."

In the next quarter of an hour, while I explained at length the importance, from his viewpoint, of taking the public into his confidence (that public which my newspapers reached ! ! !), I had abundant evidence that I was present at a secret conclave of the Treaty leaders, the first one, as I later learned, to be held after the signing of the Treaty. A dozen times while I was closeted with Collins, young, eager, serious-visaged chaps stuck their heads into the room and brought their chief close to them with a peremptory nod. A swift whispered word or two and they would be gone. Without knowing it at the time, I was witnessing the working out of a scheme to force an early adjournment of the Dail to give these leaders time to undertake a campaign of education that would result in a crystallisation of public sentiment that would compel Dail Eireann to accept the Treaty.

When I had finished stating my case I asked Collins what he wished to say for publication. For a space he sat looking at me soberly as if weighing the consequences of departing from his long established policy of silence. Then he sprang from his seat and crossed the room in three strides.

"Do you mind if I bring Mr. Griffith in?" he asked.

A moment later I discovered another quality of this man that stamped him truly big. In his attitude towards Griffith—and be it remembered that Griffith himself went on record in the Dail as being prouder of his association with Collins than of any other incident in his life—there was the limit of respectful yielding. I subsequently discovered that Collins maintained this attitude towards the lowliest of his supporters. He listened to advice from his chauffeur. But while we three were together that first night, Collins made it evident, even to me, a stranger, that his was in no sense the yielding of an inferior to a superior; it was rather the well-mannered deference of a junior to a senior equal.

Followed fifteen minutes of staccato interchange of opinions—Collins doing most of the questioning and Griffith furnishing for the most part monosyllabic replies. The discussion revolved around the advisability of making any statement for publication at that time. They talked freely, seeming to ignore the fact of my presence. Finally, Collins tore a few pages from his notebook and wrote the following:

> "At a late hour I talked with Michael Collins. He was reticent, had little to say and was reluctant to say it. He supported the Treaty and stood for it. He was not very concerned with oaths. He was concerned about getting the English out of Ireland

and having a chance of going ahead to rebuild the Irish nation. He is full of hope and buoyancy, and although he is well aware that the Treaty does not mean full freedom he states emphatically that it does give freedom to show the Irish capable of making their national status secure and strong. He says he is the practical man, and he looks forward with hope to the future with confidence in the will and strength of the Irish people to make themselves a nation among the nations. He thinks of Ireland as a home of freedom for the individual—a place where men and women shall be really free."

It was not as much as I had hoped for, but it was all he would volunteer that night. There was a great deal more I might have sent off from the cable office—and it would have been infinitely more worth while in a news sense. So far as any direct prohibition was concerned I could have done so. Neither Collins nor Griffith had asked me to treat their conversation as confidential. But experience in interviewing English and European statesmen had taught me their viewpoint in the matter. Whereas in America anything that is said to a newspaper man is properly part of an interview and so to be published, a different rule of conduct prevails on this side of the Atlantic. Frequently the so-called "interview" is written by the person interviewed. Invariably the article is edited and signed by him before publication. Fortunately for me, on this occasion I took no liberties. If up to that evening I had held the mistaken view that Irishmen were relatively as undeveloped and unimportant in statesmanship as, say, Filipinos under Spanish rule, that half-hour had quite undeceived me. Here was another George Washington—another Thomas Jefferson. And only 150 years ago an ignorant world made the error of holding them cheap!

I never did discover whether Collins granted me the interview and made his statement purposely incomplete merely to test my trustworthiness. In any event, he gave no other interview during that period until, a second time, he yielded to my persuasions.

It was the night of March 4, 1922, the night following the day of bitterest recriminations the stormy sessions of Dail Eireann had yet produced. Hour after hour, Brugha and Stack, MacEntee and Childers, Markievicz and Mac-Swiney had hurled their charges of treason at Collins and Griffith. President De Valera—ever the conciliator but more than ever this day the misunderstood, misrepresented, maligned idealist—had hotly denounced references to his Document No. 2. Having been discussed in secret session as a confidential document, he insisted it must not be referred to in public sessions of An Dail. After Griffith had disgustedly declared against this tying of his hands, but had bowed to the wishes of the Republican leader, a surprise was sprung on the Dail by Cosgrave, ablest of Collins' lieutenants. By as cunning a bit of parliamentary manœuvring as any national assembly ever saw, Cosgrave managed to read into the record the oath of allegiance to the British Crown which was contained in De Valera's Document No. 2.

The trick stung De Valera into a violent rage. In the midst of a denunciation of the methods of his opponents he suddenly sprang a surprise on his own account. Since the Treaty supporters were trying to make political capital out of his desire to keep Document No. 2 a secret, he would take the wind out of their sails by agreeing to publish it—at the close of the day's session!

True to his word, De Valera had mimeographed copies of the mysterious document distributed to the Dail and the newspaper men just before adjournment. Almost immediately Griffith was on his feet charging that De Valera had omitted parts of the original text. The uproar that followed was abruptly squelched by an adjournment. Immediately afterwards, Desmond FitzGerald—then Minister of Publicity of Dail Eireann, and generally regarded at that time as De Valera's personal Press agent—called the newspaper men together in the lobby and handed out a " Proclamation " signed by the President of the Irish Republic.

How It Happened

The first sentence showed me that it was a virulent attack on the Treaty supporters and an *apologia* as regards Document No. 2. I was sure Collins and Griffith knew nothing about it. Without waiting to read further, I made for the private room reserved for the Treaty leaders. Unceremoniously I burst in upon them and handed the Proclamation to Collins. I waited while they read it together. Their half-smothered comments as they scanned the vitriolic lines were unprintable—if human.

" Has he given this to the Press ? " asked Collins.

When I told him this was the case, he dropped into a chair and began to write feverishly. At the same time Griffith started hunting through his attaché case.

" Here is Document No. 2," said Griffith a moment later, pulling out a much-worn sheaf of papers on which were many marginal notes in lead pencil. " I will show you how it compares with the one he made public to-night."

For the next ten minutes he pointed out the paragraphs that had been deleted from the document brought forward at the session. What Griffith had charged in the Dail was amply justified. The omissions were there for anyone to see.

Collins interrupted us to ask Griffith to listen to what he had written. Immediately Griffith had approved it, Collins handed the statement to me.

" Do what you like with it," he said.

A few moments later I put the following despatch on the cable :

> " It is likely that the Treaty may be beaten [1] but that does not in any way indicate that I am without

---

[1] When Collins wrote this, his best information indicated a total of 63 votes for the Treaty—enough to give a majority of two if every eligible member of the Dail voted. But as he later explained to me, there were not a few members who intended to vote against the Treaty while secretly glad that it was sure to be accepted. To frighten these members into voting honestly Collins at all times before the vote expressed grave doubts as to the result. The wisdom of this policy of pessimism was reflected in the final majority of seven for the Treaty.

hope. Ireland is not going to be deprived of her right to live her life in her own way no matter who tries to deny or to defer that right. The Irish people have already decided that the Treaty meets with their approval as being the practical course to adopt at the present time. The Treaty has been signed by England, and surely it cannot be advanced that England is going to keep a treaty that she has not signed but is going to break a treaty that she has signed. This Treaty does give us a chance and does give Ireland a chance to work out its own future on something like fair terms. If the Treaty is beaten I have already stated that I as one of the plenipotentiaries am absolved from further responsibility. The Treaty is then dead, and those who have killed it have, of course, the position in their hands to follow their policy, and their policy is unknown to me. If the opposition throws the Treaty away they ought first to have the alternative Treaty duly signed to put against it. So far as I am aware there is not an alternative Treaty. A document has been produced as an amendment, but before that can be honestly put as a real amendment the president ought to secure the signatures of the English delegates and secure ratification of the new document by the English Parliament. Then it would be a Treaty. This course will make the new document equal to the Treaty, and even when the new document is signed and ratified by the English I am certain that plain people will scarcely see any material difference between it and the Treaty. One important thing must not be forgotten. If we offer this new document as our proposal for final settlement it commits us morally to finality. It puts a definite boundary to the march of our nation, and that must not be done, and I as one Irishman and a public representative of this country cannot agree to that.

"MICEAL O'COILEAIN."

How It Happened   19

If I had known as much about the part Document No. 2 had played in the Treaty negotiations as I know now, I could have marvelled as much as I now marvel at Collins' gallant refusal to let the people know the truth about De Valera's duplicity. In its proper place I shall tell the whole story of those long months of negotiations in London—and of the part De Valera, in Dublin, played in them.

Meantime, Collins had been engaged in writing a series of ten articles for publication in the newspapers I represented—a series intended to deal with the hitherto untold incidents leading up to the Treaty negotiations as well as the inside story of the negotiations themselves. As a matter of fact the series contained no revelations, but dealt with facts that were chiefly encyclopædic. The situation as it then existed prohibited Collins from divulging the truth. So it came about that I addressed a note to him from London reading in part as follows:

"Demands from both American and English sources have been made on me:

"(a) To persuade you to write your own story for publication in book form, or

"(b) to write a book *about* you myself,

and in the event of my failing to do the former, it looks as if I must do the latter ! !

"No one better than I knows how criminal it is to ask you to add a jot to the sum total of your days' labours, but also no one better than I appreciates your tremendous capacity for work and your disregard of personal considerations where the good of your country is concerned. I am sure, moreover, you keenly appreciate the vital importance of sparing no pains to acquaint the plain people of America and England with the truth about Ireland, and to this end nothing could compare—in point of widespread circulation—with a book 'By Michael Collins.'

.   .   .   .   .

"Then—in order to put within its covers facts which you have made plain to me you are loath to touch upon, *but which readers of both countries are hungering to have*—perhaps you would not object to my adding certain biographical data *about* you by way of an *addendum*."

In a day or two came Collins' answer, reading in part as follows:

"I have thought carefully over the proposal you make, and although I should like to meet your wishes I really cannot possibly find the time to do anything that would be up to standard, and I must, therefore, ask that you do not press me in this regard.

"In my own opinion a book about me would be of little value except it was written by somebody who was closely associated with me in the troublous times. I really don't think it could be done by anybody but myself.

"Perhaps we could talk it over when we meet again."

I went immediately to Dublin and, after several conferences with Collins, succeeded in gaining his assent to my undertaking the telling of his story. In order to give him an idea of the kind of information English and American readers wanted from him, I prepared a series of written questions covering as comprehensively as I could the whole story of Ireland's fight for freedom. These I submitted to Collins. A few days later he sent for me.

"I'm going to answer every one of your questions," he began. "What's more, I'm going to tell you things you haven't asked about. You're undertaking a big job, and it is worth while doing it thoroughly. I'll help you to do just that."

And that is how it happened.

CHAPTER II

INTRODUCING MICHAEL COLLINS

It was typical of the man that he should have postponed answering those of my questions dealing with his biography until the last. Whilst, like Theodore Roosevelt and other truly great men whom I have known, Collins was an egoist, there was a side of his character that made him as modest and almost diffident as a schoolboy.

One of the last subjects we discussed together was the matter of a proper portrait to be used as a frontispiece in this book. I asked him if there were any especial photograph which he liked.

"Not one," he replied. "It may be that my opinion is biassed, but I have never yet seen a camera's handiwork—when I have been in front of the lens—that I have not been disappointed with. But so long as a man's alive, I do not see the use of photographs of him. It's surely not what he looks like but what he does that matters."

Arguing from my publisher's viewpoint, I ventured as delicately as possible to hint that perhaps even he might fail to achieve eternal life on earth, and in the event of his failure to do so the condition which he insisted alone warranted the use of his portrait would come into being.

"In other words," he said, with a characteristic smile, " you mean I may be done in at any moment—and you want me preserved. Is that it ? "

"Well," I replied, "that may not be it, but if it is, I have your word for it that there'll be several headaches spread around."

"You may be easy about that," said Collins, slipping

into his army greatcoat and extending a hand for a farewell shake. " If they get me I'll have no complaints to make : or, if that is too much of a ' bull,' at least you can be sure that if I could speak, I'd blame nobody but myself."

And so I left the man who, in the time I had had the privilege of knowing him, had already proved himself the finest character, the most astoundingly efficient worker and the greatest natural leader of men I have ever known.

Earlier that evening I had finally wrung from Collins the story of his early life. I have his word for it that I am the only person to whom he ever confided these details. Here is the story in his own words :

" I was born in 1890 on a farm in Woodfield, Clonakilty, Co. Cork. The Irish name of the place and the name it is still known by is pronounced Paulveug. I was the youngest of eight children—with two brothers and five sisters in the home.

" My father was Michael Collins, a farmer. He was born in 1815 and lived the life of a bachelor until he was in his sixty-third year. Then, at sixty-two years of age, he married my mother—and she was forty years younger than he. When I was born my father was seventy-five years of age. My mother's maiden name was Mary O'Brien. Her native town was Tullineasky, Clonakilty. She outlived my father by ten years. He died in 1897.

" All my early life I lived in childish wonder of my father. Although I was a lad of seven when he died, he had already inspired me with implicit faith in his goodness, his strength, his infallibility. I remember as if it were yesterday an instance of my faith. It proved that I could not conceive anything of his doing that was not altogether right.

" I was out in the fields with him one day, watching him at work—a rare privilege in my kid's eyes. He was on top of a wall of bog stones, and I was on the turf below him. One of the stones, a good sized one, was dislodged under his feet and came rolling down straight at me. There was plenty of time for me to dodge it, but it never occurred to me to move. 'Twas my father's foot had done the business.

Introducing Michael Collins

Surely the stone could do me no harm. To this day I carry the mark on my instep where it crushed my foot. It was not for many a year afterwards that I was ever able to understand my father's great laughter as he told and retold the tale.

" ' Would you believe it ? ' he would say. ' There he was, barefooted, the stone rolling down on him, and him never so much as looking at it ! And when I got the thing off his foot and asked him why he had stood there and let it hit him, what do you think he replied ? He told me 'twas I who sent it down ! '

" And after his great laughter had subsided he would grow serious, and the pride of family that was in him would show itself. For he always finished by saying, ' It's a true Collins he is ! '

" On my father's side there are records of ancestors back 450 years, when they were chieftains of the tribes of Munster. Part of their slogan runs like this :

" ' Multitudinous is their gathering—a great host with whom it is not fortunate to contend—the battle-trooped host of the O'Coileain.'

" I was a reverential kid. Reverence was not only instilled into me by my father ; it seemed a natural trait. Great age held something for me that was awesome. I was much fonder of the old people in the darkness than I was of young people in the daytime. It's at night you're able to get the value of old people. And it was listening to the old people that I got my ideas of Irish nationality.

" In the matter of schooling I had the education of the ordinary farmer's son in Ireland—a kind of teaching impossible to compare with American or English systems. But at least I had the advantage of having good tutors—and of a tremendous appetite for knowledge. But it was not even a secondary-school education, as that term is understood in England. It was about as much and about as good as Irish boys generally got in those days.

"A far more valuable education was at hand in the never-ceasing talk of Ireland's destiny, the injustices from which she had suffered in the past, and was still suffering. As I grew up to young manhood the Parnell speech was the one great topic of discussion. Those were the days when every person in Ireland was thinking in terms of Home Rule. Home Rule at the early morning breakfast-table, Home Rule all the day, Home Rule by every hearthside in the evening—on such fare did the young Ireland of my generation feed and grow to manhood. It was this sort of thing that made one part of the atmosphere of nationalism.

"In our own home forgathered of an evening the people who were leaders of thought in the community. Others might have dismissed them as ' local politicians '—for one reason or another a contemptuous term—but, as a matter of fact, they were very intelligent as regards the doctrine of nationalism. And as for localism, in the sense that it is narrow and petty, one must regard the circumstances of an Irish family in that time. What was local to us in Clonakilty was in nowise different from the immediate environment of a Galway or a Connaught village.

"The early settlers of America, from New England to Virginia, thought along identical lines, even though they did so unwittingly and without realisation of their common purpose. From what I hear to-day it would seem that then there was in America more of common purpose, and in that sense of a distinctively national spirit, than there is to-day. But then their motive was a simple one—self-preservation. So with us in Ireland at the beginning of the century. A cause, an inheritance, and a need common to us all inspired us. It wasn't a thing that any man or set of men could govern. It was different from that.

"When an Irish boy in those days feasted on real bacon —to the accompaniment of his father's reminiscent comments—the spirit of nationalism was breathed into him. For the father was saying that in his youth the pigs were raised exclusively for the landlords!

Introducing Michael Collins

" With my sixteenth birthday behind me I took the Civil Service examinations—like thousands of other Irish lads of my station. For many years the British Civil Service had appeared to be the only worthwhile alternative to independent emigration. Both meant emigration, of course. Successful candidates were seldom, if ever, put in Irish posts. Theoretically, the candidate might be sent to any part of the British Empire. But experience had taught us that almost invariably our berth would be in England. Whether to keep an eye on us or to take advantage of our native ability, the powers that be staffed their London posts almost entirely with Irishmen. And I—at seventeen—wanted to live in the world's biggest city.

" Quickly, however, I discovered I was in a blind alley in the Civil Service. To be sure, it was to London I went—with a clerkship in the Post Office—a junior position that paid £70 a year. At the end of two years I resigned.

" Followed several years of other jobs, none of which satisfied my ideas of opportunity. First I took a minor post in a stockbroker's office, then a clerkship in the Guarantee Trust Company of New York at its branch in the city. But with each passing year I felt more and more convinced that London for me held as little real opportunity as did Ireland.

" Of course, I had Irish friends in London before I arrived, and in the intervening years I had made many more friends among Irishmen resident in London. For the most part we lived lives apart. We chose to consider ourselves outposts of our nation. We were a distinct community—a tiny eddy, if you like, in the great metropolis. But we were proud of our isolation, and we maintained it to the end.

" When wonder is expressed, as it often is, that I could have lived eight years in London and still have been so little known that 120,000 British troops and Black and Tans could not find me in four years of hunting me in Ireland, I can only attribute it to that policy of voluntary isolation we all observed in London. And, after all, Michael

Collins, junior clerk, could hardly be expected to have attracted any notice—especially in an English business house. It was just that fact that had convinced me there was every chance, if I remained in England, to continue to be a clerk the rest of my life.

" And then came a real opportunity !

" Queerly enough, it was preceded by another—an offer to go to America.

" It was in 1914, just before the declaration of war, that the chance came to take passage to New York. I could have gone under the most advantageous conditions, and with the one thing I had been looking for—a fair chance to get ahead. But when I laid the scheme before Tom Clarke (the Thomas J. Clarke of Easter Week) he advised me not to go. His reason satisfied me. He said there was going to be something doing in Ireland within a year. That was good enough for me. I changed my mind about going to America, and plodded along in my uncongenial job.

" It was in May 1915—after Sean McDermott had been arrested and lodged in prison to serve a four months' sentence for making a seditious speech—that I realised the climax was swiftly approaching. The British Secret Service was turning in reports from Ireland that must have been disquieting to a Government then at death-grips with the German military machine. With all the impetuosity of twenty-five I went to Tom Clarke and told him I was ready to go home and do whatever he wanted me to do. But he was not ready for me to go. The time was close at hand, he told me, but for the present I was to remain in London. I obeyed. I had good reason to obey.

" I had not forgotten what he had said to me almost a year earlier, when he had led me to turn down the offer from America. ' You should wait,' he had said then, ' for the time when we are going to do something to bring the Irish case to international notice.'

" Before the summer of 1915 was ended, however, I got the summons and hurried to Dublin. With me went fifteen of my pals—all of us with years of London living behind us.

Introducing Michael Collins

Out of that little group six were killed in the rising of Easter Week, 1916. One of these was my brother-in-law.

"It may be worth the telling at this time to point out a somewhat unusual fact of a purely personal nature. It is unusual, certainly, when one stops to consider that in forty years Ireland has lost almost half her population through emigration. Out of my family of eight, only one, my brother Patrick, voluntarily left Ireland. My sister Helen, now forty years of age, became a nun and is in a convent in Yorkshire. And there is my stay in London. But otherwise we have all elected to remain in our own country. I recall how interested Richard Croker was in this. He, himself an emigrant who eventually came back to his native land, believed the day would come when Ireland would attract immigrants. However that may be, at least I think it is just as well for the world to know that all Irishmen are not eager for the opportunity of leaving their own shores.

"As for my brother Patrick, all I know about him—and this information reached me indirectly—is that he is a member of the police-force in Chicago. Whether he is a policeman or not I have no idea. In all the years since he went to America he has never let us hear from him."

Several months prior to this—my last meeting with Collins—he had urged me to interview Eoin MacNeill, then Speaker of Dail Eireann and Professor of Ancient Gaelic History in the National University.

"You will find Professor MacNeill one of the most learned men in Ireland," Collins told me. "Also, there is no doubt that he is a fine patriot. As *Kincola* (the Gaelic name for Speaker of the House) MacNeill has held the respect of every member of the Dail; and yet his order countermanding the 1916 rising—issued by him as President of the Irish Volunteers less than twenty-four hours before the time set for the rebellion to begin—undoubtedly had a great deal to do with its speedy failure.

"So far as I know, Professor MacNeill has never explained the reason for his action. I think most of us are so sure of his staunch patriotism that we could not bring ourselves to cast the slightest aspersion on him by asking for an explanation. I for one, at any rate, however, should like very much to have it—and I suggest that for the purposes of making this tale of yours as complete as possible, you put the question to him."

And so it was a few days later that I took a jaunting-car and set out from my hotel in Dublin on a six-mile drive to the MacNeill home in Blackrock, through the lovely Irish countryside.

CHAPTER III

EOIN MACNEILL—ULSTERMAN

"THERE needs be no doubt about it whatever. I did everything in my power to prevent the Easter Week rising."

This was Professor Eoin MacNeill's answer to the question Collins had suggested I put to him. And the Speaker of Dail Eireann gave it with a degree of patent sincerity that made doubt indeed impossible. It was as if he were glad of the opportunity to go on record in a matter which he knows has been discussed in every home in Ireland for eight years. Incidentally, Lieut.-Col. Sir Matthew Nathan, Under-Secretary for Ireland at the time of the rising, and Sir Mackenzie Dalzell Chalmers, K.C.B., one of the three members of the Hardinge Commission which enquired into the causes of the rebellion, have at last their answer. (During the enquiry Sir Mackenzie Chalmers asked Sir Matthew Nathan in the witness-box if MacNeill's order countermanding the rising was a " blind." " I should very much like to know," replied the witness).

" Why I did what I did," Professor MacNeill continued, " has never been told. I have remained silent because those of my colleagues entitled to an explanation have chosen to ask for none. It has been my preference to believe they wished in this fashion to show their unquestioning faith in me. But now the opportunity has come to make all the facts known, I am glad to take advantage of it.

" As President and Chief of Staff of the Irish Volunteers I was dedicated, heart and soul, to the one great aim of that body—the achieving of real independence by the Irish nation.

As one of the founders of the Gaelic League I had done all in my power to awaken the people to a consciousness of nationality, the necessary preliminary to a successful issue of our prime ambition by force of arms. When in 1914 the Sinn Fein section broke away from the general body of the Volunteers I became leader of the seceding body. For the next two years I made recruiting speeches in all parts of Ireland and saw our forces growing by leaps and bounds. At the same time I took over the editorship of the *Irish Volunteer*, the official organ of the army.

"It must be borne in mind that conditions in Ireland in the spring of 1916 made conferences exceedingly difficult for those of us on the Black List at Dublin Castle. In my case it was exceptionally difficult, living as I was out in the country and away from my colleagues. Much was going forward that I knew nothing of—determined upon at secret meetings at which I was not present. Not until after it was all over did I come to learn the momentous decision reached by the seven men who signed and published the declaration of the Irish Republic.

"HAD I KNOWN THEIR GRIM PURPOSE I MIGHT HAVE ACTED DIFFERENTLY. I MIGHT HAVE SUBSCRIBED TO IT. AND YET I AM NOT SURE. NOT EVEN THEY COULD HAVE DREAMED THAT ENGLISH STUPIDITY WOULD TRANSFORM THEIR FORLORN HOPE FROM IGNOMINIOUS FAILURE INTO BRILLIANT SUCCESS!

"But not to anticipate myself—the Irish Volunteers had been formed and trained with a definite object known to all of us, the eventual driving out of Ireland of the English armed forces. I shared that aim with the rest. I believed it could be done. The Carson volunteers in Ulster gave us a perfect reason for being. But that anyone should be so gullible, so utterly ignorant of the facts, as to imagine for a moment that we should ever commit the senseless folly of playing England's game by armed attack against our fellow-countrymen in Ulster surprised even the most sanguine among us. The ridiculous assumption was of inestimable value to us.

"England saw us drilling, knew of our continuous

recruiting, had definite information as to our constantly increasing numbers—and let us do it without real interference. England wanted us to commit the blunder! Thus should we ourselves have settled the Irish question, from England's viewpoint, for generations to come. We should have been soundly trounced in the field by Carson's army—backed up by whatever British support might be necessary—and at the same time have ruined all hopes of a united Ireland. Because England believed we were planning to do the one thing that would vindicate her Ulster policy, our army was allowed to grow.

"In the spring of 1916 we had the men and we had the discipline in plenty for our purpose. It is true that some of us were hoping that Sir Roger Casement would succeed in inducing German officers to come to Ireland to give us the benefit of their experience, but all that was actually counted upon was shipments of sufficient arms and ammunition.

"This obviously was a vital need. Without equipment we could do nothing. But when at last word came that the shipments were on their way, Easter Sunday was fixed as the date for the beginning of hostilities—always conditional on the safe arrival of the arms and ammunition. At least this was my understanding. And that was where I was in error! I did not know that a little coterie among our leaders was inspired with an idea of the intrinsic value of martyrdom for martyrdom's sake! But I will come to that presently.

"The world knows of Casement's arrest. It happened on Good Friday. It is not so generally known that the same day a German ship carrying 20,000 rifles and 1,000,000 rounds of ammunition was scuttled and sunk by her commander in Tralee Bay to escape capture by the British. Word of both disasters reached me on the Saturday afternoon. I wasted no time in trying to prevent what seemed certain must be a ludicrous fiasco.

"By word of mouth, in hastily written despatches, and in a formal order which I inserted in the *Sunday Independent*, I forbade any movement of the Volunteers to take place. I sent a letter to De Valera among others. He was then a commandant in charge of troops at Boland's Mill. It read :

Easter Sunday,
1.20 p.m.

"Comm't Eamon de Vaileara,
   "As Comm't MacDonagh is not accessible, I have to give you this order direct. Comm't MacDonagh left me last night with the understanding that he would return or send me a message. He has done neither.
   "As Chief of Staff, I have ordered and hereby order that no movement whatsoever of Irish Volunteers is to be made to-day. You will carry out this order in your own command and make it known to other commands.
"EOIN MACNEILL."

" I had just despatched this letter when word came that my order published in the *Sunday Independent* was being questioned in various quarters as spurious. I promptly authenticated it, and added that ' every influence should be used immediately and throughout the day to secure faithful executing of this order, as any failure to obey it may result in a very grave catastrophe.'
" And all this I did without the slightest knowledge of the real plans of my colleagues. Easter Monday came as a more terrible shock to me than perhaps to any other Irishman in Ireland. Seven of our finest and our bravest leaders had put their names to the declaration of the Irish Republic, had seized the Post Office, had fired the first shots of the rebellion ! Of course, without those German arms and ammunition they must have failed in any event—had I not issued the countermanding orders—but in the resultant confusion, with our forces in all parts of the country, notably in Cork, remaining passive, it seemed that this mad act of

desperation by a mere handful of men—poorly equipped and with no support to depend upon—would constitute the most lamentable, futile gesture in the annals of Ireland's struggling centuries. Undoubtedly this would have been the case had it not been for England's stupidity!

" The truth, as I afterwards learned it, was that Clarke and Pearse and MacDonagh and the others had deliberately planned to go down to certain defeat and death. If ever seven men were animated by pure martyrdom it was these patriots. They were willing to give their lives to move their countrymen to work together in the cause they would thus ennoble. And yet how easily instead they might have found themselves a laughing stock!

" If England had only used the Dublin police force instead of high explosive shells and all the paraphernalia of war, arrested the leaders on a charge of disturbing the peace —or, perhaps trespass—and regarded the feint in its true light, the prank of irresponsible idealists not to be taken seriously, she could have led a world to join in ironic laughter! In that fashion the cause of Irish freedom could have been set back a generation. Every Irishman must thank God that England made the mistake of treating it seriously, thereby giving it a dignity with which nothing else could have invested it.

" The seven martyrs went to martyrs' deaths. Their fondest dreams were exceeded. Ireland's freedom was at last in sight!

" If it is urged that the event proves that their prevision was good and mine bad—I have no excuse to offer. Had I known their plan I am afraid I should still have disapproved it on the grounds that not a Government on earth could be so stupid as to make the ridiculous mistake of treating them seriously.

" This explanation, I trust, will establish for once and all my motive in issuing those orders."

(It may be interesting to interrupt Professor MacNeill's narrative at this point with the statement that Collins whole-heartedly supported the former in his ascribing the ultimate success of the rising to England's mistaken policy of severity in handling it. Also Collins was convinced of the sincerity of Professor MacNeill's motive in countermanding the orders for the rising.)

"I referred to the reason England permitted us to build up the Irish Volunteers," Professor MacNeill continued. "She hoped we would use that body to make war upon Ulster. Now six years have come and gone—and the truth about Ulster seems still to be as little understood as it was then. It is time the truth was told. I feel peculiarly well fitted to tell it, for I am a native of County Antrim, and was educated at St. Malachy's College in Belfast.

"I speak as an Ulsterman, if you please, but that makes me no less an Irishman. There are those who do not agree with me. In more than one section of Ireland they still talk about 'the Outlanders of Ulster.' There are folk who look upon the Black North as a diseased limb which should be cut off from the Irish social body. But the actual method proposed is as illogical as the wearing of a spiked bracelet in the case of a diseased hand. A mere artificial barrier—the most the proposed Boundary Commission could accomplish—would be no remedy if the limb were actually diseased. But, heart and soul, I am opposed to this theory of a diseased limb.

"Let an Ulster Outlander speak for that part of Ireland from which he comes. Here in Dublin there appears to be no question that I am an Irishman. Am I then an Outlander when I am among my kith and kin in the North-East? Or if my own claim to be Irish is graciously conceded, must I believe that my father and mother, my brothers and sisters down in the North, are not of my nationality?

"It is significant to note that the Boundary Commission was proposed by the English Government! Its significance will appear before I have finished. Incidentally, the Ulster Government—in one of its rare moments of proving its real devotion (?) to England—has flatly announced it will pay no attention to the Commission's findings. Once again history repeats itself. It was not so long ago—in 1886—

that Lord Randolph Churchill, father of the man to whom Lloyd George entrusted Irish affairs for the most part, made a special expedition to Ulster to assure the stalwarts of high State sympathy in England. It was then he produced the memorable phrase, ' Ulster will fight, and Ulster will be right '—IN RESISTING THE CONTEMPLATED LAW LAID DOWN BY THE ENGLISH GOVERNMENT !

" But let me assure Sir James Craig that Southern Ireland has no intention of cutting the country in two. We don't intend to do it, even if England believes it to be the one sure way of preventing a united Ireland ! This is the spirit of the people of Southern Ireland. What of the people of Ulster ?

" Why, the glens of Antrim from Glanarm to Ballycastle, and the whole mountainous district at their back, are more Nationalist than county Dublin ! The Ulster Unionist, even, is not the demon incarnate of anti-Nationalism that some raw Southerners imagine. It is a pity I am not at liberty to name business men and farmers whose confidences I have shared in trips through Ulster. Their reason for insisting I spare them publicity is self-evident. The rule of the revolver under Sir James Craig's Government has succeeded infamously well in keeping true opinion squelched. But these men have told me—and I know them to be honest men—that they pray for a united Ireland. But prayer alone is not enough. The time has come for the truth to be told. It needs only to be known—and the problem, WHICH IS NOT AND NEVER HAS BEEN A REAL PROBLEM, will solve itself !

" The truth is simple. England has done her utmost to keep flaming the hatred conceived by bigotry and falsehood at the time of the Plantation of three centuries ago. To Irishmen in the South, England's emissaries have preached the lie that Ulster Unionists are aliens. How many centuries, one may ask, does it take to make an Irishman of an alien ? What special force is at work in Ulster to prevent the immigrant there from *ever* absorbing the characteristics of Irish nationalism ?

" In Ulster England has spared no pains to foster the

feeling that the Ulster Unionist is a full-blooded Teuton and his Catholic neighbour a full-blooded Celt. She has taught both to adopt the notion that Celt and Teuton are as oil and water. But if we take the Celt to mean the race inhabiting Britain and Ireland before the Saxon and Norse invasions, and Teuton to mean the subsequent immigrants, it is absolutely certain that the descendants of the Ulster Planters are vastly more Celt than Teuton, more Celt than the Catholic Nationalists of a great part of Leinster—for the thoroughbred Englishmen is a purer Celt than almost any of the Irish people themselves.

"It is not a fact of race, but an illusion of race, that makes Ulster Unionists pro-British and anti-Irish. But it is an illusion that England has craftily created and carefully fostered.

"It is a common delusion in the South of Ireland that the Planters were all English. The fact is they were mainly Scotch. The Old-Irish Ulsterman is hardly less grave, sedate, unresponsive, taciturn, laconic, keen at a bargain, tenacious of his own, critical towards others, than the typical Ulster Presbyterian. Nor is either variety a whit more un-Irish in qualities of this kind than the Catholic Nationalist, the 'absorbed' semi-Norseman of *Fine Gall*. Is it not ridiculous to exact uniformity of type from all parts of a nation?

"There are not two Irish nations. A foreign faction —it is the happy phrase of an Ulster Presbyterian, John Mitchell—is a familiar feature in many a national history. We have in the Irish nation to-day a foreign faction. But after the Williamite settlement we were in reality two nations, and a century later only one. The fusion would have been more rapid but for the fact that during all that period, and for a generation longer, the descendants of each element adhered rigidly to their respective languages. With equal chances we should have seen all over Ireland the condition of things reported to Queen Elizabeth—'The English in Dublin do now all speak Irish, for the most part with great delight.'

"The Nationalist trend in Protestant Ulster reached its extreme point of intensity in the period of the United Irishmen. This organisation did much to bring about the ultimate division between the nation and the faction. The English Government became greatly alarmed at the rapid growth of a national bond of union between the Old-Irish Catholics and the Protestants of British descent. Catholics and Protestants alike enrolled themselves in great numbers in the United Irishmen. England accordingly took steps to work up religious animosities in Ulster, and with great success among the adherents of the ascendant religion, the Episcopalians. At the same time, England practised on the Catholics, and with no less success. It must be admitted that the lower order of Catholics in the North have at all times been prone to mere party antagonism, to meeting the silly cry of ' To hell with the Pope ' with the no less degrading cry of ' To hell with the King.'

"England was not satisfied with pitting mob against mob in Ulster. She flew at higher game on the Catholic side. It was when the Catholic world was on the verge of panic—after the French Revolution. The virtuous government of Pitt—through its pillar of Church and State, Castlereagh—had little difficulty in bringing that thorough ecclesiastic, Archbishop Troy, to believe in an alliance with the Holy British Empire in preference to the slightest sympathy with the aims of a Protestant-led and French-tainted Nationalist movement. AND WE ARE NOT THROUGH EVEN YET WITH THE FRENCH PANIC IN CATHOLIC IRELAND !

"This policy of England's has been continued with short interruptions ever since. In 1886 the English Government withdrew the whole authority of the Empire and all the forces of law and order for a period of many weeks from a riotous quarter of Belfast—establishing then the precedent which Sir James Craig adopted in 1920—on a vastly larger scale ! And down through the years, England has promised concession after concession to Catholic prelates, and never fulfilled one of them so long as the promise alone served her purpose.

"But slowly some of us were learning how far an English Government would go in playing upon Irish Catholics. We were beginning, for instance, to see through the man-against-man device of so administering education as to keep the idea of hopeless religious division ever before us. We began to see that the cause of our division was not any ingrained 'common hatred for centuries,' but was operated from above and without for the deliberate purpose of preventing good feeling between the two sections of the nation. England's policy has been immensely helped by the delusion held by most Irishmen that the anti-Irish position of the majority of Ulster Protestants is the natural and spontaneous expression of their racial and religious spirit. It is the general, unquestioning opinion. People never care to admit, even to themselves, that their prejudices are the product of deliberate manipulation by others.

"The fostering of religious feuds in Ireland by England is so much a part of the solid and irrefragable facts of history that it is surprising to find it not universally recognised. The Catholics, as a rule, have been too ready to walk into the snare, the Catholic mob habitually ready to play into the hands of these skilful manipulators. I wish I could say only the mob was responsible for the creation of the Ulster difficulty. Unfortunately, representative Catholics and Nationalists have been largely contributory to the intensity of anti-Nationalism in parts of Ulster. They have furnished precisely the evidences required to prove that Ireland is a hopelessly divided country.

"But is there no other policy towards the Ulster Unionists except to revile and disown them ? Suppose we Nationalists begin by putting our house in order, by calling off *our* dog ? Suppose we declare every man who uses anti-Protestant cries to be the worst enemy of his country's cause ? Suppose that in view of our own share in aggravating their fanaticism in the past we resolve to abstain from all acts and words of an exasperating kind in the future ? What if we perform these preliminary ablutions ?

"It must interest friends of Ireland the world over to

know that every one of these questions has been asked—
AND ANSWERED THE RIGHT WAY BY THE NEW GOVERNMENT
OF SOUTHERN IRELAND.

"Under normal conditions there are ten commercial travellers from Belfast houses going through Ireland for one going through Great Britain. On Ireland and not on Great Britain does Belfast depend for the use of her vast credit resources. The Ulster Bank, the Northern Bank, the Belfast Bank know where their business is done. And Ulster is a land of business men! Once the truth is known by Irishmen—once England's snares are recognised and so avoided—once Belfast and Dublin together see the light—that our whole problem is in fact an economic problem—when this, the real issue, is knit, I am confident that the kindly Southerners will be glad to have by their shoulders the cold and harsh-tongued men of the North."

Much more than this Professor MacNeill told me before I finally took my leave of him and started back to Dublin aboard the jaunting-car. Some of it will appear in a later chapter. Some of it cannot be told at this time. But, perhaps, in what I have set down here, he has proved himself to be what I unreservedly consider him—not only a profound thinker and a scholar, but that rarest type of Irishman—a man of moderation.

CHAPTER IV

COLLINS' OWN STORY OF "EASTER WEEK"

"SIR ROGER CASEMENT was absolutely opposed to the Easter Week rising. Of this I have abundant proof. I know that he made the trip from Germany to Ireland for the sole purpose of stopping the rebellion. I have his own statement to this effect."

So Michael Collins corroborated that part of Eoin MacNeill's story in which the Speaker of Dail Eireann told of Casement's having advised against the use of armed force at that time. This unequivocal declaration is of peculiar significance in that it is a flat contradiction of an official statement issued by the British Government following Casement's execution. Part of that statement was as follows:

" . . He was convicted and punished for treachery of the worst kind to the Empire he had served, and as a willing agent of Germany. . . . In addition, though himself for many years a British official, he undertook the task of trying to induce soldiers of the British Army, prisoners in the hands of Germany, to forswear their oaths of allegiance and join their country's enemies. . . . The suggestion that Casement left Germany for the purpose of trying to stop the Irish rising was not raised at the trial, and is conclusively disproved, not only by the facts there disclosed, but by further evidence which has since become available."

Obviously a matter of fact of this nature cannot be a matter of opinion. The record shows that it was Casement

Collins' Own Story of "Easter Week"   41

who was responsible for the attempted landing by a disguised German merchantman of 20,000 rifles and 1,000,000 rounds of ammunition in Tralee Bay. It is not denied by any Irish leaders that Casement did his utmost to persuade German officers to lead the rebellion. But listen to Collins' story.

"Casement's opposition to the rising meant nothing to the leaders in Dublin," Collins continued. "They looked upon it—and in a sense rightly—that this was simply one man's biassed view, formed as a consequence of his experiences in Germany. His outlook on the rising, or indeed on any rising, was naturally different from the outlook of men like Sean McDermott and Tom Clarke. My own opinion is that Casement had acquired a world outlook, and his mind was consequently influenced by world conditions.

"German assistance appealed to him as vital for a successful issue of Ireland's rebellion against the might of the British Empire. It is a fact—to be told now without harm to anyone—that his disappointment over his failure to induce Germany to send men to aid in Ireland's fight brought on a serious illness that kept him many weeks in bed in Munich. And let it be remembered that in this opinion he was by no means alone. I can quite understand Professor MacNeill's having shared this view. He knew—as, indeed, did most of us—that we were literally a corporal's guard planning to attack the armed forces of an Empire.

"But Sean McDermott and Tom Clarke were not waiting for German aid in the shape of MEN. Lacking them meant little or nothing to these inspired leaders. Irishmen were good enough for them. They were content to rely upon the strength of the forces at home, and their calculations were based practically entirely on home considerations. Of course, they wanted German arms and ammunition, but lacking them, they still were prepared to fight.

"If Professor MacNeill's theory that these leaders had resolved upon launching a forlorn hope to awaken the Irish people is correct, no further explanation is necessary. On the other hand, it must be obvious that to men like

Casement, the adventure appeared to be sheer madness. I am convinced that Casement's opposition would have been no less strenuous had the German arms been successfully landed at Tralee. He was under the spell of the super-efficiency of the German military machine, and could not imagine our under-trained, inexperienced amateur army being able to stand up for a moment against the English professional soldier. A few of us felt differently about it—but I think I understate it when I say that a vast majority of the Irish people at that time would have agreed with Casement.

"It is, therefore, not at all difficult for me to accept Professor MacNeill's explanation of his issuing the order countermanding the rising. Far from Casement and MacNeill being in a minority in this matter, it was we who were in the minority. With the German arms at the bottom of Tralee Bay, it must indeed have seemed an act of madness.

"The actual number of Irishmen employed in the fighting was very small. In only three places—Dublin, Galway and Enniscorthy—was there what could be called a conflict. I have always put the entire number engaged on our side at about 2,000. Of course, the countermanding order and the non-arrival of the German arms had a great deal to do with deciding the number actually engaged. It must be understood also that when I say 2,000, I refer to the number definitely under arms. There were men standing by awaiting orders in many parts of the country who would have leaped into action if the circumstances had been favourable instead of the reverse. In County Cork, for instance, if they had had arms, 2,000 men would probably have turned out.

"The British had an ordinary strength in Ireland at the time of some 30,000 to 40,000 regular troops, and, of course, they had 10,000 Royal Irish Constabulary scattered all over the country. It is difficult to say how many British troops came into action during Easter week.

"In Dublin, the British garrison numbered about 10,000. Probably all of these were actively engaged. So far as I know, we have never definitely ascertained the numbers on our side actually mobilised in Dublin on Easter Monday morning. It could not have exceeded 700, and at no time during the week through which the fighting continued could the number have exceeded 900.

"As for heroism—I saw many instances. All of our men were full of pluck and daring. Only that breed of men would have engaged in a contest where the odds were worse than ten to one against! But the incident that touched me most was an effort made to rescue a wounded comrade. Everything considered, I think it was the finest example of pure heroism I ever saw.

"There were two of them—snipers—posted under the lee of the Nelson pillar, out in the middle of O'Connell Street. The rescuer had been mortally wounded himself—unable to stand on his legs—but in spite of it, when his comrade was slightly wounded he managed to drag him across the cobblestones and into the safety of the Post Office. It was evident that the rescuer had but a short time to live, and he must have known it, for he waved the doctor aside and told him to look after his comrade. To everyone's surprise, he did not die immediately, but for several days suffered the most awful agony. Never once did he complain, and at all times he was deeply grateful for any little service rendered him. He turned out to have been a waiter in a Dublin hotel. He was not an Irishman; his nationality seemed to be Franco-Italian.

"I cannot say that I myself saw any case of specific brutality on the part of the British. I did, however, see many cases of what may be called ill-usage. For instance, a British officer abused and jostled Sean McDermott after Sean had submitted quietly to capture. Sean was a cripple. I also saw an English officer prevent one of his private soldiers from supplying water to a few of our men who had been standing some hours in the sun. But for the most part instances of physical brutality indulged in by the British were conspicuous by their absence.

"There is a form of wounding, however, that is worse

than mere physical brutality. Following our surrender and being taken prisoners we made our acquaintance with English contempt. Our captors made no effort to disguise their feeling that we were wretched inferiors, not worthy of being accorded treatment given a respected enemy. That was a pitiful thing. They honestly felt us to be almost beneath their contempt, and let us thoroughly understand it. In the batch of several hundred prisoners in which I found myself were some of our finest and bravest. The English officer in charge of us was especially abusive and insulting. He told us we were Irish swine whose place was in the pig-sty—and more of a like kind. A year or so afterwards this officer met his death in a distant part of Ireland under mysterious circumstances. The mystery was never solved.

"Not unnaturally—considering how few we were, how hopeless the contest, and how pitiful our lack of equipment and experience—there was much of a distinctly humorous nature in the incidents of Easter Week.

"Desmond Fitzgerald, for instance, was living out in Bray, to which the British had sent him the better to keep him under surveillance. His wife had gone to England on an urgent mission, leaving him and a young girl of the village, employed as a nurse, to take care of their two children. In due course Fitzgerald got word that the rising was to take place on Easter Sunday. He was in honour bound to do his bit. But there were his babies—and a mother he had no way of communicating with. The nurse, hardly more than a child herself, was no safe person to whom to entrust his children. But just the same, he risked the forbidden journey into Dublin on the Saturday night and managed to reach The O'Rahilly and explain his predicament. He wanted to do his duty, but he found himself mother as well as father to two infants! From his viewpoint, anyway, the time set for the rebellion was distinctly inopportune.

"To his credit, be it said, he managed to overcome the difficulty, and he was in the Post Office throughout the week.

"One of the most laughable things that happened was

Collins' Own Story of "Easter Week"

typical of a certain order of Irish mentality—that type which through the centuries has been responsible for our world reputation as makers of 'bulls.'

"On the Tuesday two Irish lads who had been caught red-handed by one of our patrols in the act of looting a shop were brought into the Post Office and before Tom Clarke. The old man was furious.

"'Shame on you both!' he thundered. 'To desecrate the name of Ireland in this fashion! You should be shot where you stand! Sure, shooting is too good for a looter!'

"And while the two wretched prisoners trembled under his tongue-lashing, our leader seemed to be on the point of ordering their instant execution. A minute went by and then, disgustedly and scornfully, he ordered them to be led away to the kitchen to peel potatoes.

"When Friday came, and our surrender was only a matter of hours, Clarke suddenly remembered the two looters and ordered them to be brought before him. By this time high explosive shells had smashed our stronghold into a shapeless ruin. Outside, from every quarter, machine-guns were sweeping the streets with a constant rain of fire. The looters were in a pitiable state.

"'Now then, you two,' Clarke began. 'To-morrow, maybe sooner, we're going to surrender. We're going out and give ourselves up. Every one of us may be shot. You can wait and go out with us—or you can go now. Choose!'

"Both of them spoke at the same instant. They would go then and there! And so we swung open a door and let them go. We watched them as they ran across O'Connell Street, the bullets striking all about them. To our amazement, they escaped without being hit, finally reaching the comparative safety of Abbey Street. It seemed to us that we had been witnessing a double miracle. And then one of them turned round and came dashing straight towards us! Again a thousand guns were trained on him, and again he managed to come through unscathed. We opened the door for him and he dived through it.

" ' Don't you know your own mind ? ' demanded Clarke. ' Is it inside or outside you want to be ? '

" ' Oh, sir,' came the deadly serious reply, ' I had to come back, sir. I left my insurance card in the kitchen ! '

" Important as the rising finally proved—and history will certainly give it place as being the determining factor in Ireland's fight for freedom—its importance was not immediately recognised even by those of us to whom it meant most. In many ways the experiences of that week, as well as of the preceding years of preparation, were invaluable. As a testing measure of men, it could not have been more conclusive.

" Among other lessons that I learned during this period was one it would be well if more Irishmen would take to heart. I discovered that personal bravery alone is of hardly any more use than its opposite. I hesitate to inflict hurt on any man, especially one whose only fault is one for which he cannot properly be blamed. Lack of judgment is not a thing to blame a man for. And yet it must be said that one man's lack of judgment was responsible for the hanging of Sir Roger Casement, the execution of the seven signers of the declaration of the Irish Republic, and the ingloriously speedy termination of the rebellion. The whole story must be told, but I must not tell it now. Perhaps, later on, the facts can be made known without undue emphasis on their consequences."

There was only one man in Ireland that I knew of who might merit this description. I had long had my doubts about him, and, thus prejudiced, leaped to the conclusion that it must be to him that Collins was referring. I asked Collins if this were the man. He assured me he was not.

Several months later Collins named the man and told me the whole story. The man was Austin Stack. The story in which he figured as a stupid blunderer will be told in a later chapter. But at the interview with Collins which I have just described he made it plain that he did not wish to pursue the subject then, and patently by way of changing the subject, he suggested that I next interview Arthur

Griffith, at that time the newly elected President of Dail Eireann.

"There are a few men you must know, if you are to write the whole story of Ireland's fight for freedom," said Collins. "And Griffith is one of these. I know you have talked with him, and I know you think you have sized him up—but I can assure you that you don't know him nor his measure. He is the kind that takes a lot of knowing. And if he will talk you will learn things about Ireland that no other man could tell you. It may be that Irish people and the world in general may never appreciate Arthur Griffith until he is dead and gone, but mark my words, it will come."

An odd prediction, surely. For as I write—from notes made months ago—all Ireland is paying respectful homage to Griffith lying in state in Dublin's City Hall, and a world Press is extolling his greatness in eulogistic editorials. It took his death to earn Irish appreciation and a world's encomiums. He was not the kind of man who wins applause. A thick-set, grave, monosyllabic, unapproachable type—he was not of the stuff of which popular heroes are made. But his tenacity of purpose, his indomitable will, his absolute honesty, and his love of the land to which he had dedicated himself heart and soul—these qualities at the same time enabled him to do more for Ireland than any other one man ever accomplished ; they also killed him.

There was nothing to suggest, however, that he was not in the very pink of condition the night I came upon him in a private dining-room in Bailey's chop-house in Dublin, just before the new rebellion against the Free State Government began.

CHAPTER V

ARTHUR GRIFFITH'S LAST STATEMENT

" SINN FEIN was not my exclusive creation. It is unfair to the memory of a great Irishman that this false impression should be allowed to exist. Sinn Fein was conceived by two of us—and the other man was William Rooney."

Arthur Griffith made this statement to me—so far as I am aware it was the last statement he ever made for publication—after I had asked him to tell the story of his winning his countrymen to the Sinn Fein policy of " ourselves alone." As every newspaper man who ever attempted the task knows, Griffith was by far the most difficult of all the Irish leaders to persuade to grant an interview. Only because I had sent by a waiter a message that Collins wished him to see me did Griffith consent—and presently I found myself with him in a private dining-room tucked high up under the eaves of Bailey's chop-house in Dublin, a favourite haunt of his. But at the conclusion of our talk he dashed my hopes to the ground by insisting that I delay publication of the interview—" until the facts can be told without doing damage."

At that time—it was late June—Rory O'Connor and his gunmen were in possession of the Four Courts, and every attempt to establish unity between the two sections of the Irish Republican Army had failed. Still, Griffith had high hopes of reaching a peaceful settlement with De Valera, and through him with the more radical of the Die-Hard element. In any event he insisted that there must be no publication of unpalatable facts that might jeopardise all chances of peace. There was nothing for it except compliance—obviously.

Now, however, that Griffith has gone, now that Collins' death had made it certain that the war will be carried on until law and order shall have been established throughout all the country—the story can be told "without doing damage." And in what follows I trust there will appear ample justification for my characterising Griffith as a fact merchant. In all my newspaper career I have never met a man who held facts in such superlatively high estimation.

"The Sinn Fein movement," Griffith explained, "was both economic and national. Rooney's idea—and mine— was to make Sinn Fein in this way meet the two evils produced by the Union. Primarily Ireland's need was education. Sinn Fein grew to wield enormous educational power. More than that, we saw the fruits of our labours in the growth of spiritual power among those who came into the ranks of Sinn Fein.

"Unquestionably the organisation went far in unifying Ireland. The people had been waiting for an 'Irish Ireland' policy. Sinn Fein promoted that policy. Everywhere we preached the recreation of Ireland built upon the Gael. We penetrated into Belfast and North-East Ulster, where encouraging educational work was making the national revival a living reality. And then the world war broke out.

"I do not indulge in prophecies, but the facts make clear that if Sinn Fein's work in Ulster had not been interrupted in 1914—if that work could have been completed— the freedom which the Treaty gives us would have been complete freedom. We who went to London as the nation's plenipotentiaries did not go as representatives of a united Ireland—as we should have been had our work in Ulster gone on even a short time longer. And until Ireland can speak as a united people we shall not earn and we shall not get that full freedom deserved and possessed by nations that *are* nations.

"Too much stress has been laid on two phases of Sinn Fein—neither of which was its chief characteristic. It has been repeatedly said that the Sinn Fein movement was not

D

militant, and that I was wedded to the theory of non-resistance. I have no excuses nor apologies to make for my support of the abstention policy. For Irish representatives to sit in the Westminster Parliament had been abundantly proved to be the worst thing that could happen to Ireland. But Sinn Fein was not pacifistic. The militant movement existed within it, and by its side. Those who have a mere smattering of knowledge of Irish events of the past few years must realise that this is so when they learn that two of Sinn Fein's most ardent advocates were Tom Clarke and Sean McDermott! No one will call these two mighty figures of Easter Week pacifists! Moreover, within the organisation the two movements worked in perfect harmony.

" The second over-stressed feature of Sinn Fein has been that it is a purely political machine—with the accompanying suggestion of belittlement that this charge for some inexplicable reason seems to carry. The admittedly large majority in the Ard Fheis against the Treaty was instanced as a proof of this—the fact being used to show that Sinn Fein was as narrowly partisan as the ordinary party machine—and as little concerned with the actual welfare of the nation. This is a gross libel.

" It is a fact that Rooney had little use for formulæ. He preached language and liberty. But he also inspired all whom he met with national pride and courage. ' Tell the world bravely what we seek!' he said. ' We must be men if we mean to win.' He believed that liberty could not be won unless we were fit and willing to win it—ready to suffer and die for it. He interpreted the national ideal as ' an Irish State governed by Irishmen for the benefit of the Irish people.' He sought to impregnate the whole people with ' a Gaelic-speaking nationality.' ' Only then,' he pleaded, ' could we win freedom and be worthy of it—freedom—individual and national freedom of the fullest and broadest character—freedom to think and act as it best beseems—national freedom to stand equally with the rest of the world.'

" He aimed at weaving Gaelicism into the whole fabric

of our national life. He wished to have Gaelic songs sung by the children in the schools. He advocated the boycotting of English goods, always with an eye to the spiritual effect. 'We shall need,' he said, 'to turn our towns into something more than mere huxters' shops, and, as a natural consequence, wells of anglicisation poisoning every section of our people.'

" Such was our policy. It differed not at all from that policy enunciated during the world war by many publicists in America. Just as it was urged there that Americans should be neither pro-British nor anti-British, but, on the contrary, should concentrate on being pro-American—so Sinn Fein aimed at making Irishmen pro-Irish. Only by developing our own resources, by linking up our life with the past and adopting the civilisation which was stopped by the Union could we become Gaels again and help win our nation back. As long as we were Gaels we knew the influence of the foreigner was negligible. Unless we were Gaels we had no claim to occupy a definite and distinct place in the world's life.

"'We most decidedly do believe,' said Rooney, 'that this nation has a right to direct its own destinies. We do most heartily concede that men bred and native of the soil are the best judges of what is good for this land. We are believers in an Irish nation using its own tongue, flying its own flag, defending its own coasts, and using its own discretion when dealing with the outside world. But this we most certainly believe can never come as the gift of any parliament, British or otherwise. It can only be won by the strong right arm and grim resolve of men. Neglect no weapon which the necessities and difficulties of the enemy force him to abandon to us, and make each concession a stepping-stone to further things.'

" Perhaps that is a sufficient answer to the charge that Sinn Fein was a pacifist organisation!

" Rooney spoke as a prophet. He prepared the way and foresaw the victory, and he helped his nation to rise and, by developing its soul, to get ready for victory."

"And you feel that the Treaty is, then, such a victory ?" I asked.

"Yes," came the instant answer. "It is just that. Ireland's victory is a fact ! In spite of Englishmen and sons of Englishmen—men who dare to pose as Irishmen and leaders of Irishmen—the Irish people are at last masters in their own house. And they will know how to deal with Erskine Childers and the others of his ilk.

"But let me attempt to state the bare facts of the case.

"Dail Eireann sent us to London to make a bargain with England. We made a bargain. We brought it back. The Irish people accepted it. Those are the indisputable facts.

"Our job in London was to 'reconcile Irish national aspirations with the association of Ireland with the community of nations known as the British Empire.' That job was as hard a one as was ever placed on the shoulders of men. We did not seek the job. When other men refused to go—we went. AND OUR CRITICS SHOULD REMEMBER THAT THE VERY FACT OF OUR GOING WAS ACKNOWLEDGMENT IN ITSELF THAT WE WERE PREPARED TO ACCEPT LESS THAN THE COMPLETE INDEPENDENCE OF AN ISOLATED REPUBLIC. NONE BETTER THAN DE VALERA KNEW THAT THIS WAS THE FACT.

"I signed the Treaty—not as an ideal thing—but fully believing what I believe now : that it safeguards the interests of Ireland and is everlasting proof of our right to recognition as a distinct nationality. By that Treaty I am going to stand, and every man with a scrap of honour who signed it will do the same. The suggestion that patriotism justifies or excuses a man in putting his signature to a bond of this kind—with his tongue in his cheek—is abominable. If any of the signatories to the Treaty adopts such a course he will write himself down a blackguard. The Irish people have declared emphatically that the Treaty is good enough for them, and the Irish people are our masters and not our slaves as some think. We are not dictators of the Irish people, but their representatives, and if we misrepresent them our moral authority and the strength behind us are gone, and gone for ever.

Arthur Griffith's Last Statement

"Now as to the efforts that have been made to show that certain men have stood uncompromisingly on the rock of the Republic and nothing but the Republic—the time has not yet arrived to prove that such statements are downright lies, but the time may not be far distant when the facts of the matter may safely be told. The men who have tried to make the Irish people believe this lie are the same men who have done their utmost to vilify the one man who made the negotiations possible—the man who won the war—Michael Collins. They have charged him with having compromised Ireland's rights. That is a lie.

"Every one of these detractors of Michael Collins—De Valera, Stack, Brugha, Childers—they deserve to be named—knows that Ireland's rights have never been in better hands in all Irish history. They know that in the letters that preceded the negotiations not once was a demand made for recognition of the Irish Republic. They know that if such a demand had been made there would have been no negotiations! And that is not all.

"WHILE THE NEGOTIATIONS WERE IN PROGRESS—DURING ONE OF THE MANY ADJOURNMENTS, WHILE WE WERE TEMPORARILY IN DUBLIN—DE VALERA BEGGED ME TO DEVISE A WAY TO GET HIM OUT OF THE REPUBLICAN STRAIT JACKET. I use his words.

"He was in an uncomfortable position. Nominally the leader of that section of the Dail styling themselves 'uncompromising Republicans,' he was actually the least radical of them all. Brugha and Stack—not to mention the women members of Dail Eireann—were determined that we should obtain nothing less than recognition of the Republic, even though the two men named well knew that it needed only the making of the demand for the negotiations to end abruptly. As President of the Republic De Valera felt he could not show less zeal than that of his followers. And yet he was faced with the fact that the course was worse than futile. He wanted to extricate himself from his predicament. He tried to do so—with the mysterious Document No. 2.

"That document was not written by De Valera; it was the product of Erskine Childers' brain. Three times this man who has spent most of the years of his life in the employ of his native country, England, drafted and redrafted Document No. 2. Three times we submitted it to Lloyd George. Three times he turned it down. There was nothing of a Republic in that document; it included an oath of allegiance to King George; it was not altogether unnatural—in view of its authorship—that it was decidedly more English than the Treaty itself! But let it not be forgotten that the man who now poses as an uncompromising Republican did everything in his power to saddle Ireland with an obligation very much more difficult to have met than is contained in the Treaty.

"For the same reasons that at this time I cannot allow these facts to be made public, and while they must not be made public so long as there is a chance of our settling our differences, I permitted my hands to be tied in the Dail. There I called the differences between Document No. 2 and the Treaty a quibble of words. For the purpose of the point I want to make it is enough to repeat this statement. Over this quibble of words De Valera and his followers are preparing to force the Irish people to go back to war with England. So far as my power can accomplish it, not one Irish life shall be lost over such a quibble.

"They put us in the dock—these uncompromising Republicans of the Dail. They tried us and found us guilty of treason to the Republic—THE REPUBLIC WHICH THEIR PRESIDENT HIMSELF HAD SECRETLY ABANDONED! The day will come when we shall be put on trial by the Irish people. It will be their verdict that will matter.

"We did our best for Ireland. If the Irish people had said—having got everything else but the name Republic—they would fight to get the name, I should have told them that they were fools—and then joined their ranks. But the Irish people did not do that. The Irish people are not fools!

"If a misguided, unrepresentative minority can stigmatise a whole people, if these uncompromising Republicans—whose actual and brainiest leader, Erskine Childers, is a renegade Englishman—can make it appear that the Irish people sponsor and share their madness, the world will not be fooled for long. The Irish people want peace. They want peace even to the extent of accepting alliance with England. For they see that in such an alliance Ireland can develop her own life, carry out her own way of existence, and rebuild her Gaelic civilisation. They want to end the bitter conflict of centuries—to end it for ever. If they wanted anything else they would be fools.

" Cathal Brugha said I might be immortalised by dishonouring my signature—by repudiating the Treaty. Whether I become an immortal or not is of no concern to me, and certainly to no one else. But no man who signed that Treaty could dishonour his signature without dishonouring the Irish nation. And that is a vital concern.

" Cathal Brugha also attempted to belittle Michael Collins—as a subordinate of no importance who had used the newspapers to make himself a national hero. I have gone on record that Michael Collins won the war. I said it in the Dail and I say it again. He is the man—and no one knows it better than I do—whose matchless energy and indomitable will carried Ireland through the years of the terror. If I had any ambition as a politician, if I would have immortal fame, if I longed to have my name go down in history, I should choose to have my name associated with the name of Michael Collins. Michael Collins beat the Black and Tan terror until England was forced to offer terms of peace.

" If I seem to dwell too long on the methods used by our opponents, it seems to me the facts justify me. During the long sessions of the Dail I wondered often at my very small imagination that had never visualised the heights of my own villainy. The abuse we listened to there had had no parallel since the days of Biddy Moriarity. They told us we were guilty of treason against the Republic. De Valera allowed that charge to be made—without protest.

Yet he knew, as I knew, that in one of his letters to Lloyd George he wrote this sentence:

"'We have no conditions to impose and no claim to advance but one, that we be free from aggression.

" He knew—because Lloyd George told him so at their meeting in July—that there would have been no negotiations had we insisted as a condition of the bargaining that England recognise the Republic. And still he made no move to stem the flood of abuse to which we were subjected by his followers.

" As for the attacks made upon me because of my attitude towards the Southern Unionists and the anti-Nationalists of Ulster, I hold that they are all my countrymen, and that if we are to have an Irish nation there must be fair play for all sections, and understanding between all sections. I met the Southern Unionists and promised them fair play. So far as I can control it, they shall have fair play. I hope to live to meet the Ulster Unionists upon the same basis. They are all members of the Irish nation, and their lives and fortunes are as much at stake as our own.

" THE MAN WHO THINKS WE CAN BUILD AN IRISH NATION AND MAKE IT FUNCTION SUCCESSFULLY WITH 800,000 OF OUR COUNTRYMEN IN THE NORTH-EAST AGAINST US, AND 400,000 OF OUR COUNTRYMEN IN THE SOUTH OPPOSED TO US, IS LIVING IN A FOOL'S PARADISE.

" I live in a world of realities, but that does not mean I have no dreams. I have dreamed. And I should like to make my dreams come true. But I have to face facts, and one fact is that Ireland is not equal in physical strength to England. The Treaty makes Ireland a sovereign State co-equal with the other States of the British Commonwealth. It gives Ireland essential unity because it recognises Ireland as a unit. It is for us to make that unity a fact!

" When I was a boy I was taught that the aim of Irish Nationalists was to get the British forces out of Ireland, to restore the Parliament of Ireland, and to make the Irish

Arthur Griffith's Last Statement

people sovereign in their own country. Under the Treaty these three aims have become accomplished facts. But here to-day a minority comprising Englishmen and sons of Englishmen tells the Irish people that the evacuation of Ireland by British troops is an injury to their soul, and the best way to save the soul of Ireland is to lacerate its body! That doctrine has been preached in Ireland before. I remember when I was young often hearing foolish people saying that the poorer the Irish people were the better their national spirit would be. If this were true—and De Valera has his way—we should be approaching the zenith of national spirit. But it is an absolute fallacy. In Ireland—as in any other land—the poorer the people are, the more dispirited they become.

" The men who in the name of idealism are doing their best to ruin their own country insist that we who signed the Treaty set a boundary to the march of our nation. That is a lie. By the Treaty we ended armed conflict between Ireland and England and made it possible to dwell beside her in peace and amity. As years pass it may be that changes in the relationship will come, but the Treaty insures that such changes will come by friendly agreement and not by force. No man can answer for the next generation. Meantime, we who accept the Treaty will work it honourably.

" And now one final fact: let no Irishman doubt for a moment that in signing the Treaty every one of the plenipotentiaries knew that we had got the last ounce it was possible to get out of England."

CHAPTER VI

THE AFTERMATH OF "EASTER WEEK"

"REBELLION—like any other potent remedy indulged in too often—can become a habit, a body and soul-destroying habit. It is not inaccurate to say that the senseless campaign of destruction now being waged by the madmen who have chosen to follow De Valera and the other 'uncompromising Republicans' is a direct consequence of the rising of Easter Week. It is an old story in Irish history—the story of misguided men mistaking the means for the end."

Collins thus approached the subject of the outstanding consequences of the 1916 rebellion.

"The immediate consequences," he continued, " may be divided into two parts—the consequences at home and the consequences abroad.

"The result at home was that—although not only did the British have in custody the men who had actually taken part in the fighting, but also the political activists from nearly every part of the country—nevertheless, the national spirit reawakened with marvellous promptitude. Popular feeling went entirely in favour of the insurgents, and it was thus possible for reorganisation to begin at an early date. Large and ever increasing numbers gave their adherence to the cause that was espoused in Easter Week, and more and more Irish eyes turned from the futility of representation in the British Parliament at Westminster, and of agitation there, to the utility of organisation at home and reliance on their own effort at home.

"Abroad the insurrection made it clear before people's minds that the Irish question had still to be settled, and

The Aftermath of "Easter Week"   59

had the effect of showing up Britain's claim to be the incorruptible champion of small nations. *In my own estimation the rising and the subsequent revival in Ireland, and the importance of the rising in its international character, were all inseparable from the thought and hope of a German victory.* Ireland's position at that time was to look to the Peace Conference for a settlement of the age-long dispute between Britain and herself."

"Is it your opinion," I asked, "that a German victory would have been better for Ireland than the Allied victory?"

"We thought so—then," Collins replied. "Our aim was to win our freedom. We believed that the worse England's plight was the better was our chance to compel her to grant our demand. I doubt if any of us looked so far ahead as to consider whether—our freedom once won—we could function most successfully with a triumphant Germany in the European saddle, and an England economically smashed. I think our only concern then was to win our freedom first, and let what followed take care of itself.

"We were not pro-German during the war—any more than we were pro-Bulgarian, pro-Turk, or anti-French. We were anti-British, pursuing our age-long policy against the common enemy. We were a weak nation kept in subjection by a stronger one, and we formed and adopted our policy in light of this fact. We remembered that England's difficulty was Ireland's opportunity, and we took advantage of her engagement elsewhere to make a bid for freedom. The odds between us were for the moment a little less unequal. Our hostility to England was the common factor between Germany and ourselves. We made common cause with France when France was fighting England. We made common cause with Spain when Spain was fighting England. We made common cause with the Dutch when the Dutch were fighting England.

"BASES IN IRELAND FOR GERMAN SUBMARINES?" Collins repeated my interjected question with an uplifting of his eyebrows, and a smile creeping into his eyes. For a space it seemed as if he were seeking a discreet answer. Then, the smile widening, he said, "OF COURSE NOT! WHO COULD IMAGINE SUCH A THING?"

SUBSEQUENTLY I LEARNED FROM AN INDISPUTABLY AUTHORITATIVE SOURCE THAT ON ONE OCCASION—DURING THE TREATY NEGOTIATIONS IN LONDON—WINSTON CHURCHILL AND ADMIRAL BEATTY PRODUCED AN ADMIRALTY MAP OF THE BRITISH ISLES AND SHOWED IT TO COLLINS. A RED-HEADED PIN INDICATED THE POSITION OF EVERY SHIP SUNK IN THOSE WATERS BY GERMAN SUBMARINES. BY FAR THE GREATEST NUMBER DOTTED THE IRISH COAST!

" The general mental attitude of a greater part of the Irish people," Collins continued, " was aptly described by a member of Dail Eireann, who declared—with fervent sincerity—that the day he had ceased to fight for the Irish Republic was the day he had ceased to be interested in it! I think this mental distortion goes a long way towards explaining the otherwise inexplicable madness of these irregulars now laying waste their own country. Under the leadership of men who are either fanatics or scoundrels, the Irregulars cherish the delusion that in destroying Ireland they are sanctifying her. But to return to the immediate aftermath of the rising.

" On the whole, it would, I think, be difficult to name any incident between April and December, 1916, as a ' high spot.' The one eventful thing that happened in this period was scarcely a high spot, but rather a low spot. It was the agreement of the Northern Convention of Nationalists to Partition. Aside from this one isolated incident, the Irish people responded well. A certain amount of reorganisation was effected throughout the country, and the revival of the national spirit was very marked. Just before Christmas of that year occurred probably the most important event of the whole period. It was the release of all the interned prisoners. Their release enabled us to make a really long stride in reorganisation.

" De Valera has been fond of citing the apathy of the American colonists as analogous to the lack of fervid support accorded us in those first months following the rising.

I have heard Erskine Childers liken De Valera to George Washington—and I have long suspected that De Valera does not dislike the parallel. It is a fact, of course, that only in garbled versions of history are a whole people shown to be as keenly determined in any cause as their leaders. Undoubtedly those of us who had had the wonderful inspiration that came from intimate association with such mighty Fenians as Tom Clarke and Sean McDermott were more grimly determined to win the fight they had died to win than peaceably inclined folk who lacked that inspiring association. Yet the results of the first eight months following the rising were all that could have been expected.

" The first important event of 1917 was the Parliamentary election for the North Roscommon Division. Here was an opportunity to measure the extent to which the national spirit had been revived. We seized the opportunity—and contested this election against the old Irish Parliamentary party. But let no present-day stalwart—above all, let De Valera not attempt to—forget one curious and instructive feature of that election campaign ! It was fought only five years ago—but our candidate on that occasion did not even make abstention from Westminster part of his pre-election platform. The prominent workers studiously avoided mention of this subject. As for the Irish Republic—so far as that campaign was concerned, it had ceased to exist !

" It is well to face the facts in matters of this kind and to tell the truth, however unpalatable the truth may now be to those who call themselves uncompromising Republicans. Therefore, let it be recorded that the greatest amount of support for our candidate in that election came from the Irish National League—*which did not approve of abstention from Westminster !* For the rest, our supporters were chiefly persons who had become entirely dissatisfied with the policy of the Irish Parliamentary party.

" SO MUCH HAD THE REPUBLIC OF EASTER WEEK BEEN FORGOTTEN, AND SO LITTLE HAD THE TEACHINGS YET PENETRATED INTO THE MINDS OF THE PEOPLE, THAT ALTHOUGH

OUR CANDIDATE WAS COUNT PLUNKETT—WHOSE SON HAD BEEN MARTYRED AFTER THE RISING—HE WAS RETURNED ONLY ON THE GROUND OF HIS OPPOSITION TO THE IRISH PARTY CANDIDATES! IT WAS ONLY AFTER HIS ELECTION THAT HE DECLARED HIS INTENTION NOT TO GO TO WESTMINSTER, AND THE ANNOUNCEMENT WAS NOT RECEIVED VERY ENTHUSIASTICALLY BY SOME OF THE MOST ENERGETIC OF HIS SUPPORTERS. THEY HAD ELECTED A MAN, THEY SAID, 'WHO DID NOT INTEND TO REPRESENT THEM ANYWHERE.'

"The next event of importance in 1917 was the arrest of Sinn Feiners in Dublin and throughout the country. More than forty men of influence in their communities, important local figures aside from their Sinn Fein affiliations, were deported to England. They were not actually imprisoned —and both their activities and their prestige increased rather than diminished as a result of their temporary banishment. It was but one of many similar instances of English Governmental stupidity—of England's unwitting aid in arousing the Irish people to that national unity which finally forced the ancient enemy to give us freedom. The deported forty, relieved of the necessity of pursuing their usual, personal occupations, were able to devote all of their time to furthering the aims of Sinn Fein. Their presence in England lent to their work an especial significance! But that is a story to be told elsewhere.

"Meantime, we at home were not idle. Following our victory in North Roscommon, reorganisation proceeded more rapidly than before. Two committees were now actively working—the old Sinn Fein committee and the new committee formed of members of the original committee and others who had been prominent workers in the North Roscommon campaign. As part of the reorganisation scheme a proposal was made that we should send a circular to all the public bodies in Ireland asking them to appoint delegates to a conference to be held in Dublin. Many of these public bodies did not even respond, and many of them carried the resolution to send delegates only by a bare majority. The greatest proportion of support came from the South. The

The Aftermath of " Easter Week "

conference was held, and it was decided to organise the country on the basis of abstention from the Westminster Parliament and a general policy of virile opposition against British rule in Ireland.

" While arrangements were proceeding for this conference, a vacancy arose for the Parliamentary Division of South Longford. Feeling in South Longford was not advanced politically, and the wisdom of putting forward a candidate from our side was questioned by many. However, we decided to adopt the bold course, and we put forward the name of Joe McGuinness, who was then serving a penal servitude sentence in Lewes. The election was warmly contested. Our principal appeal to the electorate was evidenced by two of our slogans—' The man in jail for Ireland ' and ' Put him in to get him out.' All of us worked hard for the felon candidate, and he was returned a winner by a majority of 27 votes.

" Once again let me emphasize a fact that cannot be gainsaid. At that election the Irish Republic was not an issue. Our uncompromising Republicans were yet to announce themselves. Joe McGuinness triumphed only because the people remembered Easter Week, and the men who died for it.

" And then followed—almost immediately—complete corroboration of our election slogan. The British Government released all of the penal servitude prisoners from Lewes ! These releases gave the final fillip to the reorganisation scheme, and were, of course, acclaimed a great triumph for our cause.

" Among these prisoners were three men who had served in the rising as commandants. One of them was De Valera. Then, as always afterwards, De Valera exercised an ascendancy over Harry Boland that amounted almost to hypnotic control. Boland's devotion to De Valera was the kind that is born of hero-worship. I am convinced Boland believed that Ireland's salvation was inseparably bound up in the person of De Valera. I have every reason to believe that Boland was absolutely sincere in this. But out of this situation arose a remarkable sequence of closely related consequences.

" Some time prior to their release De Valera and Boland and several others were being transferred from Dartmoor to Lewes. On the journey Boland managed to write a note, unobserved by the guards, and dropped it out of the window of the railway coach. He had addressed the envelope to a friend in Dublin. Curiously enough, it was picked up by an Irish girl walking along the tracks. She posted it, and in due course Boland's eulogy of De Valera—for that was what he had written—reached its destination. According to the note (and it must be borne in mind that at that time nobody in Ireland had any idea of the truth about their fellow-countrymen imprisoned in England), De Valera had been unanimously proclaimed their leader, and eventually would prove himself worthy of being leader of the whole Irish nation. The news spread like wildfire. In a week De Valera leaped from relative obscurity into first place in the hearts of the Irish people. It was exactly what had been lacking until then—a romantic figure, persecuted by the hereditary enemy—a martyred, living hero !

" Just before the releases, and while the new De Valera hero-legend was spreading throughout the country, a vacancy occurred in Clare, the constituency in which De Valera belonged. Here was another golden opportunity. With De Valera as our candidate we scored an impressive victory, winning for him a majority of almost 3,000 out of an electorate of 8,000. This victory sounded the death knell of the Irish Parliamentary party. But that was not its chief distinctive feature. It marked the beginning of public agitation in favour of the Irish Republic.

" De Valera in an English prison had obviously nothing to do with the injection of this new note in the election campaign. The talk in favour of the Irish Republic was spontaneous. At last our teachings, the lesson of Easter Week, the ultimate ideals of the men who had died for Ireland were beginning to be understood. But it is as well to bear in mind that in Clare—where the political spirit was strong and ardent—it was felt quite safe to talk about the Irish Republic. Elsewhere, however, it was not yet a topic of discussion or, where it was bruited, the talk was done in whispers!

"With the Longford victory behind us the Sinn Fein organisation had been growing very powerful, and now the Clare triumph enabled us to go ahead with such vigour that practically every other political organisation in the country was put out of existence.

"Close on the heels of these successes we determined to contest the Kilkenny election—the first borough constituency we had contested. Business interests being strong in Kilkenny, we selected as our candidate a business man—Alderman W. T. Cosgrave, a member of the Dublin Corporation. He won the election by a vote of practically two to one. Sinn Fein began to feel itself secure. It seemed as if it held political sway over almost all of Ireland.

"Our complaisance received a rude shock, however, in the Waterford election. Here the Sinn Fein nominee was defeated—the first defeat we had suffered. There were, of course, explanatory causes, but it was none the less a reverse in our fortunes.

"Finally, the outstanding event of 1917 was the Sinn Fein Convention in Dublin in October. To that first Ard Fheis there came from all parts of the country delegates from 1,500 Sinn Fein clubs. A standing committee was elected, and the machinery of Ireland's first practical national organisation was perfected. Here for the first time in Irish history was union of all the various sects and leagues—every dissentient view put aside in the interest of the common cause. But again let me emphasize the fact that that cause was not the Irish Republic. The one national policy Sinn Fein then defined was that of definite abstention from the Westminster Parliament.

"The Republic of Easter Week had not lived on, as is supposed. The real importance of the rising did not begin to become apparent until 1918. The men who are now wrecking their country—visiting insensate vengeance upon their own people for 'letting down the Republic'—know that their accusation is false. The declaration of a Republic by the leaders of the rising was far in advance of national thought. It was only after two years of propaganda that we were able to get solidity on the idea. Our real want was so simple, so old, so urgent—liberation from English occupation—it is not surprising that doctrinaire Republicanism made little appeal to the Irish people.

" The truth is best served by plain speaking. The Irish people at this moment are not wedded to the theory of a Republican form of government. There is only one reason why the Irish people have ever wanted a Republic—it is because the British form of government is monarchical! To express as emphatically as possible our desire to be different from England we declared a Republic! We repudiated the British form of government not because it was monarchical, but because it was British! If England were a Republic we undoubtedly would find a descendant of an Irish king—and establish a monarchy! So much for the inherent virtue of a Republic—as Irish eyes see it!"

Collins made it plain that the interview had lasted as long as he could afford to have it. As always, he disguised his dismissal of me with characteristic tact.

" And now I'll be getting on with the affairs of the Irish Free State," he announced. As he spoke there was that suspicion of a chuckle in his voice that always preceded his making a joke. " I suppose," he added, " I'd have no time for you at all if this were a Republic!"

" To-morrow night," he continued seriously, " I'm going to have you meet the one man who was closer in the confidence of the leaders of the rising than any other man alive to-day—Sean McGarry. There are many things he can tell you of the days before the rising, and, of them all, I am myself most anxious to hear the real story of the gun-running at Howth, and just what part Erskine Childers played in it."

CHAPTER VII

COLLINS' ESTIMATE OF ERSKINE CHILDERS

As so frequently happened during the feverish nine months of my association with Collins, his plan to have me meet Sean McGarry the following evening miscarried.

At that time McGarry was in charge of the detachment of National troops guarding the Amiens Street railway station. When I arrived at the place appointed for the meeting, I found Collins with his ear to a telephone receiver and a broad grin on his face. He motioned me towards another telephone instrument and with a gesture invited me to listen.

The amusing part of it was McGarry's deadly seriousness. For he was explaining in as technically correct military language as he knew how to use—addressing himself to the Commander-in-Chief of his army—that Irregular snipers were at the moment making exit from the station "inadvisable." Only to one who appreciated that for ten years or more Collins had been "Mick" to Sean McGarry could the humour of the conversation become fully apparent.

Eventually Collins had me meet McGarry—and it proved one of the most interesting and informative sessions of any at which I was present. And it was not until afterwards that Collins determined to go on record himself regarding the chief figure of McGarry's tale—Erskine Childers.

When Collins finally decided to expose Childers, whom he regarded as the evil genius of Ireland, he imposed the condition that it was not to be made public until every effort to effect a truce had been exhausted. He was planning then a last attempt to induce De Valera to end the senseless campaign—an effort which, it will be recalled, he announced officially the day that Griffith died.

To the very end he clung to the hope that De Valera would have the moral courage to call a halt, to disperse the brigands and turn over their arms to the Provisional Government ; but the night he took me into his confidence regarding Childers he promised that it would be a short time only before either peace came or I should be free to let the world know the truth about the man Collins held primarily responsible for Ireland's tragic plight.

Collins' murder has removed that restriction—as I see it—and more than justifies my setting down here his denunciation of the man who, Collins believed, cared for no country and served none, but was consumed with a maniacal lust for destruction.

" Of all the many men who for hundreds of years have done Ireland grievous harm," Collins began, " none has managed to deal the Irish people such an overwhelming blow as Erskine Childers. This Englishman may be sincere in all that he professes, and so far as I am concerned it makes little difference what his actual motives are. The fact remains that he has worked steadily since 1912 inflicting damage on the Irish cause. The pity of it is that those of us who have known the facts have felt that it was inadvisable to make them public. The time has come when the truth must be told.

" It may be recalled that Brugha in the last session of the Dail eulogised Childers and declared he had done more for Ireland than any other living man—the eulogy accompanying his motion calling on the Dail to pass a vote of censure on President Griffith for having called Childers a ' damned Englishman.' Brugha is dead, but Childers is very much alive. My own feeling is that Childers not only never worked any good to Ireland ; he consistently and continuously has done Ireland harm. Ten years ago, Childers—then in the English Civil Service, and with more or less influence among a certain coterie in the House of

Commons—was urging in every way at his command that the British Government should grant the Irish people a measure of freedom that was as unthinkable from an English view as it was greater and more radical than the most advanced Irishman dreamed of getting.

"Then, as at all times since, this Englishman was damning any chance Ireland might have had of winning reasonable concessions from England—by advocating an extreme course of action which must inevitably heighten English hostility against us.

"Down through the years, Childers' record shows he never once deviated from his set purpose always to be more extreme than the most extreme of the Irish Radicals. I have said it makes little difference whether he is sincere— the fact that every proposal of his has been impracticable when it has not been positively damaging being enough in itself; but that does not mean that I have not a very definite opinion as to his sincerity. Twenty years ago Childers wrote a book in which he made out a perfect case for an astounding kind of super spy—the *agent provocateur*. His ingenious scheme was nothing less than having the spy join the extreme faction in an enemy country, and lead them to excesses that would eventually bring about the desired war. That was the Childers of twenty years ago. Let us look into his activities as a champion of the cause of Irish freedom, keeping in mind this scheme he sponsored.

"Darrell Figgis went to Belgium in June 1914, and bought two thousand rifles and ammunition at Liége A Belgian sea-going tug carried the purchase to an agreed rendezvous in the North Sea, where the cargo was transhipped to Childers' yacht. Eventually we got possession of the guns and ammunition—and the whole world presently learned of the gun-running at Howth. Would anyone suggest that Childers' part in this exploit is inconsistent with his professed belief in the efficacy of his super-spy system? What practical good could be realised from our getting possession of a relative handful of weapons?

"On the other hand, the widespread publicity given to

the exploit furnished England with a new and substantial ground for dealing sternly with the impossible Irish malcontents. But even more than this Childers may have had in mind.

"At that time Carson's armed forces in Ulster were drilling and preparing to wage war upon us—at least, that is what many Irishmen honestly believed. What could suit England's wishes better than such a war? How could it be precipitated more surely than by furnishing arms in discreetly inadequate quantities to the side which, unarmed, had no choice except passive acceptance of the Ulster menace? Fortunately, for once we avoided making the error of doing what Ireland's enemies fully expected. It was for Easter Week those guns were intended, and it was in Easter Week only that they were used.

"The English zealot in Ireland's cause—what do we find him doing next? Within less than a month after the Howth gun-running, Childers was enlisting in the English Secret Service in the world war, repeating the services he had rendered his Empire in the South African war. Many times in the past few years Childers has attempted to explain in conversations with me his reasons for voluntarily aiding the nation he swore he loathed—always emphasising the fact that he had done no more than tens of thousands of born Irishmen had done, and, as he tried to put it, for the same reason—his natural love of a fight and adventure. Always he finished by saying that he was sorry, but better men than he had made mistakes.

"Then in 1917 Childers met De Valera.

"It was an unhappy moment for Ireland when this illogical, incompetent, inexperienced school-teacher came under the spell of Childers—a genius as brilliant as De Valera is guileless. It was Childers who wrote the famous Document No. 2. It is Childers who has guided practically every action of De Valera the past five years. I was strongly opposed to Childers' presence in the delegation of treaty plenipotentiaries, even as a secretary, but De Valera would not listen to my objections. There was no room for doubt

Collins' Estimate of Erskine Childers 71

that De Valera firmly believed that Childers was the only man upon whom he could depend.

"And what did Childers do in London? I risk the charge of being indiscreet in revealing what I am about to reveal—but considerations of that kind cannot weigh with me when the fate of the Irish people depends, as it does, on their knowing the truth about this man. He had told De Valera, Brugha, Stack and others in Dublin that he had a great scheme by which he could argue the British Government into recognising that there was no danger in her granting Ireland's demand for a republic. Griffith and the rest of us plenipotentiaries had no such scheme, wherefore, in due course, it was decided that Childers should have a chance of putting his scheme into execution.

"He had been most secretive about it all along, and I had no idea what it was when we went together by appointment to the Colonial Office one day last November, and there met Winston Churchill and Lord Beatty. The latter had a huge map brought over from the Admiralty at Childers' request. It showed Britain, Ireland and the European coast.

"'Now, gentlemen,' began Childers, 'I mean to demonstrate that Ireland is not only no source of danger to England, but, from a military standpoint, is virtually useless.' This announcement staggered me probably more than it did the other two. It was such ridiculous balderdash, I felt like wanting to get out of the room, but I naturally realised that I must make a pretence of standing by my colleague. Churchill and Beatty exchanged glances, and then gave Childers their attention again. 'Take the matter of Irish bases for English submarine chasers,' the latter continued. 'From the viewpoint of naval expediency Plymouth is a far better base than any port on the Irish coast.'

"'You really think so?' asked Beatty.

"Childers insisted he did, adding, 'For instance, supposing Ireland were not there at all?'

"'Ah,' said Beatty, with a smile, 'but Ireland *is* there.'

"'And how many times,' interjected Churchill, 'have we wished she were not!'

"And that was Childers' great idea, and it was all of it! The argument with which he was going to persuade the British Government to recognise the Irish Republic got no further. I never felt more a fool in my whole life. Yet to this day De Valera and others believe that Childers' scheme failed only because we of the delegation did not back him whole-heartedly.

"From my own experience in dealing with British Ministers I am convinced that nothing could more surely weaken any cause in their eyes than ridiculously stupid espousal of the cause. Lloyd George, Mr. Churchill—all of them—were responsive and reasonable so long as we put forward our points with rational argument, but Childers was a member of the secretariat, and well known by Lloyd George to be De Valera's personal representative.

"Was this merely another instance of Childers' doing Ireland grievous damage unwittingly? For my part, I find it difficult to believe that Childers ever did one unwitting act in his life, but, having said this, I repeat that it makes little difference. The only important fact that the Irish people must fully appreciate is that Erskine Childers—wittingly or unwittingly—has already done, and is now doing, his utmost to effect Ireland's ruin."

Had Collins lived he might have extended the prohibition regarding the release of this interview, but now that he is dead—and who will say that it was not Childers' brain which conceived and organised the Bandon ambush?—I take upon myself the responsibility of showing up the man Michael Collins counted worse than despicable.

CHAPTER VIII

COLLINS' PLAN OF TERRORISING TERRORISTS

"CONSIDERATION of the events in Ireland in 1918, in order to be comprehensive, must embrace two entirely distinct and different developments—one entirely political, the other wholly militant. But before I begin this part of my story I want to take this opportunity of correcting a misapprehension that exists widely regarding the part Lloyd George was playing in Irish affairs at that time. It is generally supposed that the English Premier was responsible for instituting the Black and Tan reign of terror, as well as the provocative acts of terrorisation which preceded the coming of the Black and Tans. This is untrue.

"In those days Lloyd George did not have time for Ireland—his whole attention being absorbed by the world war. The British Government's Irish policy, so far as military operations were concerned, was conceived and executed by Cabinet Ministers to whom Lloyd George had given a free hand.

"Unhappily, during the years that followed the Armistice he could not take the time to attempt to find a solution of the Irish question, counting it of less importance to England than a settlement of the European problem. For what happened then, in the period 1918 to 1921, Lloyd George had only nominal responsibility. I emphasise this fact because it seems to me high time that we who know the truth should disseminate it, and by so doing help to remove the causes of hatred and bitterness which are largely based on ignorance."

Collins made this statement to me at the outset of one

of our last meetings in Dublin—again evidencing what had come to be his greatest driving ambition—ending fratricidal strife by ending venomous and deliberate distortion of the truth.

"Taking the political events of 1918," Collins continued, "the most important incident was the South Armagh election. In this election we were at the outset confident of success, and we put up as our candidate Dr. MacCarton, who was the representative of the Irish Republic in Washington. For the second time we were defeated. Unquestionably the result of that election was a serious setback for our policy.

"Secondly, at this time, February and March, there was much talk of applying the British Conscription Act to Ireland, and arrangements were being made by us to resist it in every possible way. The Volunteers came to the decision at their Executive Council that conscription was to be resisted to the fullest extent of our military strength.

"Thirdly, the arrest of the chief leaders of Sinn Fein. There were just some half-dozen in Dublin and some few dozen throughout the country marked down for arrest who escaped the net. This, however, must not be taken as meaning that the backbone of the movement was gone. Political organisation was continued always without interference. The enemy activity up to this period had really not been very serious, and enemy activity after what are now called 'the German plot arrests' was mainly directed towards preventing public meetings, tracking down and arresting public suspects, and stopping parades, drills, training, etc., of Volunteers.

"Fourthly, towards the end of the year came the Armistice in the world war, and with it a General Election. Sinn Fein selected candidates to fight in almost every constituency in the whole of Ireland and won a decided victory at the polls. Our political machinery was altogether too efficient for the Irish Parliamentary party organisation, and the election started by our having 25 unopposed returns. Many of the Sinn Fein candidates were men who were in

Collins' Plan of Terrorising Terrorists 75

gaol or interned, and it must be admitted that the names of these candidates made an appeal in addition to the political appeal. It will be remembered that Sinn Fein immediately after the election sent representatives to London at the time of President Wilson's visit to lay a memorial of the Irish case before him.

"Paralleling our political victories were the ever increasing acts of repression practised by the British Government, although at first neither England's aggression nor oppression were more than suggestions of what was to come. During the year England had pronounced Dail Eireann, the Irish Republican Party, Sinn Fein, Cumman na m'Bann, the Gaelic League and the Gaelic Athletic Association illegal bodies. The Civil Courts were for the most part dispensed with and replaced by Courts Martial. For trivial offences severe sentences were inflicted. Possession of a card of membership in Sinn Fein earned a penalty of from six months' to two years' imprisonment. Raids by armed bands of police and soldiers began to become frequent. Gradually it was becoming apparent that England had given up trying to rule Ireland with anything less than force.

"The inevitable result of this policy—as indeed must have been anticipated by the British Government—was to drive the Irish people to meet desperate methods by desperate reprisals. The more extreme the British methods became, the more united our people grew.

"From time immemorial England had always maintained in Ireland one of the greatest and most efficient Secret Services in the world—a Secret Service which had for its corner-stone a historical and unhappy fact about the Irish people, the presence in every generation of a small minority ready to sell their country for English gold. Without the aid of these traitors, who were almost entirely corner boys, ne'er-do-wells and rogues—ragged, penniless and mentally dwarfed—England's Secret Service in Ireland would have been a far less potent factor.

"As it was, there were spies in every street bent on obtaining information that would damn their brother Irishmen.

In those days there were few public-houses in Dublin that did not shelter after nightfall a British Secret Service operative in the midst of a group of corner boys, for whom he was buying quantities of strong liquor. By the payment of a few shillings in cash and liberally plying them with drink, the operative never failed to obtain from these miserable outcasts the information desired.

"In this way the total number of English operatives represented, probably, one-tenth of the actual total of the spy organisation. Every street in every city was an open book to the English agents.

"The efforts of Dublin Castle to make the spy organisation as complete as possible did not end with these underworld ragamuffins: Irishmen in high positions were reached. Instances of this, however, were rare. But, after all, human nature is human nature, and £1,000 is £1,000—and £1,000 is very much more to an Irishman than to an Englishman or an American. A man in this country who possesses such a sum is relatively well-to-do."

Collins did not have to stress the point. I knew that hardly one member of the Provisional Government had ever been worth £1,000 at any stage of his life. The temptation that a £1,000 bribe would exert on an average Irishman—and this is true only because of the difference in his financial status—is equal to the effect of a bribe ten times as big on an Englishman or an American.

"The English Secret Service in Ireland," Collins continued, "with its unlimited supplies of money, had been unquestionably able to reach men of influence and position within our organisation. Most of these traitors met their just deserts down through all the years.

"When the Fenian leader who betrayed his comrades—the men who committed the Phœnix Park assassinations—had thought himself for all time safe from Irish vengeance, he suddenly found that the long arm of the Irish Republican Brotherhood could reach out to the farthest ends of the earth and, in the name of Ireland, mete out justice. It was only when the English ship that had carried him away with

£10,000 of English money, his reward for delivering up his colleagues, was steaming into a South African port that he was shot dead by an emissary of the Brotherhood travelling on the same ship.

" Thus every Irish youth for many generations had known in a general way of the English spy system, and how it had been always tremendously strengthened by the help of renegade Irishmen. But up to the end of 1918 we had done little to combat it.

" Griffith had won a vast majority of the best elements in all parts of Ireland to his way of thinking and to the Sinn Fein policy of moderation—urged by him for thirteen years with little success until then. But gradually he had led public opinion to believe that his was the best course for Ireland to pursue.

" The words ' Sinn Fein ' have been generally misunderstood to mean ' ourselves alone '—a mistake which even Griffith never took occasion to correct. While that is the literal translation of the Gaelic, it is not the real meaning of the phrase. To one conversant with the ancient Irish language, Sinn Fein means ' self-reliance '—obviously a very different thing. Unhappily the Irish people even yet have learned little of self-reliance. To-day they depend too much on a few leaders. What else can be expected after 700 years of subjection ? But the Irish people must acquire self-reliance and put an end for all time to their present custom of waiting for a superman to lead them into possession of full freedom.

" Other nations must understand the state of mind of the average Irishman which makes this a land where public opinion is privately expressed. For many hundreds of years this was the only way opinion could be expressed. It was still the case in 1918—with the important difference that people were beginning at last to awaken to the truth.

" The triumph of the Sinn Fein candidates was proof positive that the people were prepared to accept the responsibility involved in self-reliance. We so interpreted the overwhelming support the people gave Griffith's policy—but, unfortunately, we did not fully appreciate their inability to know how to translate their willingness into practical terms. We firmly believed that we had at the most only to point the way in order to range a united people on our side. This mistake must be borne in mind as the events of the succeeding years are recorded.

"We leaders committed the Irish people to a definite course of action. As little by little some of us began to realise that we had to depend upon ourselves in winning through to the final success of our new policy, we found it necessary to adopt more extreme measures than would have been the case had we had the active, united support of the whole people. I am making no apology for what we did in these succeeding years—I hope merely to explain the necessity which drove us.

"What we accomplished is the Treaty—a hundredfold greater result than many of us at the end of 1918 would have dared to prophesy our new policy would win for us.

"That policy was based on a recognition of the two most urgent problems with which we were faced at that time—beating the English Secret Service until it was powerless, and cleaning our own house until the last traitor Irishman had been identified and fittingly dealt with. It was a job of Herculean proportions, and until and unless it was done thoroughly, freedom could never come to Ireland. Within the inner circle of the Irish Republican Army there was no unanimity of opinion that the new policy was wise—men like Brugha and Stack, who cherished the delusion that we could by the use of force alone drive the English army out of Ireland, having no faith in Irishmen's ability to outwit English brains. Perhaps, because I, more than anyone else, disputed this admission of inferiority, it was upon my shoulders that the heavy task of solving this twofold problem was laid."

The following afternoon, in a private dining-room in the Shelbourne Hotel, where I was his luncheon guest, Collins told me the inside story of his striking terror into the hearts of the Black and Tans.

CHAPTER IX

OUTWITTING THE BLACK AND TANS

" THE English Secret Service in Ireland for centuries had broken every movement ever attempted by Irishmen to make Ireland an independent nation. The espionage staff of the British forces of control in Ireland, operating from their headquarters in Dublin Castle, was a body to which England had every right to point with pride. It was a costly organisation to maintain, but it was maintained regardless of cost—the annual total in pre-war times having been approximately £250,000. This was the expenditure when there was little or no talk of an Irish revolutionary movement. Following the outbreak of the world war, even before the Easter Week rising, the cost of administrating the spy system has been reckoned to have totalled a million pounds a year.

" From 1916 on, countless millions were spent. Secret Service money was to be had almost for the raising of an eyebrow. I always find satisfaction in the thought that much of this reckless buying of information brought cold comfort to Dublin Castle—when it was discovered that the information was nothing more than the figment of a patriotic Irishman's imagination. But with the coming of the Black and Tans in 1919, this hitherto safe and profitable form of romancing was quickly robbed of its appeal—the Black and Tans evidencing their dislike of being victimised by the torture and often the murder of their victimisers.

" The coming of the Black and Tans was England's immediate and direct answer to our establishing our own Intelligence Staff, of which I had been appointed chief."

Aware as I was of Collins' disinclination to cite instances

of cruelty on the part of the English forces, this reference to torture and murder, with which he had begun his story on this occasion, led me to anticipate that he was about to depart from his former policy of silence in this respect. But it was not to be. He refrained from citing any specific instances of Black and Tan cruelty. He made it sufficiently plain to me that it was his wish that this phase of the story be not told, to impel me, now that he is gone, to say only that I have seen photographic evidence of hideous brutality of which the Black and Tans were guilty—not to mention trustworthy eyewitness testimony of outrages committed by the army whose prime reason for being was to strike terror to Ireland.

" Before we could turn our attention to the Black and Tans," Collins continued, " we had to create our own organisation and first use it to clean English spies out of the Irish Republican Army. This alone was no easy task, but before it was finished there were left within the Irish Republican Army only men who were whole-heartedly prepared to give their lives for Ireland.

" Opposition of no mean character met our determined drive against weather-cock politicians, irresponsibles and others of similar ilk, whose presence in the Irish Republican Army, while perhaps not dangerous, was distinctly detrimental to its morale. At all stages during the process of cleaning up our own forces we had constantly to fight the unreasoning antagonism of Cathal Brugha. Poor Brugha! As Cosgrave truly said, he was a great fighter—' but not worth a damn for anything else!' I was never antagonistic to Brugha—he was fortunately not important enough to make it necessary for me to notice his hostility. However, to be just to De Valera, it is a fact that more than once he prevented Brugha's tremendous disapproval of me and my methods from leading his Minister of Defence to attempt any deed of rashness.

" Finally this part of the job was finished. Every man had been tested—tested thoroughly. First I did it myself and thus satisfied myself regarding the trustworthiness of my chief aids. Then, gradually, the finding of the true measure of each new man became automatic and in turn the cleaning out of the ranks of the Irish Republican Army of undesirables became easier and faster. Now the time had come to turn our attention to the most important part of our job—the smashing of the English Secret Service. My final goal was not to be reached merely by beating it out of existence—I wanted to replace it with a better, and an Irish Secret Service. The way to do this was obvious, and it fell naturally into two main parts—making it unhealthy for Irishmen to betray their fellows, and making it deadly for Englishmen to exploit them. It took several months to accomplish the first job—actually the most important part —and hardly more than a month to disrupt the morale of the English Secret Service, to a point at which its efficiency ceased to be the proud thing that it always had been.

"To Englishmen who knew the meaning of the appellation, the Political Section of the 'G' Division of the Secret Service meant everything that was finest and most admirable in the whole range of the British Empire's detective organisations. To gain admission into the 'G' Division was the dream of all Secret Service operatives. For the most part the personnel of this undeniably brave outfit commanded my admiration. But, as I shall have occasion to point out more than once before I finish this tale, their bravery frequently outdistanced their judgment. My own experience leads me to hold that it is wiser for those who have the selecting of men for positions in which bravery and judgment are equal requirements to choose clever cowards rather than stupid heroes.

"Within a short time after we had convinced the Irish traitors that it was best that they sever their connection with Dublin Castle, our own operatives identified six of the highest placed and most efficient English spies. It was my policy to acquaint this sextette with the fact that we knew them and had them under constant surveillance. In order to remove any doubt from their minds, I saw to it that they were furnished with typewritten reports of their own activities during the preceding twenty-four hours—several days in succession. The terror with which they hoped to reduce Irishmen to the stage of abject surrender now began to creep into their own ranks. Gradually, English operatives, who had been working night and day against us, began to see the practical wisdom of shifting their allegiance and joining our forces— to save their own skins ! Thus gradually we built up a counter spy system, operating within Dublin Castle itself.

"From this point onward, I had reliable advance information of virtually all impending events contemplated by the British. It was testing the reliability of this advance information that was largely responsible for the reputation I began to acquire as a dare-devil. For instance, one day it was told me that the Black and Tans had discovered the house at which I was in the habit of lunching every other Thursday. My information was that the Black and Tans were planning to watch the house the following Thursday, and to have a large force ready to raid it one minute after noon—the hour when I always entered it. I was not too sure of the reliability of this information, and it was absolutely necessary for me to make sure. Therefore, exactly at noon on the Thursday I rode my bicycle down the street and stopped in front of the watched house. I entered it through the basement, carrying my bicycle with me. Within one minute the Black and Tans came rushing from all directions and burst into the house. Thus I discovered that the information had been accurate and my informant trustworthy !

"It was not quite so foolhardy as it sounds, because a perfect means of escape had been previously arranged—a tunnel having been dug under the backyard into the cellar of an abutting house, through which I was able to run with my bicycle. Actually, I was on my way through the heart of Dublin a few moments later.

"But of course, in order to make this test, I had come under the scrutiny of, perhaps, two score of Black and Tans. In this connection let me refute the rumour that I resorted to disguises. I never did. I carried convincing papers, it is true, that established my identity as another man—and more than once was held up and searched by Black and Tans. But disguise was unnecessary and foolish.

"The occasion which received, perhaps, greater publicity than any other—when British soldiers surrounded the entire square in which is situated the Mansion House in Dublin, into which I had been seen to go—has been distorted in every way imaginable. A secret meeting of the leaders of the Irish Republican Army had been arranged and was being held in an inner room of the Mansion House at 3 o'clock in the afternoon. The dozen of us present all believed we had managed to get into the building unobserved. In this we were mistaken.

"Joe O'Reilly, my closest confidant, walking with two girl friends in Grafton Street that afternoon happened to overhear a British soldier just ahead of him telling a comrade that there was going to be ' a big show ' at the Mansion House in an hour or so. Joe waited to hear no more, but left the girls abruptly and took it on the run for the Mansion House. He burst in on us like a cyclone and announced the impending raid. All the others rushed out a back way and made good their escape, but I had to remain behind to safeguard invaluable documents which we had been studying, and which we could not afford just then to destroy.

"Two minutes later, the soldiers in armoured cars and afoot came rushing from all directions and quickly formed a cordon that completely encircled the Mansion House. The Lord Mayor hurried in and demanded to know what I could hope to do to avoid capture. It was easy enough—requiring only the sheets from two beds in an upper part of the Mansion House!

"With these sheets I made a rope which O'Reilly lowered down through the chimney from the roof of the Round Room and up which I climbed.

"When the British officers came swaggering in, the Lord Mayor met them and denounced their intrusion as unwarrantable. Meantime, Joe had got busy with a big germicide sprayer which he, inadvertently, most of the time pointed straight at the immaculate intruders. The Lord Mayor established Joe's identity as a cleaner, dutifully attending to the business of fumigating the Mansion House.

"For four hours they searched the Mansion House—and everything in it except the chimney in the Round Room. They were hardly to be blamed for overlooking that hiding-place—it must have seemed a waste of time, inasmuch as a blazing fire was burning in the fireplace!

"O'Reilly had lit that fire at my order. Before he had done so I had climbed the sheet rope half-way up the chimney. At this point I knew that there was a flue from a fireplace on the second floor. Climbing just above this flue I managed to get out of my clothes which I used to stuff up the chimney beneath me. The smoke did not reach me but passed out through the flue into the room to which O'Reilly had gone and opened the windows and created a draught.

"Although there was no smoke that amounted to any-thing my position was hardly comfortable, and as night came on it was a bit chilly for a man completely nude.

"Meantime, the British officers showed no intention of leaving the Mansion House until they had found me. But they were not counting on the resourcefulness of Joe O'Reilly. His cleaning operations finished, off he went on his bicycle to supper. He was allowed to pass through the cordon on the strength of the Lord Mayor's word.

"Within an hour he returned and re-entered the Mansion House—apparently to resume the fumigation of the Lord Mayor's residence. Half an hour later, when it was quite dark, a British officer hurried down the steps of the front entrance of the Mansion House and made his way quickly past the British troops stationed three feet apart.

"It was the only occasion on which I ever wore a British uniform, and the only time I ever resorted to even partial disguise. Probably no British uniform ever covered as coal-black a body!

"Where and how O'Reilly procured that uniform, I never asked. It was enough that he had had the presence of mind to go and get it, put it on under his own clothes and get it to me. Realising that he might have disobeyed one of our cardinal rules—under no circumstances to commit an act of violence except under especial orders—I deemed it wisest not to question him.

"The cordon was maintained around the Square all night and only withdrawn when the hunters became finally convinced that their information had been false.

"Meantime, Irishmen who were anxious to sell information to Dublin Castle learned that whenever they did so it became known to us immediately. Gradually, they began to realise that the very Black and Tan to whom they sold the information was one of our own agents within the Castle. If they had doubts about it, we saw to it that these were dissipated—our freeing them after their capture and after proving the truth to them, being quite sufficient to accomplish our purpose. From then on, they took the pains to acquaint others who were considering betraying us that in all probability they would offer their information to one of our men.

"Another of our more successful methods of dealing with Irish traitors was the raiding of mails. Most of the information offered to Dublin Castle was sent by post—but always with the name and address of the sender stated for purposes of reward. We had an unofficial censor who returned all except the Government mails and the would-be informers' letters. These latter we also returned to the senders, and generally a wholesome lecture was sufficient to persuade them that repetition of the offence was inadvisable.

"Almost fifty per cent. of the telegraphists in Ireland were either active members of the Irish Republican Army or employed as operatives in our Intelligence Department. From the telegraphists we got the code which was changed twice a day by Dublin Castle—immensely simplifying the work of our censor in his handling of Government messages. According to admissions made freely by Dublin Castle at this time, not one telephone message was sent or received that was not tapped by the Irish Republican Army. This may be an exaggeration—although I am inclined to think it is not. Our corps of telephone line men would certainly have resented any doubt as to the accuracy of this statement."

CHAPTER X

UNDER THE TERROR

" THE one great lesson which the Irish people undoubtedly learned from the results of our fight in the three years from 1919 to 1921, seems to be forgotten to-day. That lesson was the unbeatable essence of unity. Under the Terror we were a united people, and we smashed the Black and Tans. To-day, De Valera is doing his utmost to smash the Treaty—and if he succeeds in doing that, he will also smash the Irish nation. Are we so blind we will not see the truth ? Must we have the enemy on our backs before we will work together in the common cause of Ireland ? "

Collins thus began the continuation of his narrative of the gradual approach of Irish victory over the British Secret Service.

" One of our great concerns during the earlier stages of our fight against the Black and Tans," Collins continued, " was to keep the national spirit at the highest possible pitch. The Irish Republican Army by this time had grown to be a national body. There was not a village in Southern Ireland without its contingent of troops. Maintaining a high morale among these young soldiers helped in a large measure to ensure good morale among the civilian population. Best of all, the well disciplined army served to keep before the whole country the thought that we were at last a united people.

" Among the instruments used for this purpose, was *An t'Oglac*—a miniature newspaper published every week during the Terror by the Irish Republican Army. *An t'Oglac*—Gaelic for *The Volunteer*—was devoted to the education of the young soldiers in military matters and to strengthening their moral fibre.

"While a British army of 80,000 and half as many more Black and Tans and police left no stone unturned in their determined efforts to crush the publication—the little four-page sheet was in the hands of each soldier of the Republic every week as regularly as clockwork. It has been said that the British exerted their greatest endeavours to effect my capture, but I am sure no less gratification would have followed the destruction of our national organ. To my way of thinking, the fact that not once in three years was a single consignment of the papers ever found by the British is one of the most striking proofs of the efficiency of the Intelligence Staff of the Irish Republican Army.

"*An t'Oglac* was printed in a building less than a hundred yards distant from O'Connell Street, Dublin's main thoroughfare. In this building Pearce Beazley, editor of the paper, had his offices. The Black and Tans knew, or if they did not know, at least they had reason to believe, that Beazley was chiefly responsible for the publication of *An t'Oglac*. Furthermore, they knew that his headquarters were in the buildings mentioned. Sometimes his office was raided twice in a single day—but nothing was ever found of type or of any of the other usual equipment of a newspaper office. And without evidence of any kind, even the Black and Tans found it imprudent to arrest Beazley.

"A remarkable character—Beazley! His pluck in covering a rearguard action in the Easter Week rebellion had earned him the rank of commandant-general. A journalist by profession and an able writer in both English and Gaelic, he is to-day one of the most dependable men working in Ireland's cause. His recent journey to America resulted in a great deal of good for Ireland. Beazley was one of the men who escaped from Manchester Gaol when Austin Stack and two others also got away."

I had heard a great deal about this escape and pressed Collins for the whole story, but he firmly refused to say more about it.

"There would be no way," he protested, "of keeping it from sounding too much like self-glorification. It's for others to tell."

Wherefore I learned the details from another source. It is a story well worth the telling. Everything considered, it seems to me it must have been the most remarkable of all the hair-raising exploits which Collins engineered. Certainly it justified Mulcahy's recent tribute to Collins' "gay bravery."

Manchester Gaol is situated in the heart of the great English cotton town. On all four sides are well-lighted streets. Police patrol these streets day and night. With important Irish leaders in the gaol, the guard was unusually alert.

These were the conditions one Saturday evening—with Manchester at its busiest—when Collins arrived on the scene. At a pre-arranged moment the gaol was surrounded by men armed with revolvers, a whistle was blown, and in less than sixty seconds Beazley and his comrades were at liberty. The escape had been planned with all of Collins' usual skill. From start to finish there was not a single hitch.

A master key of the cell doors had been smuggled into the prison in a cake, and word got to Beazley to be prepared at a certain hour to release his comrades and go to a corner of the prison yard where—on a moonless night—the shadows were deepest. Those were the only instructions sent to Beazley. The other prisoners concerned in the escape were each notified separately. And so it was the quartette of Irishmen found themselves at the appointed place *inside* the prison wall. And then a rope ladder was suddenly thrown over to them. Up this they climbed and down another, at the bottom of which were Collins and his aids. Ten seconds later, a high power motor-car was speeding them away to Irish friends in various parts of Manchester.

Their escape was especially exasperating to the British Government, because they were all much wanted men. Their descriptions were published broadcast, and for weeks every port and every ship leaving for Ireland were closely watched by English detectives.

AND YET ALL OF THEM WERE BACK IN DUBLIN WITHIN FOUR DAYS OF THEIR ESCAPE!

"Beazley went back to his work of editing *An t'Oglac*, and for a long time was unmolested," Collins continued. "The fact that he was in Ireland was scouted by Dublin Castle. It was impossible for him to have slipped by the watchers at every English port! Therefore—so argued the logic of British officialdom—he must still be in England. It was not difficult, under these conditions, for Beazley to help to keep this delusion alive. He took the precaution of keeping out of sight whenever his office was raided—information of impending raids always reaching him in ample time for him to get away.

"The reason the Black and Tans could not believe that the paper was published on these premises was, as I have said, that they could never find any of the machinery necessary for the production of a newspaper. The truth did not occur to them. Yet it was simple enough. Every night of the week a few Dublin printers devoted their time to hand-setting 'copy.' They came singly, unostentatiously and set a few 'sticks' of type which they had brought with them. Immediately a page was thus set and locked in the 'form' it was carried away to the basement of a near-by building. Here, on a little hand-press, between 70,000 and 80,000 copies of *An t'Oglac* were turned off every week.

"Circulation of the paper began each Tuesday night. This was obviously the most difficult part of the whole undertaking. The Black and Tans knew that it was being sent to every town and village in Ireland, and they were bent on finding out how it was done. Discovery of the method would bring a substantial reward. But so secure did Beazley feel that he even risked meeting certain journalists every day, to inform them of the progress of the war in all parts of the country. Some of the newspaper men Beazley thus entrusted with his personal safety were Englishmen—but not once was his confidence abused.

"Many and ingenious were the methods of distribution. At one time a consignment destined for a distant part of Galway would be concealed in a sofa from which the stuffing had been removed. As often as not several hundred copies of *An t'Oglac* would be hidden in a bag of flour. The consignees of these camouflaged receptacles all knew their business. Under them were girls of the Cumman na m' Bann and boy Scouts of the Irish Republican Army. These did the actual house-to-house distributing, and thus every man of the rank and file had a copy of the paper in his possession by Friday of each week.

"For the success of the distribution of *An t'Oglac* a great deal of credit is due to the railway workers of Ireland—and not only for this does Ireland owe them much. At all times they were ready to take any personal risk and incur personal loss if it helped the Sinn Fein organisation. Frequently they went out on strike and sometimes remained out for months at a time—rather than handle munitions intended for the British forces. Time after time drivers refused to run trains in which were Black and Tans. By close co-operation with these railwaymen we were frequently able to organise a successful ambush when the foe, forced to reach their destination by road, were bound to pass a known point.

"If this citing of our ability to outwit our enemies seems to place me in the category of those who imagine that in time we could have routed them out of the country, let me dissipate that idea quickly. I hold no such opinion. English power rests on military might and economic control. Such military resistance as we were able to offer was unimportant, had England chosen to go at the task of conquering us in real earnestness. There were good reasons for her not doing so. About them I shall presently have something to say.

"At the General Election of 1918 the British Government had been repudiated by the Irish people by a majority of more than seventy per cent. The national Government was set up in a quiet, orderly and unaggressive fashion.

Under the Terror

Dail Eireann came into being. British law was gradually superseded. A loan of £400,000 was raised. At last the issue was knit. The struggle was definitely seen to be as between our determination to govern ourselves and get rid of English rule, and the British determination to prevent us from doing either.

"It was all this—this slow building up of an orderly self-government, this ignoring of English civil power—which was becoming an intolerable provocation to the British Government. Whitehall was coming to realise that ordinary methods would no longer meet the situation. Violence alone seemed to be the remedy. But England as yet thought it unwise to make these facts known.

"At first the British had been content to ridicule us. Then, growing alarmed at the increasing authority of our new Government, attempts were made to check our activities by wholesale political arrests. But neither ridicule nor arrests accomplished their purpose. The final phase of the struggle was at hand.

"For two years such violence as the British armed forces had been guilty of in their efforts at suppression, had resulted in the murder of 15 Irishmen and the wounding of nearly 400 men, women and children. Let it be remembered that in this same period there was not an instance of reprisals in kind by the Irish Republican Army.

"In this period—in the British records—there is not one authenticated case of violence used against the English military forces in Ireland.

"The only bloodshed was the work of the British. The Black and Tans had been sent to Ireland by the British Government for the express purpose of goading the people into armed resistance. This would give them the excuse they wanted. Once we arose in righteous wrath and gave back blow for blow, they could come down upon us in real earnest and swiftly beat us into impotency. That was the cherished hope of those who sent the Black and Tans to Ireland. But it was not to be realised.

"Finally, in January, 1920, and again in May and June

of that year, the people emphatically renewed their approval of our fight, in several elections. Our policy now had the virtually unanimous support of all classes. Britain felt that the moment had come for a final, desperate campaign of terrorisation.

"If there are people who doubt this, let them turn to the files of the *Times* published in London on November 1, 1920, and there read that it was 'now generally admitted' that a deliberate policy of violence had been 'conceived and sanctioned by an influential section of the Cabinet.' Of course this admission did not have the official sanction of Whitehall. Excuses, evasions and lies were still considered necessary to conceal the real object of the reign of terror which was about to begin. In August, 1920, a measure was passed in the English House of Commons, 'To restore law and order in Ireland '—which, in fact, meant the abolishing of all law in Ireland. It was preparing the ground for unbridled licence on the part of the Black and Tans.

"There can be no doubt that England went at this task with full knowledge of its brutality. This is proved by the kind of men chosen to do the work. Again, see what the *Times* had to say in this connection. In one of its leading editorials it is stated :

> 'It is common knowledge that the Black and Tans are recruited from ex-soldiers for a rough and dangerous task.'

"And just what was this 'rough and dangerous task ?' To begin with, there was the planned murder of certain leading Irishmen and officers of the Irish Republican Army. The names of these men were entered on a list 'for definite clearance.' Next, all who worked for us or supported the national movement were to be imprisoned. Finally, the general population was to be terrorised to whatever extent and by whatever means might be necessary to ensure their being kept in submission.

"To do these things England concluded that it was

wisest to pretend to have justifying causes. So we find Lloyd George in a speech at Carnarvon in October, 1920, talking about the Irish Republican Army as ' a real murder gang.' It had become ' necessary to put down a murderous conspiracy '—to ' get murder by the throat.'

" The ' murders ' that we committed were legitimate acts of self-defence forced upon us by English oppression. After two years of forbearance we had begun to defend ourselves and the life of our nation. Let it be remembered that we did not initiate the war, nor were we allowed to choose the lines along which the war developed. Let the facts speak for themselves. England made it a criminal—in large areas a capital—offence to carry arms. At the same time she inaugurated a brutal and murderous campaign against us. By so doing England forfeited any right to complain against the Irish people whatever means they took for their protection.

" Our only way to carry on the fight was by organised and bold guerilla warfare. But this in itself was not enough. However successful our ambushes—however many ' murders' we committed—England could always reinforce her army. She could always replace every soldier she lost. And that was the real reason for the coming into being of our Intelligence Staff.

" To paralyse the British machine it was necessary to strike at individuals outside the ranks of the military. Without her Secret Service working at the top of its efficiency, England was helpless. It was only by means of the accumulated and accumulating knowledge of these spies that the British machine could operate. Robbed of the network of this organisation throughout the country, it would be impossible to find ' wanted ' men. Without their criminal agents in the capital it would be hopeless to effect the removal of those leaders marked down for murder. It was these men we had to put out of the way.

" SPIES ARE NOT SO READY TO STEP INTO THE SHOES OF THEIR DEPARTED CONFEDERATES AS ARE SOLDIERS TO FILL UP THE FRONT LINE IN HONOURABLE BATTLE. AND EVEN

WHEN THE NEW SPY STEPPED INTO THE SHOES OF THE OLD ONE HE COULD NOT STEP INTO THE OLD ONE'S KNOWLEDGE!

" I know that the English spies who came to their deaths at our hands deserved their deaths. I know also that a world Press reported those murders to be the limit of cold-blooded villainy. But it is not true. We had to shake the morale of the organisation which meant to crush out the life of the Irish nation. We went at the grim business, difficult as it was, not because we relished it, but because the enemy left us no other course. And so far as it was possible we observed the rules of war. Only the armed forces, the spies and the criminal agents of the British Government were attacked. Prisoners of war we treated honourably and considerately and released them unharmed after they had been disarmed.

" Murders committed by the English forces were justified on the grounds that the perpetrators were but ' enforcing the law '—' restoring law and order in Ireland.' Murders committed by us were—murder!

" In the end the British Government awoke to realisation of the fact that its policy of violence was as futile as it was conscienceless. Eventually the day arrived when the British Prime Minister invited the Irish leaders—the ' murderers ' and ' heads of the murder gang '—to discuss with him the terms of peace.

" The fruits of that peace seemed to be within our reach in the Treaty. Is it possible that the dawn of peace is yet a long way off in the future? Are the Irish people to struggle through long years of new misery because a minority of destructive, unnatual, bitter extremists insist on proving that we are unfit and unable to govern ourselves?

" I cannot bring myself to believe that."

CHAPTER XI

THE MURDER OF FRANCIS SHEEHY SKEFFINGTON

COLLINS' disinclination to dwell on instances of cruelty practised by the British armed forces in Ireland led to my making independent enquiries. Quickly I learned in a general way of the murder of Francis Sheehy Skeffington at Portobello Barracks, April 19, 1916, by a firing squad of seven men under the command of Captain J. C. Bowen-Colthurst, Royal Irish Rifles. It seemed to be the one instance that came to every Irishman's mind when I asked for authentic cases of brutality.

The murder and a British court-martial's finding Colthurst "guilty, but insane," were extensively commented upon by the world Press, but the real story has never been published. I obtained the story from Skeffington's widow—a unique figure in Ireland to-day in that she is the only woman whose husband went to a martyr's grave who does not wear mourning, and who never tried to be elected to Dail Eireann. It seems to me to merit inclusion in these pages—if only because it is indirectly another testimonial to Collins' genius for helping others to outwit the British Secret Service.

Behind Mrs. Skeffington's reticence regarding her escape from Ireland and her trip to America by means of a counterfeit passport there is the plain stamp of Collins' handiwork. It was Collins who smuggled Mrs. Skeffington out of the country—and back again—just as it was Collins who enabled De Valera and Boland and the others to evade the British watchers and cross and recross the Atlantic without genuine passports.

In great part the facts as told me by Mrs. Skeffington are verified by the official records of the Royal Commission of Enquiry set up by the command of the King in August, 1916, at the Four Courts in Dublin.

" My husband," Mrs. Skeffington began, " was an anti-militarist, a fighting pacifist, a man gentle and kindly even to his bitterest opponents, who always ranged himself on the side of the weak against the strong whether the struggle was one of class, sex or race domination. Together with his strong fighting spirit he had a marvellous, an inextinguishable good humour, a keen joy of life, a great faith in humanity and a hope in the progress towards good.

" Several months prior to the Easter week rising my husband was sentenced to one year's imprisonment for making a speech ' calculated to prejudice recruiting.' He went on hunger strike, and was out after six days with a licence under the Cat and Mouse Act. Shortly after his release he went to the United States where, in February, 1916, *Century Magazine* published his article entitled ' A Forgotten Small Nationality.'

" Although as a socialist and a pacifist he was opposed to all militarism—even Irish—his great sympathy for and belief in the general movement for Irish freedom led him to return to Ireland where he believed he was most needed. He felt the British authorities realised perfectly—as of course they did—that he was resolutely opposed to the use of force, and therefore, in their eyes, a relatively unimportant figure. His record as a publicist for many years—as special correspondent of labour papers such as the *London Herald*, *New York Call*, *Manchester Guardian*, and as author of the " Life of Michael Davitt," and as editor and founder of the *Irish Citizen*, a pacifist and feminist Dublin Weekly— established him as a man to whom the thought of militarism was abhorrent.

" Equally well-known was his opposition to Arthur Griffith, whose ideals were anti-socialist. Altogether then, although he was openly associated with James Connolly in the revolutionary Irish labour movement and was one of

Murder of Francis Sheehy Skeffington

the founders of the Irish socialist party, he was not an undesirable in British eyes in the sense that rebel suspects were.

" Of course, neither he nor I would have been surprised had he been deported to England on his return from America. But murder without trial we did not foresee.

" My brother, Eugene Sheehy, an attorney, volunteered as a follower of Redmond for service in the British army during the war. He became a lieutenant in the Dublin Fusiliers, and later won a captaincy. My sister's husband, Professor Tom Kettle, also was a lieutenant in the same regiment and was killed in action in France in September, 1916. My father—then a member of Parliament for South Meath—supported England in the alleged ' fight for small nations.' Thus my husband and I were in a small minority in our family.

" Finally, my husband was sympathetic to the idea of an Irish Republic in so far as it made for a worker's commonwealth, but he was distinctly opposed to the use of military methods to achieve that end. I emphasise this point, because it bears directly on the fact that his murder was so completely without justification as to compel English military chieftains to admit as much officially.

" And they knew his attitude. In March, a month before his murder, my husband published an open letter to Thomas MacDonagh—one of the signers of the Irish Republic Proclamation—and made his position clear. In the course of this letter he stated :

" ' As you know I am personally in full sympathy with the fundamental objects of the Irish Volunteers. When you shook off the Redmondite incubus last September I was on the point of joining you. . . . I am glad now that I did not. For, as your infant movement grows towards the stature of a full-grown militarism its essence—preparation to kill—grows more repellent to me.

" ' High ideals undoubtedly animate you. But has

not nearly every militarist system started with the same high ideals ? You are not out to exploit or to oppress ; you are out merely to prevent exploitation and to defend. You justify no war except a war to end oppression, to establish the right. What militarism ever avowed other aims—in its beginnings ?

" ' I advocate no mere servile lazy acquiescence in injustice . . . but I want to see the age-long fight against injustice clothe itself in new forms, suited to a new age. I want to see the manhood of Ireland no longer hypnotised by the glamour of ' the glory of arms,' no longer blind to the horrors of organised murder. . . . We are on the threshold of a new era in human history. After this war nothing can be as it was before. The foundations of all things must be re-examined. . . . Formerly we could only imagine the chaos to which we were being led by the military spirit. Now we realise it. And we must never fall into that abyss again.'

" Surely there was nothing in this openly distributed document to earn British censure. On the other hand there was his arrest to prove that he was none the less offensive to the British authorities. His article in the *Century* was not calculated to improve his standing. In that article he had referred to the sentence of a fortnight meted out to a Dublin boy for kicking a recruiting poster ! As a matter of fact, subsequent events proved that his description was circulated to the military immediately after the Easter Monday rising.

" So much for my husband, and his record.

" Captain Bowen-Colthurst had had sixteen years' service in the British army. His family had settled in Ireland in Cromwell's time and been given grants of land confiscated from the Irish. At the court-martial held in Richmond Barracks, Dublin, June 6, 1916, fellow officers of Colthurst's testified to his cruelty to natives in India and to his having tortured dumb animals while on service there. After the battle of Mons, according to the testimony of Major-General Bird, Colthurst's ' eccentricity ' (which had expressed itself in his recklessly sacrificing his men and practicing cruelty on German prisoners) resulted in his being sent home from the front.

" When the Easter Week rising took place Colthurst was stationed with the 3rd Royal Irish Rifles in Portobello Barracks. The battalion's commanding officer, Colonel McCammond, was absent on sick-leave. Captain Colthurst, although not the equal in rank of Major Rosborough, was the senior office in point of service and, according to all the evidence, considered himself at liberty to ignore his brother-officers.

" If this statement seems incredible to persons who have implicit faith in the unvarying discipline enforced in all units of the British army, let it be remembered that what I have just said was stated by a British officer at Colthurst's court martial. More, it is easy to prove that there was open animosity between all the Irish regiments, as regards those recruited in the north-east and in the south of Ireland. Although they all wore the British uniform and served the same king, they were bitterly hostile to one another. Between the Royal Irish Rifles, for instance, and the Dublin Fusiliers there was constant friction. The former was an Orange regiment from Belfast.

" Through my family's connections with the British military forces I had become acquainted with Captain T. Wilson, then a despatch rider in the Dublin Fusiliers. I appealed to him—after rumours had reached me that my husband was being held prisoner in Portobello Barracks —to go there and make enquiries. He refused point blank, asking me if I wanted him to go to his death. When he realised I didn't understand the situation, he explained. He dared not go near the Royal Irish Rifles. He was a Catholic!

" So much for Colthurst and the conditions affecting army discipline in Dublin at the time of the Easter Week rising.

"When the outbreak began on Easter Monday my husband was near Dublin Castle. He learned that a British officer had been gravely wounded and was bleeding to death on the cobblestones outside the Castle gate. My husband persuaded a bystander to go with him to the rescue. Together they ran across the square under a hail of fire. Before they reached the spot, however, some British troops rushed out and dragged the wounded man to cover inside the gate.

"Throughout that day and the next my husband actively interested himself in preventing looting. He was instrumental in saving several shops; he posted civic guards, and enlisted the help of many civilians and priests. He pleaded with the crowds and persuaded them to return to their homes. But by Tuesday evening the crowds were getting out of hand. Everyone feared the worst. My husband called a meeting for that evening to organise a civic police. We met at 5.30 and had tea. I went home by a roundabout route, for I was anxious about my seven-year-old boy. I never saw my husband again.

"It was between 7 and 8 o'clock that evening that my husband passed Portobello Bridge on his way home. At this point Lieutenant M. C. Morris, 11th East Surrey regiment, was in charge of a picket. Recognising my husband from the circulated description of him he ordered his arrest. He was unarmed, carrying a walking-stick, and was walking quite alone in the middle of the road. At Portobello Barracks, wither two soldiers escorted him, he was searched and questioned. No papers of an incriminating character were found on him.

"Lieutenant S. V. Morgan, 3rd Royal Irish Rifles, the adjutant at Portobello Barracks, reported the arrest to headquarters, saying there was no charge against my husband, and asking whether he should release him. Orders were given to detain him. But the charge sheet—produced at Colthurst's court martial—showed the entry against my husband's name was ' no charge.'

"Told he was to be detained overnight, he asked that I be informed, but the request was refused. No message was ever allowed to reach me ; no notification of his death—no announcement of his first or second burial was ever issued.

"At about midnight Captain Bowen-Colthurst came to Lieutenant W. P. Dobbin, 3rd Royal Irish Fusiliers, captain of the guard, and demanded that my husband be turned over to him. This, of course, Dobbin had no right to do, but he did it. Colthurst had my husband's hands tied behind his back, and then led him out with a raiding party along the Rathmines road, the raiders firing at houses as they went along.

"Opposite Rathmines Catholic Church the column came upon two boys who had been attending the service that evening and were returning to their homes. Colthurst stopped and asked them if they did not know that martial law had been proclaimed, and that they could be 'shot like dogs.' The elder of the boys, J. J. Coade, a lad of 17, made no reply but started to walk away. 'Bash him,' Colthurst ordered, and a soldier broke the boy's jaw with the butt end of his rifle, knocking him down. Colthurst whipped out his revolver and shot him dead. The body was later carried to the barracks.

"My husband protested against this wanton murder and was told by Colthurst to say his prayers as he probably would be the next.

"Evidence as to what happened next is conflicting, although it is abundantly plain that Colthurst committed another murder a few minutes later. The official enquiry report on this subject had this to say :

> "' The evidence of the different witnesses can only be reconciled by inferring that more than one case of shooting occurred during the progress of Capt. Colthurst's party. . . . None of the evidence offered to us afforded any justification for the shooting of Coade ; it is, of course, a delusion to suppose that martial law confers upon an officer the right to take human life, and this delusion had in the present case tragic consequences.'

"All evidence of these atrocities was omitted at Colthurst's court martial. It was only against the strongest protest from the military that Sir John Simon insisted that testimony in this matter be presented to the commission holding the enquiry. But nothing was ever done about two other murders which responsible eye-witnesses declared Colthurst committed later in that week. The commission ruled that they were ' not within their scope.'

"At Portobello Bridge, Colthurst posted part of his men under Lieutenant Leslie Wilson to whom he turned over my husband with instructions to shoot him ' forthwith ' if there was any sniping at him and his raiders. Then Colthurst led his party on over the bridge and to Alderman James Kelly's tobacco shop. Before entering it they flung live bombs into the place. Then they sacked the premises and took prisoners the shopman and two editors—Thomas Dickson and Patrick MacIntyre. Together with my husband they were all marched back to the barracks.

"As it happened Dickson, a cripple, had published a loyalist newspaper, the *Eye Opener*, and MacIntyre's paper, the *Searchlight*, was also a loyalist publication. Alderman Kelly had helped to recruit for the British army. But Colthurst had mistaken the latter for Alderman Tom Kelly, a Sinn Feiner, and their combined protests were unavailing.

"Shortly before 10 o'clock the next morning Colthurst again demanded my husband from the guard, together with the two other editors. Besides Wilson and Dobbin, Lieutenant Tooley was in charge of the guard of 18 men. To them he stated he was ' going to shoot Skeffington and the other two.' According to their own testimony these subordinate officers delivered the three prisoners to Colthurst without protest. They also told off seven men with rifles to accompany Colthurst to the barracks' yard.

"This yard was about 12 feet long and 6 feet wide. As the three prisoners walked away from the firing squad, and when they had reached the end of the yard, Colthurst gave the order to fire, and all three dropped in their tracks, dead.

"The British authorities prevented my ever seeing my

husband's body, and when I attempted to have an inquest held, refused permission.

"Colthurst presently made a report of the triple murder after Major Rosborough ordered him to do so, and it was duly sent to headquarters at Dublin Castle. The report was altogether a fabrication and, subsequently, he was ordered to make a second report. Meantime, however, he kept his command without even a reprimand.

"Later in the day of the murder of the three editors, Colthurst was in charge of troops in Camden Street when Councillor Richard O'Carroll—one of the labour leaders in the Dublin City Council—surrendered. Marched to the barracks' yard, his hands above his head, O'Carroll walked to his death. Colthurst shot him in the chest. To a soldier who expressed doubt as to the effect of Colthurst's bullet, the latter replied, 'Never mind, he'll die later.' Then he ordered the unconscious man to be dragged out into the street and left there. The driver of a bread van picked him up, but the military interfered, and took him back to Portobello Barracks. Ten days later he died—in his wife's arms. They had sent for her at the last, and she arrived in time to hear him whisper a dying statement in her ear—a statement she later repeated to me.

"Three weeks later Mrs. O'Carroll gave birth to a son.

"On the same day Colthurst arrested a boy whom he suspected of having Sinn Fein information. When the boy denied it, Colthurst ordered him to kneel in the street and, as the boy raised his hand to cross himself, shot him in the back.

"In both these cases the British authorities refused to order an enquiry.

"Meanwhile, I was vainly seeking my husband. All sorts of rumours reached me: that he had been wounded and was in a hospital; that he had been shot by a looter; arrested by the police. I also heard that he had been executed, but this I refused to believe—it seemed incredible. I clung to the belief that even if he had been condemned to die, he would be tried before a jury, for martial law did not apply to non-combatants, and that I would be notified. Of course, the reason of the silence is now clear. It was hoped my husband's case would be like that of so many others who 'disappeared' and whose whereabouts could never be traced. Thirteen days after the murder of my husband and the other two editors, Mr. Tennant stated in the House of Commons in answer to a question that 'no prisoner has been shot in Dublin without a trial.'

"All day Wednesday and Thursday I enquired in vain, and Friday came without my having any positive information of my husband's fate. On Friday I tried to see a physician connected with the Portobello Barracks, but the police stopped me. I discovered I was under police supervision—as I continually was for several years afterwards. Meantime, houses were being raided and pillaged. Mme. Markievicz's home was broken into on Wednesday and all her pictures and other valuables stolen. Whole streets were ransacked and the inhabitants terrified ; the soldiers ruining everything within reach of their bayonets.

"Soldiers were everywhere selling their loot openly in the streets. Officers were shamelessly displaying 'souvenirs.'

"To allay my terrible anxiety my two sisters, Mrs. Kettle and Mrs. Culhane, agreed to try to get into Portobello Barracks. On their arrival they were immediately put under arrest and a drumhead court martial held upon them. Colthurst presided. Their crime was that they had been seen talking to Sinn Feiners. Colthurst refused to give them any information, declaring he knew nothing whatever of Sheehy Skeffington. Finally, they were marched off under armed guard and admonished not to mention what had taken place.

"That afternoon I managed to find the father of the murdered boy Coade. He told me he had seen my husband's body in the barracks' mortuary when he had gone for his son's body. This a priest later confirmed, but he could give me no other information.

"I went home shortly after 6 o'clock, and was putting my little boy to bed when the maid noticed soldiers lining

Murder of Francis Sheehy Skeffington 105

up around the house. She became terrified and dashed out the back door, carrying my son with her. I ran after them, for I knew the house would be surrounded and feared they might be shot down if seen running. As I ran down the hall a volley was fired through the front door and windows. The shots were fired without warning, and without any demand having been made on us to open the door.

"They broke in the windows with their rifle butts and swarmed all over the house, some going to the roof. Colthurst was in command. He rushed upon us and ordered us to throw up our hands. Behind him was a squad of men with fixed bayonets. The raiders numbered about 40 and included Colonel H. T. N. Allat, Royal Irish Rifles, who was later killed in the vicinity of the South Dublin Union. On this occasion, however, he exercised no command.

"Colthurst ordered us to be removed to the front room—to be shot if we stirred. For three hours they searched the house while we stood motionless, closely guarded by men with drawn bayonets, with others outside the house with levelled rifles pointed at us. The house was sacked, everything of value being removed—books, pictures, toys, linen and household goods. I could hear officers and men jeering as they turned over my private possessions. One of the soldiers (a Belfast man) seemed ashamed, and said, ' I didn't enlist for this. They are taking the whole bloomin' house with them.'

"All my private letters, including many from my husband before our marriage, his articles, a manuscript play—the labour of a lifetime—were taken. Colthurst had brought my husband's keys, stolen from his body, and with them opened his study which he always kept locked.

"Throughout the raid, Colthurst's demeanour was that of a sane man. He addressed several questions to me, and was coldly insolent in manner But he was quite self-possessed. His men took his orders without question. My sisters are certain he was sane when he questioned them at the drumhead court martial. He was not the same man, unquestionably, a friend would have found him on the golf links, for instance. But British officers are all like that. It is only on occasions like this that one sees them as they really are. Of insanity, there was no suggestion. Colthurst was simply the Englishman with the veneer removed.

"It was during this raid that he came across some papers which later he falsely endorsed as having been 'found on Skeffington's person.' This was proved at the enquiry.

"A second raid was made May 1, during my absence, and this time a little temporary maid was taken under guard to the barracks. She was held there a week, the charge against her being that she was found in my house. On this same day, Major Sir Francis Vane, the second in command at Portobello, was relieved of his command by Lieut.-Col. McCammond for his persistent efforts to have Colthurst put under arrest. He was told to give up his post and hand it over to Colthurst. Thus the latter was *promoted* six days after the murders. Later he was sent in charge of a detachment of troops to Newry, and not until May 11 was he put under 'close arrest.' Are these facts consistent with the theory of lunacy?

"Sir Francis Vane made a genuine effort to see justice done. Finding his superior officers at Portobello would do nothing, he went to Dublin Castle and saw Colonel Kinnard and General Friend as well as Major Price, head of the Intelligence department. They all deprecated the 'fuss'—and refused to act.

"By order of Colonel McCammond, bricklayers were brought to the barracks, Sunday, May 7. They removed the blood-stained bricks in the wall and replaced them with new bricks.

"Sir Francis Vane crossed to London early in May, interviewed Lord Kitchener, before whom he laid the facts, and I have reason to believe it was Kitchener who ordered Colthurst's arrest. But the order was disregarded by General Maxwell, then in command in Dublin. The net result of Sir Francis Vane's efforts was that he was dismissed from the service—by secret report of General Maxwell—deprived of his rank of major and refused a hearing at the court martial. Yet previously he had been mentioned in despatches by Brigadier-General McConochine for bravery.

"Without my knowledge my husband's body was exhumed and reburied in Glasnevin, May 8. Originally it had been put in a sack and buried in the barracks' yard. The remains were given to his father on condition that the funeral would be at early morn and that I be not notified. My husband's father consented unwillingly to do this on the assurance of General Maxwell that obedience would result in the trial and punishment of the murderer.

"On that day I managed to get to John Dillon and told him my story. Three days later he read my statement in the House of Commons in the course of his wonderful speech describing the horror he had seen in Dublin. It was that speech that compelled Mr. Asquith to cross at once to Ireland. Regarding my statement, Mr. Asquith said:

"'I confess I do not and cannot believe it. Does anyone suppose that Sir John Maxwell has any object in shielding officers and soldiers, if there be such, who have been guilty of such ungentlemanlike, such inhuman, conduct? It is the last thing the British army would dream of.'

"He went to Ireland, and found every word of my statement true, as verified at the enquiry. He found other horrors—the North Kings Street atrocity, for instance—surpassing mine. Yet the military shielded the murderers and hushed all enquiries. The Royal Commission that was appointed to enquire into the causes of the rebellion early in May did its work thoroughly, but no enquiry was permitted as to the atrocities committed by British troops in Dublin.

"The enquiry connected with Colthurst's murder of my husband and the other editors was limited in scope to the consideration of only these three murders—collateral evidence of other murders of which he had been admittedly guilty being ruled out. Witnesses were not sworn. Colthurst himself—at that time committed to Broadmoor Insane Asylum—was not present.

"Colthurst had been found insane by the earlier court martial, a wooden tribunal presided over by Lord

Cheylesmore and twelve senior officers All the witnesses were military. I was not allowed to present evidence. My counsel, Mr. Healy, declared that, ' Never since the trial of Christ was there a greater travesty of justice.'

"During the court martial Colthurst was under no restraint. He stayed at the Kilworth hotel in Dawson Street with his family, and for several weeks after he had been found ' insane ' he continued at liberty. When Dublin feeling began to run high, he was finally taken to Broadmoor Asylum to be ' detained during the King's pleasure '—but he still held his rank as captain and drew half-pay for several months. Eventually he was ' retired,' but was not dismissed from the service !

" In an attempt to force the British Government to administer justice, I went to London in July to interview editors and members of Parliament. My efforts resulted in my being sent for by Mr. Asquith, July 19. I brought with me as a witness to the interview, Miss Muriel Matters, a well-known suffragist. Mr. Asquith received us at 10, Downing Street and began by explaining the difficulties in the way of holding an adequate enquiry. The House, he said, would refuse a sworn enquiry, and that alone could be satisfactory. He wanted to know if I would be satisfied with an inadequate enquiry which was ' the best ' he could offer. I told him I should not be satisfied with any enquiry that he told me in advance would be inadequate. I told him also that if I were not satisfied I should take further action.

" I had even then in view a visit to America to tell an honest country what British militarism could do.

" Then Mr. Asquith carefully broached the subject of ' compensation ' in lieu of an enquiry. Previously proposals had been made to me, from various unofficial sources, to accept compensation, most of the arguments being based on my boy's future. Mr. Asquith put the proposition ever so delicately, but it was obviously his only object in sending for me. He was mellow and hale, with a rosy, chubby face and silver hair, suggesting a Father Christmas. But he never looked me straight in the face once during the interview !

Murder of Francis Sheehy Skeffington

I listened to his persuasive talk about compensation, and finally told him the only compensation I would consider was a full, public enquiry into my husband's murder. He finally said he would give his answer to Mr. Dillon, and so our interview ended.

"Out of this interview came the setting up of the Commission of Enquiry with Sir John Simon at its head. But Asquith narrowly restricted the scope of the enquiry as I have pointed out. My counsel was not allowed to examine or cross-examine any witness. All witnesses who might have testified damagingly to the military were either dead or scattered to points where they could not be reached. And yet the report of the commission established many important facts: the promotion of Colthurst, the dismissal of Sir Francis Vane, and the raids on my house for incriminatory evidence after the murder. Doubt was cast on the insanity of Colthurst, and grave censure passed on the military.

"Finally, let no one imagine that my husband's case was isolated, the one mad act of an irresponsible officer. It was part of an organised programme. There is evidence, sworn and duly attested, in Irish hands to-day of almost fifty other murders of unarmed civilians and disarmed prisoners —some of them boys and some women—committed by British soldiers during Easter Week. The North Staffords murdered 14 men in North King Street, and buried them in the cellars of their houses. In the British official reports two such murders are admitted. They are 'justified' in a statement made by General Sir John Maxwell at the time as follows:

> "'Possibly unfortunate incidents, which we should regret now, may have occurred. It did not, perhaps, always follow that where shots were fired from a particular house the inmates were always necessarily guilty, but how were the soldiers to discriminate? They saw their comrades killed beside them by hidden and treacherous assailants, and

it is even possible that under the horrors of this peculiar attack some of them saw red. That is the inevitable consequence of a rebellion of this kind. It was allowed to come into being among these people and could not be suppressed by velvet-glove methods.'"

Mrs. Skeffington left Ireland for America in December, 1916. She went with the fixed purpose of exposing British atrocities to the people of a then neutral country. She hoped to damage British prestige in the United States, and especially to do her best to prevent America from entering the war. As she herself has stated, she was under police and military surveillance at this time, a fact that stamps her eluding them a feat equal to some of Collins' best. This is her own story of her outwitting the British authorities.

"I managed to obtain a passport by assuming another woman's personality," she began. "With the help of her Scottish family I learned to dress and make up like her in every way. I cannot give further details on this point as others are involved and our fight for independence is not yet over.

"My first goal was a Scotch port from which it had been arranged I was to take ship for an American port. The boat I took for the Irish Sea crossing did not, as was usual, stop at Liverpool for mails. Ordinarily all passengers were questioned and searched at that port, but I was unfortunately spared that ordeal as a result of a submarine scare which caused us to make a wide detour away from the English coast.

"Before starting on the journey—perhaps the more risky because I insisted on taking my boy with me—I had carefully arranged an alibi to account for my absence from Dublin. I let it be generally known that I had fallen ill and had gone to the home of a friend in the country to be nursed. Letters I had prepared were posted by this friend every day while I was on the high seas and in America.

"Providence again came to my aid—although it did

not seem so at the time—when my seven-year-old son developed diphtheria on the eve of our departure from the Scotch port. It was necessary to put him in a hospital at once, and there he was isolated for ten weeks under the assumed name which I had adopted. Finally, when he was released, to my astonishment he was not only very changed in appearance, but had acquired a strong Scotch accent!

" To further my chances of eventual success, and realising that I could be of no use to my boy while he was in the hospital, I returned to Dublin. I had recovered from my ' illness,' and resumed my former occupation as a teacher. Thus I put the sleuths off the scent. My second trip across the Irish Sea—in possession of the false passport—was a relatively easy matter. At Liverpool the authorities subjected Greeks, Americans and Irish aboard the boat to a rigorous examination, but my Scotch passport and passable ' burr ' let me escape with a question or two.

" The most difficult part of my task was travelling in Ireland itself. There was, of course, no chance of my leaving from the port of Dublin. I had to go north by a roundabout route, during the course of which I adopted a series of disguises. At one stage of the journey I was an elderly invalid; at another I was a touring actress. These were necessary transitions from my own identity to that of the Scotch woman named in my passport.

" Of course the passport was bogus, but, like my make up, it was good enough to deceive the authorities who examined it. The turning out of those bogus passports is a story by itself which, one day, perhaps, can be safely told. But as yet no one in Ireland knows how soon bogus passports may again become vitally necessary!

" My little boy was obviously an invalid, and as such an object of compassion—a fact that served to distract attention from me. Also I encouraged him to chatter in the hearing of the British authorities, and his suddenly acquired Scottish burr was better for my purposes than a dozen passports!

" I remained in the United States for eighteen months,

lecturing on 'British Militarism as I have known it.' In this period I addressed audiences in every large city from New York to San Francisco, and from the State of Washington to Texas. I spoke at women's clubs, at universities, including Harvard, Chicago and Columbia, at peace and labour conferences, and, of course, Irish assemblies. I was arrested in San Francisco for speaking against conscription *for Ireland* after America had entered the war. But I was not detained nor even charged.

" For several weeks I lobbied Congress and the Senate, and obtained an interview with President Wilson. I found him sympathetic but guarded.

" The British in America were not idle at this time. They tried many times to put an end to my activities. Once their agents attempted to get me into Canada by inducing me to board the wrong train out of Buffalo. They approached me as an Irish reception committee. A stranger put me right just as the train was about to pull out of the station. Had I remained aboard, I should have been deported to England the moment I was in Canada.

" The American people were very kind to me. Individually and collectively they are extremely warm-hearted, hospitable and sympathetic. I made many enduring friendships with Americans that have stood the test of time. I found American women especially helpful—women like Jane Adams and Mary McDougall of Chicago, Alice Park of Palo Alto, and Katherine Lecky and Dr. Gertrude Kelly of New York. If for any reason I had to live outside Ireland, I should choose the United States as a second home.

" Having readopted my own personality as soon I landed in America, the task of returning to Ireland was no easy matter. At last, after much difficulty and delay, I obtained a passport from the British under restrictive conditions. It permitted me to go to Liverpool only ; I should not be allowed to go to Ireland, but must remain in England. I told them I was willing to chance their being able to keep me in England, and so took passage to Liverpool, where I arrived in July, 1918. There I was closely examined by the military who threatened me with dire penalties if I failed to report regularly to the police or tried to leave Liverpool. These threats I naturally ignored.

"First, one of my sisters obtained permission to come to Liverpool and take my little boy back to Dublin. Then I disappeared for a fortnight—with the help of friends, a fast car, and some disguises. Eventually I landed in Ireland—at the end of July—as a stowaway in a tramp steamship. For two nights and a day I hid in the pitch dark, grimy hold without food or water. We landed south of Dublin and, after some delay, I was smuggled ashore, clad in ship's dungarees, in the small hours of the morning.

"The British still believe I managed to elude them by disguising myself as a nun, and nuns were searched regularly for weeks before it was discovered I was back in Ireland.

"Almost as soon as I resumed my ordinary life—having in the interim transacted some special business which I cannot divulge at this time—I was arrested and deported to Holloway jail in London for the duration of the 'disorder' in Ireland. I hunger struck, was released, and finally permitted to return to my home.

"By this time Colthurst had been released from the insane asylum 'cured.' So far as I know it is the only case on record of a man found guilty of murder but insane, who has ever obtained his release from an English criminal lunatic asylum. It was the fact that he had been released that undoubtedly led the British authorities to permit me to return to Ireland. Public opinion in England itself was aroused. It was going too far—Colthurst at liberty and his victim's widow imprisoned!

"Since then I have been arrested several times; my home has been raided several times, and on one occasion I suffered concussion of the brain as a result of having been clubbed with the butt end of a rifle in the hands of a Royal Irish Constable.

"The last I heard of Colthurst he was occupying a minor official post in Essex. His stay in the Broadmoor Asylum lasted about eighteen months—from July, 1916, to February, 1918. His release was effected by a campaign conducted by the *Morning Post* and the *Spectator*, both of which newspapers insisted—quite correctly—that he was not insane. I go further, and declare that he never was insane! So far as I have been able to discover, no formal steps were ever taken to establish his restoration to sanity.

" His family no longer live in Ireland. Some of his property—he owned some castles in Cork—was burned to the ground last year. It would seem to be fairly safe to assume that Ireland has seen the last of Captain Bowen-Colthurst.

" One final word about Adjutant Morgan, the only Catholic in the Royal Irish Rifles, and the only man at Portobello Barracks who treated my husband kindly. Very shortly after my husband's murder he was removed from the regiment, deprived of his adjutancy, and sent to the front ' under a cloud.' There he was killed in 1917."

CHAPTER XII

CHILDERS' OPINION OF AMERICANS

DURING one of the early sessions of Dail Eireann, after the signing of the Treaty, I approached Erskine Childers and asked him to tell me the truth about his share in the famous gun-running exploit at Howth, July 26, 1914. He took a day to consider my request, and then sent me the following letter :

> " I am afraid I shall hardly be able to do what you ask of me. I should have no control over the articles, and as the Hearst Press is, I understand, strongly Free State, it might be better if the matter was obtained from that quarter."

Not satisfied with this misstatement of fact, I sought out Childers and assured him that he would of course have " complete control over the articles " in that they would be published exactly as he wrote them. The fact that a statement from him would be welcomed by the Hearst newspapers was the best evidence that his charge of bias was unjustified.

" That may be true," Childers admitted soberly, " but the fact remains that all America is more English than England herself, and an Irish appeal in the United States is useless. Why, there is a fringe along the New England coastline where the people sing night and morning—in their hearts—' God Bless the King ! ' And from the seat of your Federal Government to the distant cities of the Pacific coast there is a childish fear of England—the result of propaganda seduously spread by England's workers. None of you stops to realise it is the old story of the lion and the whale—but that is exactly what America and England are. It is ludicrous—this idea that England would fight America. But England's might is ever kept uppermost in the minds of the American people. And American publicists do quite as much as Englishmen to keep alive the false sentiment that alliance between the two countries is of equal, mutual advantage.

"Most of your newspapers are worse than the London *Morning Post*—worse in their lick-spittling attitude towards the British Crown and their contempt for everything and everybody not of English ancestry. Your huge trade interests are truly soulless. To make an appeal to the American people on a basis of idealism is hopeless. Your President Wilson found that out. America is the most materialistic people in the world to-day. Your worship of success is surely a contemptible national policy—but it is America's dominant characteristic.

"Your Ambassador at the Court of St. James wears knee breeches! Such truckling to England is disgusting. But what American is going to say that in so doing your Ambassador is not faithfully reflecting the mental attitude of a great majority of the people he represents? What other nation sends with such eagerness so many of its nationals to be presented at the English Court each year? Where else is so much newspaper space devoted to the ecstasies of those who have had this priceless honour conferred upon them?

"Why, your well-read American won't even discuss the revolutionary war! They are actually ashamed of it! Most of the American people are pleased that American school-books distort the facts of that fight that smashed British rule in America. It is a thing not to be talked about in most American circles. 'It's not done'—that most abominable of all England's abominable catch-phrases—it is enough to tell present-day Americans to ensure their not doing it!

"But even in revolutionary times there was always a fifty per cent. minority against George Washington. America would never have won her independence if it had not been for the stubbornness of one man. Washington did not lead a people inspired by love of freedom—he compelled an unwilling people to follow him. And to-day an England-loving America is ashamed it ever happened!

"This is why I do not care to address the American people on any subject whatsoever. Perhaps this explanation makes my reason plain."

I watched him shuffle away down the corridor of the National University building—an undersized, emaciated, unhappy figure—and wondered what sort of American woman must be his wife!

It was as a result of this interview that I persuaded Collins to do what was necessary to obtain all the facts of the gun-running at Howth. And eventually he arranged the three-cornered conference with Sean McGarry—the one man left alive in Ireland to-day who was closest in the confidences of the Easter Week leaders. At Collins' bidding Mc-Garry told us the following tale:

"In the summer of 1914 there was an army of 80,000 men up in Ulster, led, armed, and drilled by Carson, and pledged to resist by force the enactment of Home Rule. This was all unlawful—this open defiance of the laws of the English Parliament to which Ulster professed the limit of loyalty. But the English Government let this announcement of rebellion pass unheeded. They had let those troops prepare for war for two years and done nothing at all to stop it.

"We, in the South, looked on during these two years, and then we reached the conclusion that what Ulster could do we could do. We were not altogether unmindful of the fact that we outnumbered the Carsonites by about four to one! So we made up our minds to arm and drill on our own account, NOT TO ATTACK ULSTER, but to be able to face the English Government with the only argument she has ever understood! And then what happened? Within a month the Government, which for two years had allowed the Carsonites to get in all the arms they wanted, issued an order prohibiting the importation of any arms or ammunition into Ireland!

"Naturally we both started gun-running. Ulster had had two years' start, but she still wanted more arms and ammunition. She got them! Perhaps the *Fanny* will be remembered by some—the yacht that steamed right through 'watching' British warships and landed her cargo of guns at Larne after the newspapers had told of her coming for two weeks previous! The *Fanny* came in and went out and never a word from the gunboat patrols. Larne, it may be necessary to state, is in Ulster!

"Meantime, the gunboat patrols off Dublin and Wicklow, as well as the western coast, had nothing the matter with their eyesight. We knew the difference, never fear. But it had nothing to do with the fact that we had to have arms.

"It was July 26, 1914—when everybody was talking about Austria's ultimatum to Servia—that we managed to unload 2,000 rifles and a goodly supply of ammunition at Howth. A route-march had been called for that day (it was a Sunday) and about 1,200 of the Dublin Volunteers took part in it. Perhaps a dozen of us, all told, knew what was the real purpose of that nine-mile route-march!

"Word came to me the day before to get a boat and go out in the bay to meet Childers' yacht. So on that Saturday afternoon I went over to Howth with two others, and tried to bargain with boatmen for a launch. But there was a storm, and never a boat could we get. Finally, we persuaded one old fellow to take us out and have a run around the harbour—to see if it was as rough as it looked! He was on the point of casting off the lines when, unfortunately, he caught sight of a revolver sticking out of one of our pockets! That was enough for him! We hadn't been too convincing in our explanations for wanting to make the trip anyhow—and when he guessed the truth—that we intended to keep him out in the bay, once we got him away from shore, he quickly put his engine out of commission! He wasn't wanting to be a hero in the least!

"On we went to Dunloacharie, and again met with no success. Not a boatman would go outside in the storm, and not one of them would hear of us going alone. Up in Bray, however, Willie Cullen managed to get a boat—an open motor boat—and he it was who finally picked us up at Howth, after a wild night out by himself in Dublin Bay. So far as I know, Willie Cullen's name has never even been mentioned in connection with the gun-running, but it is my opinion his bravery ought to be made known. Without him and the boat I don't know what would have happened.

"Well, we met the Childers' yacht all right, and, to our surprise, we found a woman steering it! The woman turned out to be Mary Spring Rice—daughter of the then English Ambassador in Washington! [1]

"We showed the way in to the pier in our motor boat, after assuring Childers that the English patrol boat was not in the neighbourhood—a whisper that we were going to run guns in to Wexford having sent it off on a false scent. Before we had made fast the Volunteers—doing exactly what the Ulstermen had done at Larne—had taken possession of the pier, advised the police and harbour officials it was best for them to remove themselves from the immediate neighbourhood—advice they all decided was sound—and were all ready for us. While we were unloading the rifles and several cases of ammunition another 300 of the Volunteers arrived, making our total about 1,500 men. The job finished, we started back to Dublin.

"Of course, Dublin Castle had been notified before ever we left Howth, and at Clontarf, on the outskirts of the city, we met a force of police and soldiers. Our rifles were unloaded. A parley took place. They demanded the surrender of the guns. We refused. The soldiers—a company of the

---

[1] Authentic records of the Howth gun-running exploit have established that there was a woman aboard Childers' yacht, and that she was at the wheel when it came alongside the pier at Howth, but until now her identity has remained unknown.

King's Own Scottish Borderers—were ordered to charge us with fixed bayonets. Two of them in the excitement fired at us One of our men was bayoneted. Then the English commander called another parley. By this time there was only the front rank of our force anywhere in sight! The rest of us, interested only in saving the guns—had disappeared across the fields! And so not one gun was lost!

"Then came the tragedy in Bachelor's Walk—when the British troops, marching back to their barracks, were cursed and stoned by a crowd composed chiefly of women who had heard rumours of a massacre of the Volunteers at Clontarf. The soldiers fired without warning—and killed one man, two women, and a boy. Nobody was ever punished for that, although it ought to be remembered that this was not only before we had begun to use armed force—two years before, in fact—but also before the world war had made killings the order of the day.

"The only other important thing about the gun-running at Howth—which I think most certainly should be emphasised—is that about one week later ERSKINE CHILDERS ENLISTED IN THE BRITISH SECRET SERVICE!"

Collins suggested to McGarry that he should continue the narrative to include what he personally new about Sir Roger Casement's activities in connection with gun-running from Germany. It was interesting to note Collins' intense desire to acquire information on points outside his own immediate jurisdiction. He explained to me in an aside that after his arrival in Ireland in 1916 he had had little opportunity of enquiring into matters not directly concerned with his own duties.

"The one big point about the Germans that I think should be told," McGarry continued, "is that they did not let us down in 1916. Casement always felt that they did, but he admitted to me that they never actually promised to send *men* to help us. That was what Casement most wanted—not having too much faith in us because of our inexperience as soldiers—and Germany might have sent men if the war had gone her way instead of against her. I had a letter from Casement when he was ill in Munich, early in 1916, stating that he had a kind of conditional promise from Germany regarding men for Ireland. It was that if they won a decisive advantage on either the Eastern or Western front they would send us men.

" Of course, this influenced our plans to no little extent. We knew that such aid from Germany would be at best temporary. We had to arrange to be in a position to make our move coincide with the arrival of the Germans—and carry through our plan of campaign while we had them with us. So it was that the rising was originally set for Easter Friday. It was Tommy O'Connor who carried the word from us to Casement."

The casual references to communications between Ireland and Germany, and McGarry's calm statement that the Germans were planning not only to make the trip to Ireland—but, later, to make the return journey—provoked an interjected query from me. Was passage between the two countries as easy as that?

McGarry looked at Collins—obviously seeking his advice before making answer. But Collins did not return his glance. Instead, he turned his face towards me—and grinned! It was quite as if he had put it into words. It *was* a foolish question!

"Anyhow," McGarry continued, "there were many things to be done. We sent a messenger to America on one of the American liners to tell our friends there that we were going to start on Good Friday. Tommy O'Connor came back from Germany and explained that the Germans were going to send in guns to Tralee—but the ship would not make it in time for us to start on Good Friday—the nearest they could figure the time of its arrival being between Good Friday and Easter Sunday morning. This meant rearranging everything.

" In the midst of our work of notifying commands all over the country, back came our messenger from America and reported that everything there was moving as well as could be wished, and all plans made for the Good Friday rising! Within an hour that messenger was heading back to New York! It was vitally necessary for him to let our friends know that the date had been altered from Good Friday to Easter Sunday. The ship on which he was making the second journey was delayed for five days in the English Channel—as a result of a German submarine scare; and that was very bad for us.

"If it is not plain enough without my saying it, I'll explain that naturally one of the most important things our messenger had to do in New York was to get word to Casement in Germany. Except on this occasion we had been able to communicate in this way without any trouble at all— but this time things went wrong. Owing to the lateness of our messenger's arrival in New York, his message, wirelessed from there to Germany, found Casement gone! He was in the submarine on his way to Tralee Bay—and he did not know that we were planning to begin the rising on Easter Sunday with or without aid in the form of German soldiers!

"The disguised German merchantman that was bringing the arms to us was stopped and searched three times, but every time Captain Spinlow, her skipper, bluffed the British and was allowed to continue on his way to Tralee. But when, finally, he was actually in the bay at Tralee, he found himself surrounded by British patrol boats—and there was nothing for it but scuttling the ship. This he did, and down to the bottom went 20,000 rifles and a million rounds of ammunition!

"And this happened only a few hours before Casement walked into the trap! I have every reason to believe that Casement had become obsessed with the idea that we were being fooled. When he went to Berlin from Munich, he heard that we were planning to start the rising—because we were counting on the aid of German *men*. And he believed our cause was hopeless without their aid. I know this was his fixed idea. To prevent us from attempting what he thought was the impossible, he insisted on hurrying to Ireland in a submarine. The world knows the price he paid for that trip!"

CHAPTER XIII

THE TRUTH ABOUT THE TRUCE

"SEVEN months before England granted the truce of July, 1921, she wanted very much to withdraw the Black and Tans from Ireland and end the murderous war which she had begun to realise could never be won. A truce would have been obtained after the burning of Cork by the forces of the Crown—in December, 1920—had our leaders acted with discretion. There is every reason to believe that the British Government were minded to respond favourably to the endeavours of His Grace, Archbishop Clune, who attempted to mediate; but the English attitude hardened through the too precipitate action of certain of our public men and public bodies."

Collins thus began an exposition of the events leading up to the ending of hostilities. So far as I am aware, England's desire for this earlier truce is not generally known.

"Unhappily," he continued, "several of our most important men gave evidence of an over-keen desire for peace while tentative proposals were being made and considered. So it was that, although terms of truce had been virtually agreed upon, the English statesmen abruptly terminated the negotiations when they discovered what they took to be signs of weakness in our councils. They conditioned the truce, then, on surrender of our arms; and the struggle went on.

"British aggression continued; our defence continued. It was now war to the death in very truth!

"Of course, in these seven months preceding the truce, there were many instances of unofficial 'feelers' put out by men on both sides—much visiting back and forth by well-meaning but unauthorised persons. Friends of Ireland from America frequently tried to intervene on our behalf, but those of us actually in the fight played no part in these conversations. We had no time for talk!

" The attitude of those of us who eventually took part in the Treaty negotiations was the same—in 1920 in Ireland as it was in 1921 in London. It is no good to have confusion of thought about this. We were fighting as Irishmen had always fought—for freedom! We were fighting for freedom from English occupation, English interference, English domination! But there was no thought in our minds as to what especial label might be attached to the freedom—if only we could win it. In other days we had struggled to win Repeal of the Union, Home Rule, or some other form of devolution. But it was not these labels that mattered; our fight was essentially a struggle to win for ourselves as large a measure of freedom as possible. And so we were fighting—not for a republic—but freedom! We felt—and those of us who believe in the Treaty still feel—that freedom for Ireland is of vastly greater consequence than the form of government under which we shall enjoy our freedom.

" When charges of treason are directed at us now—it is as well that our aspirations of 1920 be kept in mind. I said at a meeting of Dail Eireann that the Treaty gives us freedom—not the ultimate freedom which all nations hope for and struggle for—but freedom to achieve it. AND I WAS AND I AM NOW FULLY ALIVE TO THE IMPLICATIONS OF THAT STATEMENT!

" Returning to the fight as it was being waged at the beginning of 1921—the most important phase of it was our gradual realisation of England's desire to call a truce. This was the more important because it had never been possible for us to be militarily strong, nor to do more by force alone than to make England uncomfortable. Now, at last, we discovered that we had grown strong enough to make England *too* uncomfortable. More than this—we discovered that while England expatiates on the futility of force (by others) it is the only argument she listens to. Above all, the valiant efforts of Irishmen under the Terror—their deaths—these finally awoke the sleeping spirit of Ireland.

" That spirit was once more flaming—and with cause. For the people saw in England's desire to end the reign of terror the true worth of the young men who had gone to their deaths that peace might come to their country. There had been—on rare occasions—regrettable acts on the part of individual Irish soldiers, but such acts had been so few as to be negligible, and when they did occur they were the outcome of terrible and incessant provocation, and were foreign to the whole nature of the Irish resistance. The normal conduct of our soldiers proved them to be chivalrous, courageous, and enduring—and with an unsurpassable devotion to the ideal of freedom. Let me cite an instance.

" In June, 1921, a party of four Volunteers of the East Clare Brigade, engaged in cutting wires on the railway at Meelick, were surprised by a party of 30 English soldiers with two machine guns. Fire was opened by the enemy at close range. The commander of our little force was atop a telegraph pole and had time to shout a warning an instant before the firing began. His men jumped to cover while he dropped off the pole behind a low bank beside the railway. Two of the four managed to make good their escape, but the other two—Lieut. M. Gleeson and Commandant C. McCarthy—were killed.

" As they ran across a field McCarthy fell wounded, and Gleeson went on without noticing it. But on reaching a place of safety and finding his comrade missing, he immediately started to retrace his steps. Presently he saw him lying in the open field across which an English machine-gun and about a dozen rifles were pouring a hail of lead at about 100 yards range. At the same time Gleeson saw a party of five English soldiers scurrying around the field to cut off their retreat. It must have been as evident to Gleeson as it was to my informants, who were looking on, that no power on earth could save McCarthy, but it was equally evident that Gleeson preferred going back and dying with his comrade to leaving him. Racing down the field, straight into the fusillade of bullets, he knelt beside McCarthy and lifted him on to his back—with his right hand busily firing his revolver at the pursuing soldiers, as he carried his comrade up the field. Another moment and Gleeson fell, badly wounded—while McCarthy collapsed a few yards further on.

" When the British troops came upon Gleeson they found him still unconquered. With his last breath he fired his last cartridge at them. That was the performance of an Irish boy of 20 years of age WHO HAD NEVER BEFORE BEEN IN ACTION ! According to the British officer in charge—a Lieut. Gordon of the Royal Scots—who had been through the world war—Gleeson was the bravest man he had ever seen ! His men, however, apparently did not share his opinion. They frightfully mutilated the body—as also that of McCarthy.

" In the same brigade area, at about the same time, ten of our soldiers, exhausted after a forced march, were attacked by a strong patrol of Constabulary. Eight of our ten lads had never before been in action, and were unnerved by fatigue and the suddenness of the attack. How they were saved by the bravery and resourcefulness of their officers is worth telling.

" They had started to cross an open field when the Constabulary, numbering twenty-two, suddenly swept up behind them in lorries and opened fire. It was a roasting hot day and our men were completely played out. The Constabulary were, of course, quite fresh. Our men dashed to shelter under orders of their commander, who himself stood his ground to cover their retreat. Almost immediately one of the others came running back to his commander, and insisted on remaining with him. He was Brigade Police Officer Thomas Healy. As these two men slowly retreated—firing at their pursuers, and delaying them—Healy at last sank to the ground in a state of collapse. He had not been wounded. His death was due to heart failure. He was a native of Tralee and had been a member of the R.I.C., from which he had resigned a year earlier.

"Meantime the others were becoming so exhausted they could hardly stand, their commander, having now to cover the retreat alone, being obliged to order, coax, threaten, and appeal to them to keep moving. Here then, was one man fighting twenty-two men, with eight of his own command useless as combatants. He was a good shot, however, and managed to bring down more than one of the enemy at 500 yards range. The pursuit lasted half an hour—all of it up hill—but in the end the Constabulary withdrew. After almost superhuman efforts, the commander had succeeded in saving all of his men except Healy.

"These were typical deeds. And as they became known among the people there was no stemming the tide of rising national spirit—victory was at hand! But there was another unifying cause—and one I choose to state merely in general terms. During the reign of terror 274 Irishmen were assassinated in their homes or while in custody.

"Torture of Irish prisoners in a vain attempt to force them into a betrayal of their comrades had occurred in thousands of cases. Brutal assaults upon suspected men had been almost the invariable rule in raids by Black and Tans on Irish homes. There is proof in plenty to substantiate these statements, but I prefer you obtain it elsewhere."

Accordingly I sought this proof in other quarters—and quickly found there was indeed plentiful sworn evidence of the truth of what Collins had said. Of many that I have seen and read the following sworn statements are typical:

THE SWORN STATEMENT OF MARY MAGEE, OF CORROGS, NEWRY, CO. DOWN.

"I, Mary Ellen Magee, of Corrogs, Newry, co. Down, do hereby solemnly declare that the statements made herein are the truth, so help me God.

"On Wednesday, June 8, at or about the hour of 8 o'clock in the evening, I heard voices (which I afterwards found to be those of Special Constabulary) speaking to my brother, Stephen Magill, at the door of our house. They were asking him was his brother in the house. Before he could reply, my brother, Owen Magill, walked out to the side of Stephen. They were only a few feet from the door when I heard the order, ' Hands up ' and the next thing I heard was a volley of shots. I ran to the door and saw my brother Stephen falling, and my brother Owen ran to me and said to me ' I'm done.' I took my brother Owen round to the back of the house and helped to bandage his wound, which was in his right side. He was quite conscious and did not appear to be seriously wounded. My brother Stephen was shot through the heart and died in a few minutes. His wound appeared to be caused by an explosive bullet as the gash in his breast was almost two inches in diameter.

" When the Specials left, we took my brother Owen into the house and he undressed himself and went to bed. At about 10 p.m. the Specials returned and enquired for my brother Owen, who was wounded. They told him they were going to take him to hospital and they told me the same. My father was in the room with my brother at the time ; the Specials kicked him out of the room and abused him badly. My father is aged 78. Then my brother walked out of the house with the Specials, and as far as I know, walked over two hundred yards to the military lorry which was in waiting. They did not allow my brother to put on his coat, but took him away in his shirt and trousers. As far as can be ascertained, my brother was dead when he arrived at the hospital.

" The Specials returned on June 10, and raided our house. They knocked down a stack of hay, and threw clothes and other things on the yard. On Sunday, June 12, they again returned. Neither my father nor myself were in the house at the time. They broke open the door and tossed everything over the house, pitching beds, clothes, and everything here, there, and everywhere They again returned on June 18.

" On the occasion of their visit on June 8 they followed me through the fields, and threatened to shoot me if I did not tell them where my wounded brother was, he having hid himself under the bed when he heard they were coming the second time. This is a true statement of all the main facts of the case.

(Signed) "MARY ELLEN MAGEE.
"*June* 20*th*, '21."

THE SWORN STATEMENT OF LAURENCE MCGIVERN, OF DRUMREIGH, CO. DOWN.

"I, Laurence McGivern, of Drumreigh, Rostrevor, co. Down, was employed as a servant with Patrick J. MacAnuff, of Shinn, Ardaragh, Newry. On the morning of June 5, the house was raided by military between the hours of 3 and 4 a.m. They ordered me out of bed and asked me questions I knew nothing about. They then asked, Did I know who I was speaking to. I said no. They then said they were Royal Irish Constabulary, and made me repeat these words after them. One of them hit me and knocked me down. I got up and two of them ordered me out. I refused, as I said I was bare-footed, but they made me go, and took me across the lawn and ordered me not to look behind at the crowd of military behind me. They then gathered around me, made me put my hands by my sides, and hit me with their fists. They knocked me down and kicked me in the back and sides, and used the ends of their rifles on my head and face. An officer came out of the house, and asked (by the way) what had happened. The reply was that I fell on my face. He lifted me, knowing well what had happened; but he took me into the house and helped my master to put me to bed. I was then unconscious for some time and am now at home unfit for work and under the doctor's care. I am twenty years of age.

(Signed) "LAURENCE MCGIVERN."

(This raid had a tragic sequel a few days later when a

party of British forces again raided the house in search of Patrick MacAnuff. His sister, Theresa MacAnuff, who was on a visit from Broadford, England, rushed to a window when she heard the soldiers breaking their way through the house, and called for help. She was ordered by the raiders to desist. She continued to call, and was thereupon shot dead.)

LETTER WRITTEN BY PATRICK TRAYNOR,
106, BOTANIC ROAD, GLASNEVIN, DUBLIN.

" Rath Internment Camp, Curragh,
" Co. Kildare.
" 10*th June*, '21.

" DEAR ——

" The following account of my treatment with a view to extracting information by British Intelligence Officers whilst I was a prisoner in Dublin Castle, should be published.

" From March 30 to April 20 I was a prisoner in the Castle, and in all was interrogated by British Intelligence Officers on 33 occasions.

" During each interrogation with a view to extracting information, I was treated by these Intelligence Officers with the utmost cruelty. My fingers were bent back until they nearly tipped the back of my hands. My arms were twisted, a red-hot poker was held to my eyes, and threats to destroy my sight were made. I was kicked and threatened with shooting. On several occasions I was taken to a dark passage, under the canteen, which leads to the cells, and badly beaten. The doctors here can testify to my condition on arrival.

" On one occasion an officer asked me if I would care to see a priest, and upon my saying ' Yes,' a ' priest ' was sent to see me. This ' priest,' I afterwards discovered, was a member of the Intelligence Staff in Dublin Castle and an ordinary civilian.

" Love to all,
" Yours affectionately,
" PADDY."

SWORN STATEMENT OF EDWARD DORAN, BALLY-MACGEOUGH, KILKEEL, CO. DOWN.

"I am a farmer and live at Ballymacgeough, co. Down. I was arrested on May 10 and taken, with Thomas Fearon, James McDermott, Thomas Cunningham, and Edward Cunningham to Newry Military Barracks. We were all placed in the same cell there. About an hour after our arrival a police officer came in. I saw him strike Thomas Fearon. He took me to a guardroom where there were forty constables and placed me with my back to the wall. He took up two or three empty cartridges off the floor and said : ' See where your friends have gone.' He then put his head out of the door of the guardroom and said, as if speaking to somebody in the yard : ' Don't close that grave. We'll put them all in one.' He then turned to me and said : ' What are you in the I.R.A ? ' I said : ' I don't recognise your right to ask me any question.' He hit me with his open hand on the face. He repeated his question. I refused to answer. He then struck me with his clenched fist on the cheek, loaded his revolver and said he would give me three minutes to answer.

"At the end of about three minutes, he said, ' I'll let you off if you will answer me one question. Who is your commandant ? ' I said nothing. He said, ' Are you going to answer that question ? ' I said ' No.' He then rushed at me and commenced to beat me with his clenched fists about the face. He knocked me down once. He cut my face and gave me two black eyes. Whilst he was beating me, a Black and Tan officer came in, got beside me and struck me, knocking me down. The officer then took up his revolver and watch, and, looking at his watch, said, ' My lunch has got cold with you and I am going to finish you now if you don't answer my question.' As I still remained silent he asked me, ' Are you going to answer?' I said, 'No.' He gave me a kick on the thigh. Then he stood back from me and fired a shot. The bullet passed close to my head. The plaster fell off the wall behind me. He showed me a mark on the wall and said, ' Do you see how it missed you ? ' A sergeant then took me out to the yard, and as I was passing the officer on the way out he (the officer) gave me a kick on the thigh again.

(Signed) " EDWARD DORAN."

"*Dated this 25th day of June, '21.*"

In the course of the interview Eoin MacNeill granted me he described his experiences with the Black and Tans. He said :

"It was at an early hour that the Black and Tans smashed into my house and arrested my eldest son—then about 12 years of age—and me. They took us in a lorry down into the village of Blackrock, where there were several other lorries standing. Apparently their occupants were raiding houses in the vicinity. Our captor stopped his car and ordered us down into the road. Then he pointed to a blank wall on which had been scrawled, ' Up the Republic,' and, producing a bucket of whitewash and a brush, held them out to my son and ordered him to whitewash the wall.

"My boy looked up at me to see if I would allow him to do this, and I told him not to touch the brush or the bucket. ' Oh, you won't let him do it, eh ? ' said the Black and Tan. I replied that I certainly would not. ' Very well, then,' said he, ' you do it yourself.' I refused. Setting down the bucket and brush, he produced a revolver and pointed it at me. He told me if I did not do as he ordered within one minute he would fire. But when I did not move, he finally put his revolver back in his holster, and gruffly ordered us into another lorry.

"This was the only bad treatment accorded me at any time while I was a prisoner in the hands of the British. In the English jail where Griffith and I were fellow prisoners, every possible consideration was shewn us."

The Truth About the Truce

When I reported back to Collins that I had found ample testimony to support his general statement that the Black and Tans had been guilty of acts of extreme cruelty—he made no comment. All he had to say in that connection, he explained, he had already said.

"Even after the truce had been declared," Collins continued, "I was not in favour of bringing these matters forward. A truce presupposes the possibility of a return to the conditions which existed before it was declared. I could see no good purpose served by doing anything to make worse the conditions that had been so barbarous. I am still inclined to doubt the wisdom of reopening a subject that cannot be done justice to unless one goes into details of indescribable infamy. However, the fact remains that exaggeration in this connection is impossible."

CHAPTER XIV

THE INVITATION TO NEGOTIATE

" THE excuse offered by the British Government for the brutish insensibility of the Black and Tans was that they were meting out to murderers just retribution. Mr. Lloyd George was ' firmly convinced that the men who are suffering in Ireland are the men who are engaged in a murderous conspiracy.' At the London Guildhall he announced that the police were ' getting the right men.' A demand for the truth about English repression in Ireland was beginning to make itself heard in all parts of the world. It was becoming ever more difficult to convince the world that the premeditated murder of Irishmen constituted legitimate acts of self-defence."

Collins thus began the story of events leading up to the Treaty negotiations.

"At length, when the Terror, growing ever more violent and, consequently, ever more futile, failed to break the spirit of the Irish people—failed as it was bound to fail—concealment was no longer possible," Collins continued. "The true explanation was blurted out when Mr. Lloyd George and Mr. Bonar Law declared that their acts were necessary to destroy the authority of the Irish national government which ' has all the symbols and all the realities of government.'

" But this announcement had an unexpected consequence. In the opinion of responsible men in the other States of the British Empire, such destruction had no justification. They expressed their opinion in emphatic fashion. They convinced British statesmen that it was essential for England to put herself right with the world—the Irish slate had to

The Invitation to Negotiate 135

be cleaned. So declared the Premiers of the Free Nations of the British Commonwealth—then assembled at the Imperial Conference in London. There was only one course for the British Prime Minister to take—to invite us, whom he had called ' murderers ' and ' heads of the murder gang,' to discuss with him terms of peace. The invitation was:

> " To discuss terms of peace—to ascertain how the association of Ireland with the community of nations known as the British Empire may best be reconciled with Irish national aspirations."

The world knows that we accepted that invitation.

" What is not known—except only by those few of us who had to take the responsibility of accepting or refusing the invitation—is the searching of our hearts and minds, the weighing of every consideration, the honest effort some of us made to put aside scepticism in order that the decision might be the fruit of our combined best judgment. There was much in our immediate path that undeniably prejudiced us as to the possibility of obtaining a generous peace from England. Beyond that were more than seven centuries of English misrule of Ireland. In our councils were men who believed—and who still believe—that to try to make a bargain with England could result only in Ireland's getting the worst of it.

" I have always believed that Mr. Lloyd George foresaw the inevitable at least a year before his colleagues even considered the possibility of granting Ireland freedom. I base my belief on the fact that while the Terror was at its height the British Cabinet passed the Government of Ireland Act, 1920—better known as the Partition Act. In my opinion, Mr. Lloyd George intended the Act to allay world criticism. As propaganda it might do to draw attention away from British violence for a month or two longer. At the end of that period—most of the English Ministers mistakenly believed—Ireland would have been terrorised into submission. That desired end gained, a chastened nation would accept the crumb of freedom offered by the Act. Britain—her idea of the principles of self-determination satisfied—would be able to present a bold front again before the world.

"It seems to me this must have been what was in the mind of the British Cabinet in passing this measure. Certainly it was not asked for by Ireland. Nobody representing any Irish constituency in the British Parliament voted for it. We of the South took advantage of its election machinery only to repudiate the Act and to secure a fresh mandate from the people. Otherwise the Act was completely ignored by us. In the Six Counties almost one-fourth of the candidates were returned in non-recognition of the Act, while Sir James Craig himself said, referring to himself and his friends, ' we accept the Parliament conferred upon us by the Act *only as a great sacrifice.*'

"I believe there was an understanding between Mr. Lloyd George and the Orange leaders. The Act entrenched them—or appeared to—within the Six Counties. No doubt, both the British Prime Minister and Sir James Craig had it in mind that if a bigger settlement had ultimately to be made with Ireland, at least the Act put them in a position from which they could bargain. In any ' settlement ' the North-East was to be let down gently by England. Pampered for so long, they had come to be able to dictate to and to bully the nation to which they professed loyalty. They were to be treated with tact in regard to any change of British policy towards Ireland.

"This much I was convinced of from the moment the Lloyd George proposal of peace reached us. In our councils I urged this view. I held that England now realised that both the Partition Act and the Terror had alike failed to achieve what had been expected of them. Ulster's usefulness to England had ceased to be potent enough to prevent Irish freedom, but I urged that we should not be unmindful that Ulster could be useful in another way. She could buttress England in England's determination that, while agreeing to our freedom, Ireland must remain associated with the

British group of nations. England's insistence upon this association as a minimum was based on her conviction that her own national safety can be assured by nothing less. In this view I HAD THE COMPLETE SUPPORT OF DE VALERA NOT ONLY DURING THESE PRELIMINARY CONFERENCES, BUT AT ALL TIMES DURING THE PROGRESS OF THE NEGOTIATIONS !

"What seemed to me to be our chief concern was so to make our moves that Britain would be obliged to give us the maximum limit of freedom. And from the outset I was convinced that that maximum limit would be bounded by association with the British Empire. I anticipated what subsequently turned out to be the fact. Britain must represent to us that the North-East would never acquiesce in more, while representing *to them* that in such a settlement they would be preserving that which they professed to have at heart, the sentimental tie with the nation to which they were supposed to be attached.

"In those preliminary conferences, a few of us held that any settlement which did not include *the possibility* of a united Ireland—which was not predicated on the living truth, THAT EVERY IRISHMAN IS FIRST AN IRISHMAN WITH RIGHTS THE SAME AS THOSE OF EVERY OTHER IRISHMAN—would be unacceptable to us. It was not so much the Partition Act itself that mattered—it was an even more formidable legacy that England would leave us, PARTITION OF VIEW. That is there, and it has to be dealt with. It is for us, to whom union is an article of our national faith, to deal with it.

"For the most part De Valera—at first—seemed to be in accord with the views voiced by Griffiths and me. As, little by little, Childers wormed his way into our councils, however, De Valera's attitude gradually changed. From beginning to end Stack and Brugha were unqualifiedly hostile to the whole idea of entering into negotiations with England. Yet for a long time we had all been agreed on the fundamental wisdom of no coercion for Ulster. Likewise we were one in our conviction that a divided Ireland could never be a free Ireland.

"It was—and, more's the pity, it still is—this serious internal problem which led some of us to argue for the attainment of the final steps of freedom by evolution rather than by force. If we could obtain substantial freedom by consenting to association with the British Empire, it would at least give us time to teach the North-East to revolve in the Irish orbit and to get out of the orbit of Great Britain. We held that in acquiescing in a peace which would admittedly involve some postponement of the fulfilment of our national sentiment—by agreeing to some association of our Irish nation with the British nations—we would be going a long way towards meeting the sentiment of the North-East in its supposed attachment to England.

"Against these councils the uncompromising Republicans raised up the objection that by consenting to bargain with England before she recognised the Republic—we should be letting the Republic down. But De Valera, himself, pointed to the fact that this was not an issue to be argued then. Mr. Lloyd George had already made it clear that no such recognition would be granted. Furthermore, it was pointed out that were the Irish Republic a recognised fact, we should have to use our resources to coerce North-East Ulster into submission. None of the conferees was prepared to sponsor such a course of action. We had long since concluded that coercion—even if it succeeded—could never have the lasting effects which conversation on our side, and acquiescence on theirs, would produce.

"Our position at this time, as it appeared to me, was one of greater strength than ever before in the history of Ireland under English rule. From the English view-point, peace with Ireland had become a necessity to the British Cabinet. Already Mr. Lloyd George—in 1921—had made a peace offer to De Valera. That offer had not been acceptable to the Irish people. Referring to it, Mr. Churchill, at Dundee in September of the same year, had said :

" ' . . . this offer is put forward, not as the offer of a Party Government confronted by a formidable opposition and anxious to bargain for the Irish vote, but with the united sanction of both the historic parties in the State, and indeed all parties. It is a national offer.'

" Undoubtedly it was a national offer, representing English necessity to put herself right with world opinion. It had, at last, become essential that England find a way of peace with Ireland or a good case for further, and what unquestionably would have been more intensive, war.

" The important factors in the situation were known to all of us. We knew the Dominion Premiers were in England fresh from their people. They were able to express the views of their people. The Washington Conference was looming ahead. Lloyd George's Cabinet had its economic difficulties. England's relationships with foreign countries were growing increasingly unhappy. Recovery of the good opinion of the world had become indispensable. BUT I FOUGHT THE STUPID NOTION THAT WE WERE STRONG ENOUGH TO RELY ON FORCE ALONE.

" England wanted peace with Ireland, true ; but if Ireland made impossible demands we could be shown to be irreconcilables and then England would again have a free hand for whatever further measures of force might be necessary ' to restore law and order ' in a country that would not accept the responsibility of doing so for itself. I was under no delusion that the offer indicated any real change of heart on the part of England towards Ireland. In this respect I was entirely at one with the uncompromising Republicans. But I held that then, as always, England's difficulty was Ireland's opportunity, and we should be fools to fail to seize it merely because behind the offer was no sincerity of good will. It seemed to me to make no difference that an awakening conscience had nothing to do with the English offer. It is true that there were stirrings of conscience felt by a minority of Englishmen—the minority that had opposed England's intervention in the European war. They were the peaceful group averse to bloodshed on principle. They were opposed to the killing we had to do in self-defence quite as much as they were opposed to the aggressive killing of our people by the British agents sent to Ireland for that purpose.

" I urged that we waste no time in considering this phase of the situation. Pacifists the world over are almost without any political power and have very little popular support. The point was that peace had become necessary to England. It was not because she had repented in the very middle of her Black and Tan terror. IT WAS NOT BECAUSE SHE COULD NOT SUBJUGATE US! It was because she had not succeeded in subjugating us before the world's conscience awakened and made itself felt.

"We had ample evidence of this. There was, for instance, the frank admission of Lord Birkenhead in the British House of Lords early in August:

> " ' The progress of the coercive attempts made by the Government have proved in a high degree disappointing.'

" From every side came proofs that world sympathy was with us—passive sympathy for the most part. If we had done no more—and we had done much more—this winning of world sympathy was itself a great asset in the proposed negotiations with England.

" What it was never possible to make the more extreme of our conferees appreciate was that we had not beaten AND NEVER COULD HOPE TO BEAT THE BRITISH MILITARY FORCES. We had thus far prevented them from conquering us, but that was the sum of our achievement. And in July, 1921, we had reached the high-water mark of what we could do in the way of economic and military resistance. I suppose there are Irishmen who will go to their graves still cherishing the notion that continuation of the struggle would have ended in an overwhelming victory for Irish arms. It is a pity, but it is a fact. To such men figures mean nothing. They will not see.

The Invitation to Negotiate

" But even some of these uncompromising Republicans had their moments of sanity. Some of them, at least, are on record as recognising our inability to beat the British out of Ireland. See what Mr. Barton had to say in *The Republic of Ireland* in its issue of February 21, 1922 :

" ' . . . it had become plain that it was physically impossible to secure Ireland's ideal of a completely isolated Republic otherwise than by driving *the overwhelmingly superior* British forces out of the country.'

And yet Mr. Barton—after he had put his signature to the Treaty—talked at a session of Dail Eireann about having signed ' under duress ' ! Before we went to London to negotiate, Mr. Barton knew, as did we all, that the element of duress existed and would continue to exist so long as British power lasts.

" I have explained how we considered every phase of the situation before finally deciding to accept the offer. I WANT TO MAKE IT ABSOLUTELY PLAIN THAT AT THE CONCLUSION OF OUR DELIBERATIONS WE HAD ABANDONED, FOR THE TIME BEING, THE HOPE OF ACHIEVING THE IDEAL OF AN ISOLATED REPUBLIC. FOR ANY OF THE MEN WHO PARTICIPATED IN THOSE CONFERENCES TO PRETEND OTHERWISE IS ABOMINABLE ! WE ALL CLEARLY RECOGNISED THAT OUR NATIONAL VIEW WAS NOT SHARED BY THE MAJORITY IN THE FOUR NORTH-EASTERN COUNTIES. WE KNEW THAT THAT MAJORITY HAD REFUSED TO GIVE ALLEGIANCE TO AN IRISH REPUBLIC. WE KNEW THAT THEY WOULD NOT YET ACQUIESCE IN ANY KIND OF ISOLATION FROM BRITAIN. BEFORE WE UNDERTOOK THE TREATY NEGOTIATIONS WE REALISED THESE FACTS AMONG OURSELVES. HAD WE NOT REALISED THEM—HAD WE NOT ACCEPTED THEM AS FACTS—THERE WOULD HAVE BEEN NO NEGOTIATIONS. LET THERE BE NO DOUBT ABOUT THAT.

" It is true that before we accepted the invitation sent by Mr. Lloyd George we endeavoured to get an unfettered basis for the conference. And after negotiations had been begun—as I shall presently point out—we continued to try. Document No 2 was an instance of this endeavour. But we did not succeed. Again and again we asserted our claim that the plenipotentiaries could enter such a conference only as the spokesmen of an independent sovereign State. It was a claim Britain tacitly admitted in inviting us to negotiate at all, but the fact remains that we finally went to London without recognition of our nation as an independent sovereign State. We went—and in going WE ADMITTED THAT THERE WAS A POSSIBILITY OF THE IRISH PEOPLE RECONCILING 'IRISH NATIONAL ASPIRATIONS' WITH 'ASSOCIATION OF IRELAND WITH THE GROUP OF NATIONS KNOWN AS THE BRITISH COMMONWEALTH.' Let us not fool ourselves about that.

"Those who cannot, or who will not, look these facts in the face blame us now, and more than blame us. They find fault with us because in agreeing to some kind of association of our nation with the British nations we were not able, by the touch of a magic wand, to get rid of all language of Empire. That is not a fair attitude. We like that language no more, perhaps less, than do those who wish to make us responsible for its preservation. It is Britain's affair not ours, that she cares to preserve the prevarications of obsolete feudalism. The British Empire is what it is. It is what it is with all its trappings, its symbols of monarchy, its feudal phraseology, its obsolete oaths of allegiance—its king a figurehead having no individual power as a king—maintaining the unhealthy atmosphere of mediæval subservience translated into modern snobbery. But these are things that are not to be dissipated by the waving of a magic wand!

" MOREOVER, THE RESULT OF OUR DELIBERATIONS SPEAKS FOR ITSELF—WE ENTERED INTO NEGOTIATIONS WITH THAT EMPIRE AND ITS LANGUAGE IS THE LANGUAGE WE HAD TO SPEAK.

"It is not any verbiage about sovereignty which can assure our power to shape our destinies. The important

The Invitation to Negotiate

thing is to grasp everything which is of benefit to us—to manage things for ourselves—to make such a constitution as suits ourselves—to make our Government and restore our national life along the lines which suit our national character and our national requirements best. *It is now only fratricidal strife which can prevent us from making the Gaelic Ireland which is our goal."*

CHAPTER XV

THE TREATY NEGOTIATIONS

"My going to London as one of the plenipotentiaries was in spite of my conviction that any other Irishman, would serve the cause of Irish freedom better than I—at least, so far as the Treaty negotiations were concerned. For three hours one night, after the decision had been made to send a delegation to London, I pleaded with De Valera to leave me at home and let some other man take my place as a negotiator. But it was no use. My arguments seemed to fall on deaf ears. I had no choice. I had to go."

This statement Collins made to me many months after he had told me the inside story of the Treaty negotiations—and in view of all the circumstances it was, perhaps, one of the most astounding things he ever told me.

"Of course we all knew," he continued, "that whatever the outcome of the negotiations we could never hope to bring back all that Ireland wanted and deserved to have—and we therefore knew that more or less opprobrium would be the best reward we could hope to win. But as Arthur Griffith has told you, we went when others refused to go—because it was a job that had to be done by somebody. For my own part, I anticipated the loss of the position I occupied in the hearts of the Irish people as a result of my share in what was bound to be an unsatisfactory bargain. And to have and hold the regard of one's fellow-countrymen is surely a boon not to be lost while there is a way to avoid it. But this consideration was not at all what moved me to try to keep out of the negotiations.

"The point that I tried to impress upon De Valera was

The Treaty Negotiations

that for several years—rightly or wrongly makes no difference—the English had held me to be the one man most necessary to capture because they held me to be the one man responsible for the smashing of their Secret Service organisation and for their failure to terrorise the Irish people with their Black and Tans. Brugha has spoken of this English legend as having been altogether of newspaper manufacture. What difference does that make? The important fact was that in England, as in Ireland, the Michael Collins legend existed. It pictured me a mysterious active menace—elusive, unknown, unaccountable. And in this respect I was the only living Irishman of whom this could be said. If and as long as the legend continued to exert its influence on English minds, the accruing advantage to our cause would continue. Bring me into the spotlight of a London conference and quickly would be discovered the common clay of which I am made! The glamour of the legendary figure would be gone for ever.

"Whether De Valera underestimated the advantage of keeping me in the background—whether he believed my presence in the delegation would be of greater value—OR WHETHER FOR MOTIVES BEST NOT ENQUIRED INTO HE WISHED TO INCLUDE ME AMONG THE SCAPEGOATS WHO MUST INEVITABLY FAIL TO WIN COMPLETE SUCCESS—is of little importance. The only fact that may appeal to the careful reader as significant is that BEFORE THE NEGOTIATIONS BEGAN NO DOUBT OF DE VALERA'S SINCERITY HAD PLACE IN MY MIND!

"As I have before stated, I objected to the presence of Childers in the secretariat because, as I have already pointed out, I considered him at least altogether too radical and impractical and, at worst, an enemy of Ireland. But just as I failed in my plea to be kept off the delegation so De Valera would not listen to Childers' exclusion. His argument was that, aside from whatever truth there might be in my view that the menace I constituted was of advantage to us, Ireland needed her ablest advocates at the conference table—and he insisted I belonged in that category. As for Childers—and here I am convinced he was quite sincere—he said he considered him the most brilliant constitutional authority Ireland had ever had, and his presence in the delegation an essential of success.

"So my wishes were thwarted. Instead of being kept in the background—against all eventualities—to be offered in a crisis as a final sacrifice with which to win our way to freedom—I had to walk into Whitehall and deal, face to face, with the heads of the British Empire. AT THE VERY MOMENT I WAS SHAKING HANDS WITH MR. LLOYD GEORGE ON THE OCCASION OF OUR FIRST MEETING THERE WAS STILL IN EXISTENCE THE DUBLIN CASTLE REWARD OF TEN THOUSAND POUNDS FOR MY CAPTURE, DEAD OR ALIVE! SUBSEQUENTLY I REMINDED THE BRITISH PRIME MINISTER OF THIS INCONGRUOUS STATE OF AFFAIRS—BUT THAT DID NOT HAPPEN UNTIL I HAD DISCOVERED THAT HE KNEW HOW TO LAUGH!

"From beginning to end the English plenipotentiaries dealt candidly, fairly, sympathetically. Much criticism has been directed at Griffith and me because frequently we went into conference alone with Mr. Lloyd George and Mr. Churchill. It seems to me the point is not well taken. I have never heard of anyone's criticising De Valera for having conferred quite alone with Mr. Lloyd George a few months earlier. There are inevitably details in the course of negotiations of this character which are best discussed by a few men, rather than by dozens. It comes to this: confidence in the negotiators. And if, as Brugha charged, we were bungling amateurs the fault lies with those who sent us as their plenipotentiaries.

"It would be poor return for the treatment accorded us in London to overstep the bounds of strict ethics by divulging anything of the negotiations which in any way could prove offensive to the English participants. I have no intention of doing so. But with that said, there are certain points which I may shed light upon without committing that unpardonable offence. And, to begin with, there is one matter that I can deal with without any breach of confidence or without any departure from etiquette.

"It has been charged that we signed the Treaty under duress. It has been said we signed the Treaty under a threat of 'immediate and terrible war.' That is not true. It was Barton who first made this charge—and by his own statement proved himself a man who could be successfully threatened ! BUT BARTON—CHALLENGED TO QUOTE THE EXACT WORDS USED BY ANY OF THE ENGLISH PLENIPOTENTIARIES IN FRAMING THE ALLEGED THREAT—ADMITTED THAT IT HAD NEVER BEEN VOICED IN WORDS ! Nevertheless, Barton, having signed the Treaty, opposed it and gave as his justification his having acted under a threat which was never made ! It is time this kind of thing received the attention it merits.

"Surely I have made it plain enough that British armed force could wipe the Irish nation out of existence. Is it necessary to labour a self-evident fact ? No one but a madman would question it. And in that sense, then, there was, during the negotiations as there has always been as between England and Ireland, the element of duress present. Nobody doubts that had we been able to do it we should have beaten the English out of Ireland—as our simple right. Our acceptance of the truce, our consenting to negotiate—yes, and in the same sense our signing of the Treaty—all these proved that there existed the element of duress. Had we been able to do it we should have whipped England decisively—and then the Treaty negotiations would have been conducted in Dublin, and we should have been a conqueror nation announcing terms of surrender to a vanquished foe ! The only reason that did not happen was because we could not make it happen ! What good end is to be served by pretending otherwise ?

"I dwell on this point because in many quarters this charge of duress has been interpreted to mean that we plenpotentiaries were subjected to personal duress. Of course, this is nonsense. Obviously there was not, and could not have been, any personal duress. But the unfortunate impression that individual members of our delegation were directly threatened has found lodgment in the minds of men not conversant with the fundamental rules of conduct of negotiations between two sovereign States. Of frankness there was plenty. Plain speaking was to our liking. And there was little of subtlety and drawing of fine distinctions. Meantime, however, the weeks dragged along, and we could see small chance of arriving at any possible agreement.

" Time after time—duly reported in the world Press—we adjourned the conference, and went back to our colleagues in Dublin—with nothing that was encouraging to report. It was during the first of these return visits that De Valera brought forward the first rough draft of what later came to be the ' Mysterious Document No. 2.' Its right to the title lay in the fact that it was not of De Valera's composition. Put forward by him as his alternative to the proposed Treaty, it was, in fact, the work of Erskine Childers. I had little difficulty in guessing the identity of the author as soon as I read it. Dominionism tinged every line of this production. No Irishman who understood the tradition and the history of Ireland would have thought or written of his country's aspirations in the terms used in this document.

" Under the terms of this document Ireland, by our own free offer, was to be represented at the Imperial Conference. Thus our status would have been taken from a Constitutional Resolution passed at an Imperial Conference ! It was quite clear that the outlook of the author of the document was bounded entirely by the horizon of the British Empire. BUT DE VALERA WAS INSISTENT THAT WE CARRY THE ALTERNATIVE PROPOSAL BACK TO LONDON AND THERE SUBMIT IT AS OUR IRREDUCIBLE MINIMUM !

" We did so. The English delegates turned it down flatly. We brought it back to Dublin, and it was revised and amended—and again we took it to Downing Street. Again it was turned down. And again we returned to De Valera with the twice-rejected document. But a third time revisions and amendments were made, and a third time we presented ourselves in London with the Childers' compromise. When Mr. Lloyd George let us understand that further repetitions of this kind could mean only the final breaking up of conference, we shelved Document No. 2—shelved it for once and all, as we thought. But that was an error.

" Meantime, I had come to have what I believed—and believe—was a clear understanding of the basic facts of the situation. And when the opportunity arose I made it quite clear to the British representatives that my stand was different from that of the author of the thrice-rejected proposals. I stated that Ireland was a mother country, with the duties and responsibilities and feelings and devotions of a mother country. This simple statement had more effect on the British delegates than all the arguments about dominion status, or all the arguments basing the claim of our historic nation on any new-found idea. I told them that Irish nationhood springs from the Irish people, not from any comparison with any other nation, not from any equality—inherent or acquired—with any other nation.

" In the course of our conversations Griffith and I soon learned that the imposing conferees were primarily men who dealt in facts, men to whom facts appealed. In this respect they were like ourselves. In the Mansion House in Dublin there was much of fine idealism—and almost as much of impractical dreaming. In Whitehall there were no illusions —and idealism had no place. But in Whitehall, at least, we knew where we stood.

" As I have said, I hesitate to do anything that can be construed as a breach of etiquette, but to make my point quite clear I must risk the charge by citing two instances of this downright frankness which characterised the English statesmen with whom we dealt.

" It happened during the conference between Mr. Churchill and Lord Beatty and Childers and myself—in the Colonial Office—to which I have already referred. In my embarrassment over Childers' failure to produce anything approaching a reasonable idea to back up his statement that he could prove that Ireland was of no concern to Britain, I searched my mind for something to say that would at least make mycolleague's impracticability less glaring. It will be remembered that Childers had insisted that Plymouth was a better base for submarine chasers than any Irish port! While Lord Beatty was pointing to the map and thus flatly disproving the truth of this assertion, I had an idea. Pointing to the French coast I suggested that Havre, for instance, would have made an excellent base for the British forces engaged in hunting submarines.

"'Quite so,' replied Lord Beatty. Then he smiled, and added, ' BUT WE CAN'T TAKE A *FRENCH* PORT !'

" If that constitutes duress, I'll admit that we were under duress. But to my way of thinking it is plain talk, right talk, and the kind of talk I prefer my opponent to use.

" The other instance of this willingness on the part of the Englishmen with whom we were dealing to say what they mean was furnished by Mr. Lloyd George. I think he will have no objection to my quoting him. As I have already stated, I know he can laugh !

" It was in the midst of our consideration of the defence clauses in the British proposals. Mr. Lloyd George made it quite clear to us that the British people could not, or would not, for the sake of their own safety, allow any Irish Government to build submarines. England did not mind if we built a dreadnought or two, a battleship or two—although these concessions do not appear in the signed Treaty. In fighting for vital concessions we were not weakening our position by claiming anything so obviously useless as the right to build and man a few capital ships ! It must be apparent to everyone that to do such a ridiculous thing would be to play England's game.

" We could indulge our vanity—if we were foolish enough to waste public funds in such a manner—by having an infant navy that could never mean anything at all to the British sea power—BUT WE COULD NOT HAVE ONE SUBMARINE ! SUBMARINES ARE CHEAP TO BUILD AND REQUIRE FEW MEN TO OPERATE THEM ! SUBMARINES ARE A REAL MENACE TO ENGLAND !

" I fought my best to try to argue the point. 'After all,'

I said to the British Prime Minister, ' Ireland could never hope to wage an aggressive war against England.' Restricting our offensive armament seemed to me on a par with muzzling a Skye terrier.

" ' Submarines,' replied Mr. Lloyd George, ' are the flying columns of the seas.' He looked at me straight as he said this, and slowly a twinkle came into his eyes. Then he spoke again. ' And I am sure,' he said, ' there is no need for me to tell you, Mr. Collins, how much damage can be inflicted by flying columns ! We have had experience with your flying columns on land ! '

" There was nothing to be said then ! He knew what he was talking about. More than that—he knew that I knew !

" But De Valera and Childers saw nothing disadvantageous to us in this prohibition of submarines. Perhaps it would be more nearly accurate to say that De Valera did not visualise the potential value of Irish submarines—and that Childers did ! In any event, Document No. 2 conceded this British claim fully. Document No. 2 gave way to England on a point that really mattered ! This cannot be stated too emphatically. Such a concession to British necessity, real or supposed, was nothing but rank dishonesty. LET US AGREE—SINCE WE MUST—THAT WE SHALL NOT BUILD SUBMARINES, BUT DON'T LET US PRETEND THAT WE ARE DOING IT FROM ANY MOTIVE OTHER THAN THE REAL MOTIVE !

" With the Treaty finally signed, what was the position ? After 750 years, Ireland was about to become a fully constituted nation—the whole of Ireland as one nation to compose the Irish Free State with a Parliament to make laws for the peace, order and good government of Ireland, and with an Executive responsible to that Parliament. This is the whole basis of the Treaty, and it must be borne clearly in mind that the Treaty (and a treaty, be it remembered, is between equals) is the bed-rock from which our status springs, and that any later Act of the British Legislature derives its force from the Treaty only. We have the *constitutional* status of Canada, and that status being one of freedom and equality we are free to take advantage of that status. In fact, England has renounced all right to govern Ireland, and the withdrawal of her forces is the proof of this. With the evacuation, secured by the Treaty, has come the end of British rule in Ireland. No foreigner will be able to intervene between our Government and our people. WILL IRISHMEN CONTINUE TO INTERVENE BETWEEN OUR GOVERNMENT AND OUR PEOPLE ?

" The Treaty we brought home gave us the freedom we fought to win—freedom from British interference and domination. The Black and Tans are no more. The regular British Military Forces are gone. The Royal Irish Constabulary is only a memory in the twenty-six counties. And these are the results of the Treaty. And we knew that December night when we boarded the train, bound for home, that these were to be the results of our many months of arduous labours. If it were not a triumph for the cause of Ireland, at least it was a greater measure of success than any of us had dared hope. And it seemed that the Irish people resident in London considered it a triumph. For at the station there were thousands of them —men, women and children—waving the tri-colour and cheering us and singing happy folk-songs. It was a heartening sight. Was it only a forerunner of our greeting in Dublin ? We all wondered.

CHAPTER XVI

THE MISGUIDED ONES

" Our arrival with the signed Treaty in Dublin, on a grey, cold December morning, was in a sense prophetic of what was to follow through all the bitter weeks of the Dail sessions. Here were no signs of jubilation. There was no one at the station to greet us. And yet the newspapers had acclaimed the Treaty as a triumph. Even the few people abroad at that early hour seemed strangely apathetic. Had our four months of hard work meant just nothing at all to the people whom we had tried to serve ? It appeared so."

Collins spoke with an unaccustomed note of sadness in his voice. Although at this time he did not make reference to it, I recalled an earlier confidence of his—the real ambiton he hoped one day to realise. When I tell it, there should be no longer any doubt as to the kind of man this young, inspired Irishman was. He hated politics. He hated intrigue. He hated everything that was not constructive. What he wanted above anything else—and I can say this because I have his word for it—was to see his country awaken to the meaning of good citizenship and so permit him to lay down the heavy burden of being the leader of a people asleep and ignorant. And when that day came Collins hoped he might be able to set himself up in business —a little business in which he could never have to be afraid of becoming rich !

That was a very real fear in Collins' mind—perhaps the only fear he ever knew. On two different occasions it became my duty to acquaint him with opportunities offered him by American interests through me. One of them involved his receiving a sum of money greater than the total of his life's earnings—to be paid to him for writing a series of articles for American publication. He agreed to write the articles BUT FLATLY REFUSED TO ACCEPT PAYMENT FOR THEM!

"Would you think of offering your President Harding payment for such a thing?" he asked soberly. Collins had no "side," but he was Chairman of the Provisional Government, and he held that any act unworthy of that office must reflect on the dignity of the Irish nation.

The other offer I presented to him called for his leaving the responsibilities of government to others and making a journey to the United States where a lecture tour had been tentatively arranged for him. He shook his big head emphatically. It was out of the question, he insisted. And when I explained to him that in six months of lecturing he could do more for Ireland's cause in America than he could ever accomplish in any other way, he was still adamant in his refusal even to consider it. I asked him if he had any idea how much money he himself could earn by such a tour. The question seemed to strike him as very humorous. He grinned, and shook his head. I told him he would be the richer by at least a million dollars.

"That settles it," he said with a chuckle. "I'll keep away from America. A million dollars would ruin a better man than I am!" And he meant it! But returning to Collins' story of the homecoming of the envoys.

"The lack of jubilation among the people," he continued, "was dispiriting enough, but it was nothing compared with the open hostility we faced in the Cabinet drawing-room of the Mansion House. Awaiting us there were De Valera, depressed, gaunt, solemn; Stack, his eyes blazing, his fists tight clenched; Brugha, the personification of venom; Mme. Markievicz, more nearly hysterical and more vituperative than ever she was in any session of the Dail. These and others faced us, and one of the first words of greeting told us that we had made ourselves 'Partners of the Empire '—referring to the phrase used by the Lord Chancellor of England in felicitating Ireland.

"Before that first conference ended Griffith and I realised what we must expect from these men and women with whom all through the years we had fought the fight for Irish freedom. From colleagues they had suddenly changed into savage, relentless enemies. And yet, then—as always ever since—Griffith and I hoped against hope that we could persuade them of their error. IT IS ALL VERY WELL FOR CRITICS OF THE POLICY WHICH GRIFFITH AND I ADOPTED TO DECLARE THAT THE MENACE THIS MISGUIDED MINORITY CONSTITUTED SHOULD NOT HAVE BEEN MET BY KID-GLOVE METHODS—BUT THE IRISH PEOPLE NEEDED, AND STILL NEED ABOVE ANY OTHER, ONE THING—UNITY—AND UNITY IS NOT TO BE ACHIEVED BY KILLING ALL THOSE WHOSE OPINIONS MAKE UNITY IMPOSSIBLE. HARMONY does not spring FROM MURDER. THERE ARE FEW MEN IN THE WORLD WHOM YOU CAN BRING TO YOUR POINT OF VIEW BY KNOCKING THEM DOWN.

"Griffith and I held that the Treaty healed an age-old tragedy, the first act of which was played in Dublin in 1172, when Henry II. of England compelled Ireland's tribal kings to swear fealty to him. But the little group of men and women facing us in the Mansion House held a different opinion. They told us—and for the most part they were sincere—that the Treaty we had signed was the most infamous document any Irishman ever signed; that every martyr's widow, and most of the army leaders, considered we were guilty of treason. It was they—at first—who held the floor, and had their say. But finally I had my chance.

"'In signing this Treaty,' I told them, 'we have laid the foundation of peace and friendship with the people at our side. What I have signed I shall stand over in the belief that, if it brings Ireland no other blessing, the ending of the conflict of centuries is the finest thing that ever happened for the Irish people.'

"This I told them, but it served to lessen their hostility

not at all. Stack, I remember especially, was incensed because Griffith had ' forgotten ' the meaning of Sinn Fein —which he mistranslated as ' Ourselves Alone.' Neither Griffith nor I made answer to this charge—nor, indeed, to any of the charges. Unexpected as was this vitriolic condemnation of us, and as little prepared for it as we were, we both grasped the essential point that recriminations were useless and worse than useless.

" De Valera showed us a telegraphed appeal to the Irish people sent from London that morning by Art O'Brien, head of the Irish Self-Determination League. ' Be not misled into thanksgiving without cause,' the telegram read. ' Complete sovereignty is a claim which no nation can forgo. And until it is met in our case we of the Irish race cannot and will not rejoice.' This was, at any rate, less vicious in tone than the rest, and we quickly made it plain that we expected no acclamation of joy that might properly follow a national triumph. We asked and wanted no throwing up of hats, no fervid demonstrations of any kind. We did ask and did want calm, deliberate, FAIR consideration of the results of our labours in London.

" Of the 121 members of Dail Eireann, 112 were veterans of the war and men who had served at least one term in an English jail. Many of them have been arrested and imprisoned three and even five times. A few have served prison terms as many as nine times. And to these Teachtæ of the Dail we submitted the Treaty with its oath of allegiance, ' That I will be faithful to His Majesty King George, his heirs and successors by law.' We knew how hard it was going to be for these men, who had suffered so much at the hands of England, to take that oath. BUT WHO IS GOING TO SAY THAT THEIR DIFFICULTY IS ANY MORE PAINFUL THAN OURS ?

" I talked with these men, and tried my best to reason with them. The world knows the result. A majority of seven in Dail Eireann brought the Treaty into being. But the minority left me in no doubt as to where I stood in their estimation. Few of them chose to say it openly, but all of them held that I was not the same man who told the young Volunteers at Rathfarnham that ' Irish freedom is coming because of the men who have died and because of the men who are still prepared to die.' I was the same man. I am the same man. And I say now what I said at Rathfarnham, with the difference that now I say Irish freedom HAS come!

" Of course, the Dail discovered that there was a serious split in the Cabinet at the first of the secret sessions in December. De Valera had just motored back from the West. Brugha was on hand fresh from an inspection of the army that had taken him all over Ireland. Both were convinced that the vast majority of the people would support them in any move they made. And, for a few days, this was a fact undoubtedly. The people still hailed De Valera as their leader. They applauded him when he told them, ' We have counted the cost, and we shall not quail even though the full price of our freedom has to be paid.' Brave words, truly ! Applauded certainly ! But sanity was yet to prevail.

" Brugha told us in one of the secret sessions that we had fallen to the magic of Lloyd George. Mme. Markievicz held us in scorn because we had proved ourselves incapable of matching swords with ' the Welsh wizard.' De Valera referred to his own fears—fears that led him to abstain from taking part in the negotiations. He admitted his fear that he might succumb to the British Prime Minister's cunning, and then, apparently on the verge of tears, declared that this is what had happened to us. The man who had taken the measure of Woodrow Wilson and Georges Clemenceau had outwitted us. This is what De Valera told the Teachtæ. IT WAS NOT THUS.

" The truth, as I have tried to make it plain, is that Lloyd George was well informed. The militarists in Whitehall were pressing for an immediate onslaught by sea and land. They believed—and many of them still believe— that the late Lord Salisbury spoke accurately when he said that ' the Irish are no more fitted for self-government than the Hottentots.' What Ireland needed—declared these advocates of ruthlessness—was twenty years of resolute government! Lloyd George did not believe this. I repeat: he was well informed. He knew we had organised on a national scale and could count on 3,000,000 men, women and children to do their part of the task of fighting the British armed forces in guerilla warfare. He knew the British garrison in Ireland, all told, numbered 150,000 men. He knew what it would mean to conquer the Irish people. He did not want to have to do it.

"Lloyd George knew that the Terror had failed; that it had been not only non-deterrent but had actually swelled the patriotic fervour of the youth of Ireland. He knew that the morning they hanged young Kevin Barry 550 young men of Dublin enrolled themselves in the army! He knew that we were smuggling arms and ammunition into Ireland throughout the truce. He knew we were recruiting and drilling. He knew our ramifications were world-wide. There were evidences of this close at hand. The raids for machine-guns on Chelsea and Windsor Barracks were such evidences. The Irish Office in Whitehall had proof that as much as five pounds had been paid for a high-explosive detonator—and five times as much for a service revolver! The British Prime Minister had accurate information as to the intended recipients of the 600 ·45 calibre Colt automatics discovered on the docks in Hoboken! He knew the planned destination of the 355 lbs. of T.N.T. seized in the home of a coal-miner in Newcastle.

"But he knew more than this. He knew that Ireland's freedom was absolutely dependent on the good-will of Britain. He made *us* know it! He made us see the common sense of entering into friendly relations—a course dictated, if by nothing else, by the instinct of self-preservation. He put clearly before us the indisputable fact that our economic interests are identical. It was our task to convince our people that these were the facts.

"To many Irishmen the Treaty had come as a crushing disappointment. There is no gainsaying it. They had believed that in some magical way we of the delegation would be able to make possible the rebirth and regeneration of the Gaelic State on a stupendous scale. Anything less than this seemed impossible to accept. Yet we could not for ever live in dreamland. The reality of the situation had to be made plain from Cashal down to Kerry. Griffith voiced the urgent need of unity on the part of ' all sections of the Irish nation in raising the structure and shaping the destiny of our new Free State.' And already the people began to understand.

" De Valera at first insisted that the Treaty would never be accepted by the people. He declared that ' the terms of this Agreement are in violent conflict with the wishes of the majority of this nation.' But little by little he began to realise that this was not the case. Whereupon he sponsored the remarkable policy of saving the people from themselves by preventing their expressing their will ! To me it would have been a criminal act to refuse to allow the Irish nation to give its opinion as to whether it would accept this settlement or resume hostilities. But in the initial stages of the fight within the Cabinet De Valera and his followers seemed capable of making a plebiscite impossible.

" Our difficulty then—as it is still—was to make plain to the people that the task of making a noble Irish Ireland lies in the people themselves. It cannot be stated too often that our people for hundreds of years have been subjected to the de-nationalising influence of Anglicisation. The task before us, having got rid of the British, is to get rid of the remaining influences—to de-Anglicise ourselves. There are many among us who still hanker after English ways, and any thoughtlessness, any carelessness, will tend to keep things on the old lines—the inevitable danger of the proximity of the two nations.

" It is no restriction nor limitation in the Treaty that will prevent our nation from becoming great and potent. The presence of a representative of the British Crown—*depending upon us for his resources*—cannot prevent us from doing that. The words of a document as to what our status is cannot prevent us from doing that. . . . One thing only can prevent us—and that is disunion among ourselves. Can we not concentrate and unite not on the negative but on the positive task of making a real Ireland, distinctive from Britain—a nation of our own? The only way to get rid of the British contamination and the evils of corrupt materialism is to secure a united Ireland intent on democratic ways, to make our free Ireland a fact, and not to keep it for ever in dreamland as something that will never come true, and which has no practical effect or reality except as giving rise to everlasting fighting and destruction. Destructive conflict seems almost to have become the end itself in the minds of some—some who appear almost to be unheeding and unmindful of what the real end is.

" In those early days of the year we clung hopefully to the belief that our political opponents must sooner or later cease their opposition and accept the will of the people, which was daily becoming more and more overwhelmingly in favour of the Treaty. At that time Ireland was perhaps the only country in Europe which had living hopes of a better civilisation. We had an unparalleled opportunity of making good. Much was within our grasp. Who could lay a finger on our liberties? If any power menaced us we were in a stronger position than ever before to repel the aggressor. We had reached the starting-point from which to advance and use our liberties to make Ireland a shining light in a dark world, to reconstruct our ancient civilisation on modern lines, to avoid the errors, the miseries, the dangers into which other nations with their false civilisations have fallen.

" The only way to build the nation solid and Irish is to affect the dissentient elements in a friendly national way—by attraction, not by compulsion, making themselves feel welcomed into the Irish nation in which they can join and become absorbed as, long ago, the Gerladines and the de Burgos became absorbed. The old Unionists, Home Rulers, Devolutionists—and now the uncompromising

Republicans—we had to have them all, and we tried to win them all. We are still at it. If with each passing week our efforts seem to be more and more futile—if the soul-destroying pessimism which is gradually settling down over our people cannot be dissipated—at least it will not be because those of us enlisted in the cause of an Irish Ireland have not used every means in our power to put an end to internecine conflict.

"The English Die-Hards said to Mr. Lloyd George and his Cabinet, 'You have surrendered.' Our own Die-Hards say to us, 'You have surrendered.' There is a simple test. *Those who are left in possession of the battlefield have won.*

"Yes—we had won. We had won our freedom. next we had to consolidate our gains to prove ourselves worthy of the victory. And as the weeks lengthened into months and our opponents became ever more bitter and more extreme, we began ourselves to wonder if in the end the Irish people—in order to be able to live in peace—would consent to remain in dreamland, to be led by dreamers! We wondered, but we did not cease doing our best to prevent this national tragedy. We have not ceased—and we shall not cease. The fight must go on until it is won. It will go on until law and order have been established in every square mile of the 26 counties. To that we have dedicated ourselves."

CHAPTER XVII

DISHONEST TACTICS

"THERE were 1,200 of us in the internment camp. Almost every man of the lot had done his share in digging the tunnel through which a few of us would be able to make our escape. By mutual agreement this number was fixed at thirty. If a greater number attempted it the escape would be foredoomed to failure. The point was—how to nominate the lucky thirty. Every one of us knew in his heart that our return to the army meant more to Ireland than that of any other man! That was only human, of course. The selection was not safely to be left in our hands. Only some one less self-interested ought to name the thirty.

"Among ourselves we discussed our various leaders—to find one upon whose judgment we could all rely. Brugha, as titular head of the army, was objectionable to many of us. De Valera likewise was voted down. Finally, Collins was proposed. Not one man of the 1,200 had any objections to him. And so we left our fate in his hands. We did it because we had implicit trust in him."

This little story was told me several months after the signing of the Treaty by Desmond Fitzgerald. I tell it here to make clear the wonderful hold Collins had on all classes of Irishmen. In their eyes he was the embodiment of honesty and fair dealing. But in the case of De Valera there was also a kind of blind faith on the part of hundreds of thousands of Irish people which accounted for his very real power in Dail Eireann. They are a simple people, the Irish. They must have an object of devotion. And once a national hero has won their affection, it is neither easy nor wise to attempt to disillusionise them. And this

Dishonest Tactics

fact must be borne in mind while considering Collins' steadfast refusal to tell the Irish people what he himself had discovered—THAT DE VALERA'S "IDEALISM" WAS NOT GENUINE.

"The unnatural campaign of destruction being waged by the uncompromising Republicans," Collins said at one of our last conferences, "had its beginnings in the bitter fight in the early sessions of the Dail. For a long time I struggled with myself to keep from believing the evidence of my own eyes and ears, but finally I had to realise that the man we had made President of the Republic was capable of resorting to dishonest methods. Griffith came to this conclusion before I did, but in the end we were both of one mind. Also we saw eye to eye as to the inadvisability of making this deplorable fact known among the people. No good end was to be served by such a course. We felt that we were strong enough within the Dail itself to remove De Valera as a potent factor of disruption. But now the time has come to establish the grave charge I have made.

"De Valera would not head the delegation that went to London. Every member of the Cabinet and every Teachtæ of Dail Eireann wanted him to conduct the Treaty negotiations, and many of us pleaded with him not to remain behind. But he was immovable. The reason he gave was twofold. First, he said, it was beneath his dignity, as President of the Irish Republic, to leave his country; and, second, he could not afford to put himself in a position in which he might do his nation irreparable harm by a chance word across the conference table. He insisted his value to the Irish people would be greatest by remaining in Dublin, and from that distance guiding us in our task.

"I for one accepted what he said as being his sincere belief, although I differed from him. But when he persisted in forcing us to present to the British delegation Document No. 2—after we had told him time and again that it meant the breaking off of the negotiations—a doubt of his sincerity began to form in my mind. Subsequent developments have removed that doubt. There is no longer any doubt about it. De Valera was animated by only one purpose—the collapse of the negotiations to be effected by our stubborn unreasonableness!

"De Valera's alternative contained very little that was not in the Treaty, and little that England could have objected to, but for that very reason our insistence on its supplanting the Treaty merited the unequivocal refusal our insistence met. Besides that, De Valera's document was loos in its construction. In the application of its details we should have been constantly faced with conflicting interpretations leading to inevitable discordance. But such considerations meant nothing to De Valera. HE NEITHER EXPECTED NOR WANTED HIS ALTERNATIVE ACCEPTED!

"He stated that England had never kept a treaty, and would not keep this Treaty. He used this argument in support of his contention that his Document No. 2 should have been forced upon the British Government. Yet a blind man can see the fallacy of such an argument. England, said De Valera in effect, would not keep the Treaty which she had signed—and would keep a treaty she had not signed! The truth is that De Valera, under the malignant influence of Childers, had reached that point of paranoia at which persecutory delusions become fixed. He would effect the ruin of his own country before he would admit that peace and friendship between Ireland and England were possible. AND YET HE IS THE MAN WHO ACCEPTED IN THE NAME OF THE IRISH PEOPLE THE ENGLISH INVITATION TO FIND A WAY FOR THE TWO NATIONS TO LIVE SIDE BY SIDE IN AMITY. I SAY—AND I CHOOSE MY WORDS DELIBERATELY—THAT HIS ACCEPTANCE OF THAT INVITATION WAS A DISHONEST ACT.

"Of course it has been abundantly established that Document No. 2 was not of De Valera's authorship, to begin with. And it is fact that cannot be controverted that De Valera claimed its authorship. It is relatively unimportant, but it is an added proof of my charge. As to the differences between the Treaty and this alternative, such as there are, they all bespeak the dishonesty of purpose of their author. There is, for instance, the definite stipulation in Document No. 2 for Britain's ratification of the alternative. And hand in hand with that fact is De Valera's vehement protest against the British conferring on us of the rights and powers of the Treaty. That is not honest.

"Under certain clauses of the alternative Ireland is committed to an association so vague that it might afford grounds for claims by Britain which might give her an opportunity to press for control in Irish affairs as ' common concerns,' and to use or to threaten to use force. The Irish people would never have agreed to commit themselves to anything so vague. We know that there are many things which the States of the British Commonwealth can afford to regard as ' common concerns ' which we could not afford so to regard—one of the disadvantages of geographical propinquity. We had to find some form of association which would safeguard us—as far as we could be safeguarded—in somewhat the same degree as the 3,000 miles of ocean safeguard Canada.

" De Valera knew when he accepted the British Prime Minister's invitation to discuss ' association with the British Commonwealth ' that that meant association of a different kind from that of mere alliance of isolated nations. For him to have suggested otherwise was dishonest. More than that, the association of the Treaty is less equivocal than the association proposed in Document No. 2. The external association mentioned in Document No. 2 had neither the honesty of complete isolation—a questionable advantage in these days of warring nationalities when it is not too easy for a small nation to stand rigidly alone—nor the strength of free partnership satisfying the different partners. Such external association was not practical politics.

" De Valera and Childers laboured long over the framing of an oath which they knew had to be incorporated in any agreement that would be acceptable to Britain. Their first essay read as follows :

" ' That for the purposes of the association Ireland shall recognise His Britannic Majesty as head of the association.'

Here merely is recognition as precise as that given in the Treaty—but it met with such disapproval that De Valera and Childers shelved it in favour of another, namely:

> " ' I do swear to bear true faith and allegiance to the Constitution of Ireland and to the Treaty of Association of Ireland with the British Commonwealth of Nations and to recognise the King of Great Britain as head of the associated States.'

This alternative oath was discussed by the Dail for many long, weary days in private sessions. De Valera attempted to explain that the King of Great Britain might fairly be regarded as a managing director—a mere name in common usage these days when industrial concerns are amalgamating and entering into agreements. The King of Great Britain would thus occupy the same relative position towards the associated States as a managing director occupies towards associated businesses. Now a managing director is one who manages and directs. Whatever the practical value of royal prerogatives, no modern democratic nation is managed and directed by one ruler. This talk of a managing director was as nonsensical as it was dishonest.

" Throughout the Childers document there are dangerous friction spots—which obviously were to be avoided by any one with Ireland's interests at heart. Ireland, being the weaker nation, could not fail to suffer if a misleading clause had to be interpreted. As for the defence clauses, I have already told how De Valera and Childers gave way to England on the only point that really mattered—agreement not to build submarines. It will not do for them to say submarines would be of no use to us. Childers, with his experience in the Royal Navy, knows better. I cannot believe that De Valera is so ignorant as not to know better. IF HE BELIEVES WHAT I HAVE TOLD HIM MORE THAN ONCE, HE DOES KNOW BETTER!

" But without going into tiresome details I want to state again that from beginning to end this document is for the most part a repetition of the Treaty WITH ONLY SUCH SLIGHT

VERBAL ALTERATIONS AS NO ONE BUT A FACTIONIST, LOOKING FOR MEANS OF MAKING MISCHIEF, WOULD HAVE THOUGHT IT WORTH WHILE TO HAVE RISKED WRECKING THE TREATY FOR.

"As an improvement on the Treaty, Document No. 2 is not honest. It may be more dictatorial in language, but it does not contain in principle a great 'reconciliation with Irish national aspirations.' It merely sought to attach a fresh label to the same parcel, or, rather, a label written of purpose illegibly in the hope of making believe that the parcel was other than it is.

"What is this idealism that is supposed to be animating De Valera and his followers? Without attempting to answer that question, let me point to its proven consequences. We are back in slavery! At the very moment that we had been lifted out of the worst slough of destitution these idealists began their senseless, wicked campaign, the underlying purpose of which is to destroy us as a nation! We were turning our eyes towards the light of liberty, and beginning to lift our heads as Irish men and Irish women, with a land of our own, and with traditions and hopes of which no nation need feel ashamed—and then from East to West, from North to South, a handful of desperate madmen brought down upon the people all the wicked anguish of fratricidal strife! They have done and are still doing their best to prove true the degrading lie that what is English is respectable, and what is Irish is low and mean! BUT THEY WILL NEVER SUCCEED IN THAT.

"Let a world who stands by now and expresses scorn of a people who permit outrages to be practised upon them by a negligible minority understand that this is not fair to the Irish people. Let the world remember that there have been only brief intervals between long periods of starvation —periods in which we could reflect upon our condition and awaken to the cause of our miseries. The presence of the English had deprived us of life and liberty. An infamous machine was destroying us. Now that it has gone, the ravaging effects remain. National consciousness is not an over-night growth. Of patriotic fervour there is no lack, but a people must be schooled for generations to know how effectively to put their patriotism to practical ends.

"The history of 700 years must be reversed before we shall know the meaning of national freedom. And first of all we must acquire the habit of standing together. Already to a large degree the advantages of the Treaty have been irretrievably lost. Our very national life is being threatened by this continued disunion. The country is too small to stand a big cleavage in the national ranks. The opposition as represented by De Valera and his Irregulars has already proved nearly fatal to the national interests. If De Valera succeeds in his opposition, he will undoubtedly destroy the nation as a whole. BUT DE VALERA WILL NOT SUCCEED! THAT IS THE ONE EVENTUALITY—AND PERHAPS THE ONLY ONE—WHICH WILL NEVER HAPPEN SO LONG AS THERE REMAIN ALIVE SANE IRISHMEN.

"When, during the Terror, England issued the order I have already referred to, making it a criminal offence for an Irishman to be in possession of arms, it was held to be a death-blow to our fight for freedom. Yet to-day we are faced with a greater misfortune—disunity among ourselves. Until now I have refrained from speaking plainly about those men who are leading the nation into black chaos—but nothing less than the brutal truth will serve now.

"More than once in Ireland's history has an Irish army been betrayed by Irishmen. Once, for instance, the Volunteers were betrayed—by Grattan—who, when it suited his purpose, spoke of them as 'an armed rabble.' The old saying that the only real lesson of history is that the lessons of history are never learned, is peculiarly applicable to some of the Irish people to-day. If De Valera has his way, the Irish army of to-day will be rendered useless, as were the armies of 1652, 1691 and 1782. BUT DE VALERA WILL NOT HAVE HIS WAY. THE NATIONAL ARMY IS THE PEOPLE'S ARMY, AND IT WILL BRING THE PEOPLE WHAT THEY MOST DESIRE—ABIDING PEACE.

"Finally, let there be no doubt anywhere that the vast majority of responsible opinion in Ireland is absolutely against De Valera and his followers. See what the bishops of Ireland said at a general meeting, held in St. Patrick's College, Maynooth, April 26, 1922:

> " ' The condition of the country is a subject of the deepest distress and humiliation. On the great national question of the Treaty every Irishman is entitled to his own opinion, subject to truth and responsibility to God. It is a national question to be settled by the national will and ascertained by an election. It is painful to have to use the language of condemnation, but principles are being openly defended which are in fundamental conflict with the law of God. The army as a whole, and still more a part of the army, has no moral right to declare itself independent of all civil authority in the country. Such a claim is subversive of all civil liberty. The army more than any other order in society, from the nature of its institution, is the servant of the nation's government. . . .
> " ' We appeal in the name of God, of Ireland and of all national dignity to the leaders on both sides, civil and military, to meet again, to remember old fellowship in danger and suffering, and if they cannot agree upon the main question to agree upon two things at all events—that the use of the revolver must cease, and the elections, the national expression of self-determination, be allowed to be held free from all violence.'

" To this appeal Griffith and I responded whole heartedly. The result is known by the world. The Military Executive that was set up in the Four Courts was the answer of the extremists who clung to De Valera's idealistic (!) pronouncement that Ireland was theirs ' for the taking '—clung to it as greedy vultures cling to a carcass. The die was cast. It was now only a question of weeks, perhaps days, before the people's army would have to go forth and defend the people's rights. It was heart-sickening. But the fact remained."

CHAPTER XVIII

THE ULSTER PROBLEM

"WHEN a people have struggled for 750 years against subjection it is perhaps not strange that the one dominating characteristic of such a people should finally come to be antagonism. And antagonism has come to be an ingrained quality of many Irishmen. Among ourselves in the 26 counties there is hardly less of antagonism between the labour group and those not so labelled than there is between the so-called Republicans and those who support the Treaty. The agreement with the British Government has removed Ireland's one great inspiration for unity, and has made many Irishmen forget that after all we are every one of us—Republican extremist and moderate Free Stater, radical labourite and idealistic Separatist—IRISH!"

Collins thus introduced his narrative of the two years' reign of violence in Belfast one night while he lay ill at the house of a friend in Dublin. He told me the story only after he had become convinced of the uselessness of further conferences with Sir James Craig.

"Mistaking the means for the end is perhaps the greatest blunder a man can make," he continued. "Unhappily it is a blunder of which many Irishmen are guilty. In some instances fighting for freedom has come to mean fighting for fighting's sake. Bringing the victims of this delusion to realise their folly constitutes the gravest problem confronting the Free State Government. For it is this spirit of suspicion and hostility animating opposing groups of Irishmen that is largely responsible for the situation in Ulster. If unity is impossible among us of the South, how can we expect understanding and reconciliation with Ulster?

"The semblance of unity which we managed to manufacture at the recent session of the Sinn Fein Ard Fheis was artificial in the sense that it was but temporary and for expediency, but it would be a mistake to imagine for a moment that that unity would not become very real and absolutely effective if either Britain or Ulster attempted to take advantage of any apparent split between the four opposing groups. It has always been so—in Ireland. Enemies of to-day are brothers in arms to-morrow—instantly an outsider seeks to exploit either to his own end.

"*I have every reason to believe, however, that neither Britain nor Ulster has any thought of trading on our disunion. Those of us who negotiated the Treaty are convinced of the good faith of the English signatories. This in itself precludes the possibility of any aggressive action on the part of Ulster. Whitehall invariably shows Belfast the way. The bitterer our quarrel becomes, the more virtuous will be the attitude of both Britain and Ulster.*"

(In the light of subsequent events this prophecy is of unusual interest in so far as it proves the great insight of the Irish leader. At the time he gave me this interview massacres of Roman Catholics were of daily occurrence in Belfast. The pogrom had been uninterrupted for two years. With the outbreak of the civil war in Southern Ireland the atrocities in Ulster ceased as if by magic!)

"Before I take up the situation in Ulster, therefore, I want to emphasise the one factor that is worrying us more than any other—the disunion that exists within our own parties. Divergencies of opinion among supporters of the Treaty are almost as great as the gulf that separates the Free State party as a whole and the Republican party. There is an unbridgeable chasm between the uncompromising extremism of the radical wing of the Republican party and its moderate adherents.

"De Valera is a moderate at heart. An idealist, he is at the same time less radical than many of his followers. Proof of this can be adduced. To do so I shall lift a corner of the veil of secrecy that covered the three-hour conference that took place just before the opening of the Ard Fheis between the leaders of the two parties. At that conference De Valera and Stack met Griffith and me in an attempt to find a common ground on which to appeal to the 3,000 Sinn Fein delegates for unity. As I think I have already made plain there is no follower of De Valera—not even excepting Cathal Brugha—more bitterly hostile to the Treaty than Austin Stack. Yet an agreement was reached—and reached in the face of Stack's violent opposition. To prove De Valera's moderation it is necessary to reproduce a portion of our discussion in the conference.

" ' I have a clear majority of 600 in this Ard Fheis,' said De Valera.

" ' You have not,' I told him.

" Stack insisted that their majority was quite 600—and a blind man could have seen the chip on his shoulder.

" ' You're wrong,' I told them. And before they could say anything further I showed them how wrong they were. I told them they had a majority of more than a thousand!

" In spite of this admission of mine we reached an agreement not to take the vote which I acknowledged would see us beaten by two to one. The reason De Valera consented to forego this victory was simple. He knew that that Ard Fheis was as typical of the Irish nation as Tammany Hall is typical of New York State. As well expect Tammany to endorse the Republican candidate for President as to expect the Ard Fheis to vote to disestablish the Irish Republic. A vote in the Ard Fheis would leave the situation in the country unchanged. No good could come from taking a vote then. I drove the point home with a paraphrase of the alleged threat of Mr. Lloyd George (which he never voiced) about ' immediate and terrible war.'

" ' If you force the issue here,' I told De Valera, ' it will mean that we shall go to the country and have an immediate and terrible election!' "

" Even Stack smiled. But his opposition to any kind of agreement was not in the least abated. He was still dissatisfied even after De Valera had managed to persuade us to postpone the General Election for three months. That agreement was popularly supposed to be a victory for De Valera. Actually it earned him the displeasure of all the extremists among his followers. His moderation, as then expressed, accounts for the ascendancy to-day of Rory O'Connor. De Valera is less than ever the real leader of those who oppose us. He wishes more than ever that some way could be devised to get him ' out of the Republican strait-jacket ' !

" It is a pity, but it is true, that De Valera finds himself in an inextricable position for all his desire to get himself out of it. Recently he qualified an earlier statement of his by saying that whereas he had stood on the rock of the Republic, he now felt he held a stronger position in that he was standing on the rock of Right. The truth is he knows that rejection of the Treaty will not bring the Republic into practical being any more than it has ever been a practical entity. He knows, moreover, that the Republican ideal is as dear to us who support the Treaty as it is to himself. He knows the achievement of that complete independence which a recognition of the Republic would bring to Ireland is much more nearly certain of being won through the medium of the Treaty than by its rejection. He knows that we who oppose him will work to make Ireland strong enough to declare her independence—strong enough to force world recognition of her status as a soverign State.

" He knows these things—but his followers do not. And the pity is that he has not the moral courage to tell them ! He is a leader who does not lead, but is forced to adopt a course insisted upon by his followers. And I have gone into this purely domestic business in order the more clearly to set forth the actual facts regarding the situation in Ulster. For, curiously enough, there is a perfect parallel there.

" Sir James Craig—like De Valera—is powerless to control his followers. The madmen responsible for the bloody warfare on defenceless Catholics in Belfast and elsewhere throughout the North-East counties have gone about their slaughtering with complete disregard of their own authorities. They are continuing their murdering with absolute impunity. I came to a realisation of the truth during the visit of Sir James Craig to Dublin—at that conference after which it was announced that ' a serious situation ' had arisen over the question of the Boundaries Commission. It was not at all the matter of the Boundaries Commission that brought the conference to an abrupt end. It was not our disagreement over this subject that made Sir James Craig walk angrily out of the City Hall.

" Time after time Craig declared that Lloyd George had tricked Ulster. Each time my only reply was a demand to know what he was going to do to end the slaughter of Catholics in Belfast. Each time Craig evaded the question. Finally, I told him that there was no use of our continuing the discussion because he had satisfied me that he could not guarantee, much less control, the actions of his followers. His public announcement that Ulster would never abide by the findings of the Boundary Commission was, perhaps, his way of refuting this charge of mine. It seems to me hardly a refutation!

" Before I take up the details of the atrocities in Belfast I must make one further reference to Sir James Craig. I foresee the possibility of the end of his nominal leadership in Ulster—and the consequent opportunity for the Free State Government to take that situation in hand.

" If we can achieve unity in the 26 counties, if by setting a good example among ourselves we can prove our capacity for self-government, there will be a favourable reaction in the North-east. Of even greater value will be the changing of public opinion in England. By our own efforts I believe we can influence the sentiment of the British Government, which has been historically pro-Ulster, and make it favourable to Ireland as a whole. To bring this about there must be an end of Irish hatred of England. There must be an end of references to the English as ' the enemy.' So long as the British Government acts in accordance with the spirit of the Treaty we must deal with them in the same spirit. Our hope of a United Ireland is based largely on a growing realisation by the British Government that it is to their own best interests to give the Free State Government a chance to prove our good faith toward the North-East Once we can accomplish this there would follow necessarily the withdrawal of English support from Craig. The records are the best proof that Irish unity is impossible with Craig in power in Ulster.

"And now we can examine the records and determine whether this is a fair statement. For everything that has happened in Ulster since the pogrom against Catholics began—July 21, 1920—Sir James Craig, as head of the Ulster Government, is responsible. Let us look at the official figures. Here are the total for two years:

Killed	447
Wounded	1,796
Driven from employment	9,250
Driven from homes	23,960
Now homeless in Belfast	3,800

"All these figures refer to Catholics. In the same period no Protestants were driven from their employment or their homes. As for reprisals, here is a table that shows the comparative numbers of killed and wounded on both sides during the first six months of 1922:

	Catholics.		Protestants.	
	Killed.	Wounded.	Killed.	Wounded.
January	8	20	4	13
February	28	70	17	27
March	42	58	22	38
April	26	37	15	36
May	46	103	29	63
June	20	57	8	33
Totals	170	345	95	210

"These figures are misleading inasmuch as the killing and wounding of Protestants have not been in all cases the work of Catholics. We have indisputable proof that uniformed specials and armed mobs of Protestants have frequently numbered their own kind among their victims. This has been an unavoidable feature of the rule of the revolver in the streets of Belfast. One of the most recent outrages illustrates the inevitability of such mistakes on the part of the Ulster gunmen.

"At the intersection of two of the busiest streets in Belfast a lone gunman took possession of an office and throughout an entire afternoon terrorised the neighbourhood. He fired at every passer-by, and before his murderous work had completely emptied the street he had killed five men and wounded seven others. Of these twelve there were only three who were Catholics. From his position he could not possibly have identified any of them by sight. SUCH INSENSATE BLOOD LUST IS HIDEOUS ENOUGH—BUT HOW MUCH GREATER THE INFAMY OF A GOVERNMENT THAT PERMITS SUCH A THING TO HAPPEN WITHOUT TAKING ANY STEPS WHATEVER TO INTERFERE WITH THE MURDERER!

"A Mrs. Fitzpatrick, living in her own home at 5, Parkmount Terrace, Belfast, was driven into the streets with her three young children on the night of July 18. She was the only Catholic left in the locality. Nine weeks earlier her husband had to escape from the house by the back way when word reached him that a crowd of loyalists were coming to kill him. Since then he has never dared return to his home. This was the notice served upon Mrs. Fitzpatrick:

> "'As these premises are required for the Southern loyalists, who are homeless, you are required to clear out, or, without further notice, means will be taken to have you removed.'

According to information that has reached us Mrs. Fitzpatrick's house has remained unoccupied ever since. There is no record of the arrival in Belfast of any 'Southern loyalist.'

"More recently the *Belfast Telegraph*—consistently a mischief-maker and inciter of the pogromists—printed an account of an alleged attack by Sinn Fein gunmen from the Oldpark Road upon Royal Ulster Constabulary in the Marrowbone district. The facts are these :

"Two drunken specials in civilian clothes appeared at the Brickfields in the afternoon of July 19 and approached a crowd of Catholics—expelled workers—who use the fields for recreation purposes. The specials drew revolvers and shouted, 'Hands up, you —— Fenians!'

"Then they searched the Catholics, and finally took a boy off across the Brickfields. After going a short distance with them the boy started to run away. The specials, very much under the influence of drink, chased him and fired shots at him, but he escaped. Soldiers on duty in the neighbourhood opened fire and wounded one of the specials, Isaac Bradley, in the groin. Later all the male inhabitants of the Marrowbone were rounded up in the Brickfields and searched.

"In the evening of the same day members of the R.U.C. were making enquiries in Ardilea Street when they were fired at by the loyalists in Oldpark Road. The police saw five men armed with a rifle and revolvers between Cliftonville and Oldpark roads, and gave chase. The men escaped pursuit, but the Marrowbone was raided and searched from end to end for the ensuing twenty-four hours.

"Orange newspapers safely count on the ignorance of the outside world regarding the location of Catholic quarters in Belfast—but it is high time that attention was called to the fact that Sinn Fein gunmen would hardly choose a Catholic community like the Marrowbone in which to fire upon their own friends!

"Outside Belfast the rule of the revolver is almost, if not quite, as much in evidence. There was the case of a Mr. Owen Donnelly, of Whitehouse, whose daughter was married recently to a Mr. Anderson of the same village.

M

Mr. Anderson was formerly a Protestant who became a Catholic shortly before the marriage. On the wedding-day he was visited and threatened by two specials, and a few days later his father-in-law received the following letter:

> "'I want to let you know that we know the game you have been playing these few months as regards W. Anderson. You rushed the thing, got him to turn, and paid him to do it.
>
> "'You think you are clever, and we know you are the boss of the Sinn Fein Hall as well, but we know all and the clothes you are wearing will not save you. We have seen you miles away from Whitehouse, so you are easy got. It might be days and it might be weeks, but we will get you when we want you so you may prepare to meet your God. You will not get any letters from us again, but we will send you a bullet quick and sure. Take heed and don't treat this as a joke. We have men away after Anderson. At present he is in Coalisland so we will get him, we never fail. Sinn Feiner beware, for this is your last chance, so get down and say your prayers, but vengeance is ours. You will not lead any more good Orangemen into the ranks of the damd old Fenians.
>
> "'FROM THE 6-COUNTIES COMMITTEE to a rebel bastard and leader of young men from the Protestant Faith.'

"Since his receipt of this letter Mr. Donnelly has remained in Whitehouse—and as yet the threat remains a threat.

"The lying propaganda promulgated by the Belfast Press has gone a long way towards misleading world-opinion. In order to carry out the extermination of the Catholic minority in the North-East it was necessary to make it appear that the 90,000 unarmed Catholics in Belfast were making war upon the 280,000 Orangemen and non-Catholics, most of whom are armed and well supplied with ammunition. To illustrate the methods of the propagandists the slaughter of children in Weaver street last February is pertinent.

"There were the usual playing children in Weaver Street when two strange men appeared and held a whispered conversation with the police on duty. The policemen went into an adjoining street and ordered the children who were playing there to go into Weaver Street. Then they drove all the children to one end of the street. Presently the two strange men appeared again and threw a bomb into the midst of the children—killing and wounding more than twenty of them—all of them Catholics. Five of the wounded died, and most of the survivors are maimed for life.

"THE PRINCIPAL CONTINENTAL PAPERS—INCLUDING THE LEADING CATHOLIC PAPERS IN ROME—REPRESENTED THIS AS A CASE OF BELFAST PROTESTANT CHILDREN BEING BOMBED BY SINN FEINERS. THAT WAS THE STORY SENT TO THE WORLD BY THE BELFAST PRESS ASSOCIATIONS.

"Another attempt made by the propagandists has been to show that civil war has been raging in Belfast. The facts give the lie to this statement. The population of Catholic males between sixteen and sixty in Belfast is about twenty thousand. Of the forty-nine thousand armed special constables in the Six-County area, there are twenty thousand in Belfast. There are ten thousand soldiers in Belfast. There are three armed men, therefore, to keep in order each two unarmed Catholic males between sixteen and sixty years of age. Surely it is not necessary to say more.

"Recently the Ulster newspapers have diverted their activities from incitements of the pogromists into the more profitable channels of incitements of the Irregulars and armed bandits throughout the rest of Ireland. The issue of the 'Fenian Irregulars' War Bulletin' for July 21, containing altogether less matter than one column of an ordinary newspaper, has no fewer than seven extracts from the Orange Press. Erskine Childers, De Valera's director of publicity, seems proud to reprint the gloating of these Ulster newspapers over the alleged victories of the Irregulars. He copies also—in the columns of his *Poblacht na h'Eireann* —their advice to the Irregulars as to how best to carry on guerilla warfare.

"Changing conditions have resulted in a change of methods on the part of these propagandists. Formerly the prime object was to make reasonable the Ulster denials that pogroms and persecutions ever took place in Belfast, and that Orangemen were forced to act in self-defence by the provocative aggression of Sinn Feiners. Now they bolster up this lie by attempting to show that the peace that reigns in Belfast is the direct result of the departure of the Sinn Fein gunmen for the South—to join the ranks of the Irregulars. This, they urge, leaves the majority of the Ulster Catholics free to do what they have hitherto been restrained from doing by these gunmen—recognising the Ulster Government! I KNOW OF NOT ONE INSTANCE OF ANY SUCH RECOGNITION!

"Is it possible that the real reason for this industrious spreading of falsehoods is to be found in the wording of a supplementary estimate for the British Civil Service, issued July 20, 1922? It deals with an item of £2,250,000 for a grant in aid to the Six-County area, as a contribution towards abnormal expenditure—'*not to be audited in detail.*' It is not enough that this is one of the supplementary estimates which generally escape the notice of the British taxpayer. It is well to take the added precaution of keeping well hidden the fact that this 'abnormal expenditure' is caused by misgovernment that is without parallel since the penal days!"

CHAPTER XIX

THE REBELLION: ITS CAUSE AND COST

" WHILE critics at home and abroad were accusing the Provisional Government of being too lenient with the radical Republicans, at first led by Rory O'Connor and his lieutenants, we were, in fact, awaiting the moment when we could safely adopt sterner methods. Unity was still our goal, as it must always be our goal. By inopportune action against the rebels in the Four Courts we might easily have split the country wide open. Irishmen were not to be called upon to shed the blood of Irishmen until the provocation had become intolerable."

Even while Collins was making this statement to me—one night in July, in my bedroom in the Hotel Shelbourne—the reports of rifle and revolver shots reached us through the open window, emphatic proof of that intolerable provocation.

" To explain our long endeavour to save the country from the misery of fratricidal strife," Collins continued, " it is necessary to go back to the early part of May when individual members of the I.R.A. signed the following statement, and had it published :

" ' We feel that on this basis alone can the situation best be faced, viz.:

" ' 1. The acceptance of the fact—admitted by all sides—that the majority of the people of Ireland are willing to accept the Treaty.

" ' 2. An agreed election with a view to

" ' 3. Forming a Government which will have the confidence of the whole country.

" ' 4. Army unification on above basis.'

"Following the publication of this document, there came from the Director of Publicity, Republican Forces, Four Courts, a reply that stated that ' Any agreement upon which the army can be united must be based upon the maintenance of the Republic.'

"Then came the adoption by the Dail, May 3, of a motion to appoint a committee ' to consider and discuss the statement issued by the army officers on May 2.' The members of this committee were Sean Hales,[1] P. O'Maille, James Dwyer, Joseph McGuiness, Sean McKeon—representing the Free State party—Mrs. Clarke, P. Ruttledge, Liam Mellowes, Sean Boylan, Harry Boland—representing the Republicans. At the first meeting of this committee it was recommended that hostilities should immediately cease, and steps were taken to effect this. After a conference at the Mansion House the following day between leading officers of both sections of the I.R.A., it was announced that a truce had been declared as from four o'clock that afternoon with a view to giving both sections of the army an immediate opportunity of discovering a basis for army unification. Then, May 10, it was announced that the conference had concluded without reaching an agreement.

"The Dail adjourned after receiving a promise from the committee that a fresh effort would be made to find a solution of the difficulties. At the resumed sitting of the Dail, May 16, further reports of the peace conversations were presented indicating that a basis of settlement satisfactory to all parties had not yet been reached. It was then that I approached De Valera with a suggestion that he and I find a way out of the *impasse*. Out of our conference came what has been called the Collins-De Valera pact. The terms of that agreement were as follows :

"'We are agreed :

"'1. That a National Coalition panel for this

---

[1] Brother of the man who commanded the detachment of 200 Irregulars who ambuscaded the Collins' cavalcade at Bandon, where Collins met his death.

third Dail, representing both parties in the Dail and in the Sinn Fein organisation, be sent forward on the ground that the national position requires the entrusting of the Government of the country into the joint hands of those who have been the strength of the national situation during the last few years, without prejudice to their present respective positions.

" ' 2. That this Coalition panel be sent forward as from the Sinn Fein organisation, the number for each party being their present strength in the Dail.

" ' 3. That the candidates be nominated through each of the existing party Executives.

" ' 4. That every and any interest is free to go up and contest the election equally with the National-Sinn Fein panel.

" ' 5. That constituencies where an election is not held shall continue to be represented by their present Deputies.

" ' 6. That after the election the Executive shall consist of the President, elected as formerly; the Minister of Defence, representing the army; and nine other Ministers—five from the majority party and four from the minority, each party to choose its own nominees. The allocation will be in the hands of the President.

" ' 7. That in the event of the Coalition Government finding it necessary to dissolve, a general election will be held as soon as possible on adult suffrage.'

This agreement was submitted to Dail Eireann, May 20, and was agreed to unanimously.

"World opinion—as voiced in newspaper editorials and in expressions of private individuals which reached me —condemned me for entering into this pact with De Valera. In the light of what has happened since, the condemnation may appear to be justified. Yet I cannot bring myself to believe that it was not my duty to have done what I did,

In my official capacity as Chairman of the Provisional Government, I had no right to evade the duty I owed the Irish people—and the paramount responsibility resting upon me was to make any sacrifice that might spare the Irish nation from civil war.

"As to my own personal views—whatever I may have anticipated is beside the point."

Collins would not say more than this. But I had already learned from another source—and had amply corroborated it—just how much faith Collins had in the efficacy of his pact with De Valera. I tell it here because it is very well worth the telling.

Collins met Harry Boland on the street—one day shortly after the public announcement of the pact. Everywhere in the ranks of the uncompromising Republicans there was bitter disappointment over the "surrender" of their leader. It was being openly charged that De Valera had shaken hands with a traitor. In all fairness to Boland, it should be added that he was not of those who openly charged Collins with treason, although his affiliation with the extremists had prevented his actively repudiating their charges. As they came face to face, Collins opened the conversation.

"Boland," he began, "if De Valera and the rest of you uncompromising Republicans believe what you say—that because I support the Treaty I am guilty of treason—and you have the courage of your convictions, there is only one decent thing you can do. You know what a traitor deserves. Why don't you have me killed?"

"Now, Mick, be reasonable," replied Boland. "You know we can't afford to have you killed. Look at the disastrous reaction among the people who believe in you. We wouldn't dare take the responsibility of such a thing."

"Nonsense," said Collins. "You know better than that. The best thing the Irish people do is forget—and forget quickly. Within a week they would have forgotten me. Besides, you and those with you have openly charged that I am guilty of treason. There is only one punishment fitting

The Rebellion: Its Cause and Cost

that crime and no considerations of any kind should sway you from executing that punishment—no consideration, that is, unless, maybe, there is nobody among you that dares try it.

"I am altogether serious, Boland. You know what has to be done if a diseased body is to be made well. You must get at the central nerve tissue and destroy it. Also you know well that I am the pulse of this movement which you call treasonable. Destroy me and your idealistic colleagues can go ahead with the Republic without domestic opposition worthy the name."

When I related this story to Collins—as I did do when he refused to talk about his personal views of the value of the pact with De Valera—he chuckled. It was a characteristic of his, very much like a peculiarity of Theodore Roosevelt's, which bespoke his vast amusement. But the tale did not draw his fire; and I was determined to make sure that in eight months I had not completely misunderstood my man.

"But surely," I expostulated, "you don't mean to tell me you have decided to become one of those anæmic, maligned, martyrs-for-martyrdom's-sake persons! You don't mean you are prepared to put up your hands and be shot down in cold blood!"

"Ah, sure," came the quick reply, the smile widening and the chuckle more pronounced, "if they try it, there'll be several of them that will have headaches!"

Then, resuming his narrative, Collins dissected the motives actuating the leaders of the rebellion.

"It is not a pleasant thing to have to say," he began, "but there is no doubting that from the moment De Valera found himself beaten in the Dail and had to resign the Presidency, his wounded vanity led him straight into the arms of the bitterest of his followers. At any time before the outbreak of actual hostilities he could have stopped the rebels' preparations with a word. But he had forgotten Ireland in his own hurt—and to smash the machinery of the Government in which he did not have the controlling voice became an obsession with him. I have never seen anywhere in print a reference to a remarkable statement that De Valera made the third day of the private sessions of the Dail—Friday, December 16, 1921. On that occasion he said :

> "'I have been President of the Irish Republic ; I will never accept any lesser office in any Irish Cabinet.'

"De Valera cannot escape the responsibility of this revolt. In that one sentence lies the reason for his, first, fomenting civil war and, now, taking part in it. Of the remaining fifty-six members of the Dail who voted against the Treaty more than two-thirds have told me that they are delighted with the prospects of a peaceful Ireland. Not ten of the minority Deputies to-day approve of the senseless campaign of murder and destruction that is being waged by De Valera and his followers.

"Study of the mentality of the Irregular leaders with whom De Valera has chosen to associate himself, robs of any surprise their ambushing of the funeral cortège of a dead Volunteer. Such acts of desecration are but the natural development of the war policy worked out by leaders warped by vanity and egotism, and carried out by pliant followers who, from the very nature of their organisation, must necessarily include the rag-tag and bobtail of society—professional irresponsibles who, when war seemed unlikely, used the camouflage of an irregular armed force either to live without working or to get rich quick at the expense of the community.

"When De Valera spoke glibly about wading through blood, he paved the way knowingly for what was to come. He paved the way for the recognition in his organisation of an under-world section of his countrymen to whom could be left the work of promoting disorder and decay. He so twisted the minds of many Irish youths that they now regard as a 'stunt' the wholesale destruction which marks

The Rebellion: Its Cause and Cost

their track through the country. De Valera paved the way.

"Our intelligence staff was meantime not inactive. We knew what was going forward as a result of secret conferences in the Four Courts. When we made our attack on the rebel headquarters it was because we had in our possession proof that Rory O'Connor had perfected his plans for the opening of a general offensive in all parts of Ireland—and with the promise of De Valera to take an active part in the hostilities. Stack and Brugha and Childers were active participants in these conferences and, like De Valera, had important posts to fill the moment the fighting began.

"During the far-too-long-protracted period of discussion of the Treaty it was frequently pointed out that the time for talk was ended, and that the next phase must be one of hard work and constructive statesmanship. It was plain that if the development of our natural assets was to be delayed by unscrupulous, incompetent, or merely silly men and women, the assets of the nation, her cities, her soil, her many natural resources and capabilities, would be seriously injured. Few of us then foresaw the waste and destruction of mad war. It is the wickedest sin of those now in arms against the Irish nation that for the most part they are without any realisation of their sin. From injuries that were merely malicious and spiteful in the beginning, their destructive operations are now conducted on a basis of sheer lunacy.

"At whatever cost, there must be a return to sanity. The realisation must be brought home: that the looted shops, the burned town and city areas, the broken roads and railways—all the items of the wild orgy of destruction —must be paid for by the Irish taxpayer. The cost of this campaign of appalling carnival of crime is more than a million pounds a day—and this is a dead loss, never to be recovered. Ireland must be saved at no matter what cost. This is the people's war, and the people must win.

"It is the people's war because it is their homes and lives and fortunes that are being ruined. And so they are with their Government in the effort to suppress this revolt with the utmost speed. The people know that resources spent now in pursuit of victory will be economy if they ensure that wild destruction of all resources must cease. The victory of the people must be as sudden and as complete as possible. When the fighting ceases it must have ceased for once and all, and the will of the people be proved supreme beyond further question. There must not be any qualification of this, no shadow of doubt about it at all.

"THERE CAN BE NO TALK OF COMPROMISE, BECAUSE NO COMPROMISE IS POSSIBLE IN THE PRESENT CASE. WHEN WE HAVE PEACE IT MUST BE A REAL PEACE UPON WHICH WE CAN BUILD UP CLEAN AGAIN FROM THE SOUND AND SOLID FOUNDATIONS OF THE PEOPLE'S WILL.

"I promised in an earlier talk to dwell at greater length on that idea of the preference one should have for a wise coward as contrasted with a stupid brave man. I regret to say that, in the interim, facts have been brought to my attention that make me question the honest courage of the stupid man I had in mind.

"He is Austin Stack. I do not even now impute his bravery. But until recently I had faith in his honesty. His stupidity was amply evidenced at the time of the capture of Sir Roger Casement. In that crisis Stack lost his head completely, and was guilty of blunders a clever coward would never have committed. Let it be borne in mind that Stack to-day is one of the leaders of the Irregulars. He is actively engaged in leading bands of men against their fellow Irishmen—killing, burning, looting. Yet, as recently as last May—the sixth day of that month, to be exact—Stack made a speech in Bridgeport, Conn., in which he made the following statement :

"'I would rather that the proposed Free State was beaten by what is called constitutional means than any other. We propose to fight this election and defeat the Treaty at the polls. That is the only way the Treaty can be beaten without bloodshed.'

It was all fours with other speeches of other Republicans during this period. For the greater part these men proclaimed that a war against brother Irishmen was unthinkable. In view of their subsequent actions it is clear that the speeches were uttered with the object of lulling the people into a sense of false security until such time as the rebels were ready to strike. Meantime arms, explosives, and means of transport were being piled up in various areas, notably in the Four Courts and in Cork.

"Austin Stack has personal bravery in no small degree. I regret to have evidence of his dishonesty. Yet no man who knows him will ever believe that Stack could ever prefer a contest to be won in any fashion other than by fighting. Constitutional means never had any appeal for Stack. But in America, perhaps, he was influenced by the same considerations as caused J. J. O'Kelly, at Philadelphia, at about the same time, to make this statement:

> "'Nobody in the U.S. need have any fear that the opposing sides in this matter of the Free State will not conduct themselves properly. Any discussion they may have will be in keeping with the dignity of our race.'

It may be mentioned in passing that Stack and O'Kelly were members of a Republican delegation hastily despatched to America to try to bolster up the waning cause of the Republic.

"The cost of the revolt has already reached staggering totals. No man can tell how many more millions of treasure, how many more lives, the campaign of destruction may yet cost. But of one thing the Irish people may be sure. The fire that is testing our souls will make us the purer for it—when once again peace has come. And this is especially true of the young manhood represented by the national army.

"Our army, so long as it exists for honourable purposes only, will continue to draw to it honourable men. It will call to it the best men of our race, as the Athenian army did—men of skill and culture. And it will not be recruited as so many modern armies are, from those who are industrially useless. It has not been so recruited, and it will not be. For our army will continue to exist only for the defence of our liberties, and of our people in the exercise of their liberties.

"An Irish army can never be used for the ignoble purposes of invasion, subjugation, and exploitation. But it is not only upon our army that eventual victory of a self-governing Ireland depends. It depends more upon the extent to which we make ourselves invulnerable by having a civilisation which is indestructible. That civilisation will be indestructible only by its being enthroned in the lives of the people, and having its foundations resting on right, honesty, and justice.

"Our army in the field will deal with the ne'er-do-wells upon whom De Valera now depends. But in the final analysis our army is secondary in maintaining the peace that must be won. Its strength is but the strength of our real resistance—the extent to which we build up within ourselves what can never be overthrown nor destroyed—the extent to which we make strong the spirit of the Irish nation."

CHAPTER XX

THE FUTURE OF IRELAND

"WITH the Union came national enslavement. With the termination of the Union goes national enslavement—*if we will*. Freedom from an outside enemy is now ours, and nobody but ourselves can interfere with it. Complete national freedom can now be ours, and nobody but ourselves can prevent us achieving it. We shall no longer have anyone but ourselves to blame if we fail to use the freedom we have won to achieve full freedom. We are now on the natural and inevitable road to complete the work of Davis and Rooney, to restore our native tongue, to get back our history, to take up again and complete the education of our countrymen in the North-East in the national ideal, to renew our strength and refresh ourselves in our own Irish civilisation, to become again the Irish men and Irish women of the distinctive Irish nation, to make real the freedom of which Davis sang, for which Rooney worked, for which Tom Clarke and Sean McDermott and their comrades fought and died."

This was Collins' considered answer to my question as to his opinion of the future of Ireland. It was early in the series of interviews that he took up this subject, introducing it in characteristically humorous fashion.

"Sure, there's not a man on earth with sufficient prevision to dare guess what the morrow will bring to Ireland. Indeed, few of us appreciate what is happening to-day—and a bare minority who know the truth about Ireland's yesterday. With conditions what they are, a man would be rash to venture a prophecy about the future of this country, but for the self-same reason it is impossible to tell a comprehensive story of Ireland's fight for freedom—if ever '*Finis*' is put at the bottom of any page of it. So perhaps, after all, it is as well to make the end of the tale a forecast which may well prove wrong before the type is set.

"The known facts naturally provide a basis for anticipating what the future has in store for Ireland, and they may be briefly stated for this purpose. The British have given up their claim to dominate us. They have no longer any power to prevent us making real our freedom. That much is an accomplished fact.

"The freedom which has been won is the fruit of the national efforts of this generation and of preceding ones. The efforts of resistance made by the nation were the expressions of what had been robbed from the nation. But these efforts have not been continuous. With the Union came upheaval. The seat of Government was transferred to England. With Catholic emancipation, and the 'right' it gave to representatives of the Irish people to sit in the foreign parliament, the national spirit was invaded. People began to look abroad. The anglicisation of Ireland had begun. The English language became the language of education and fashion. It penetrated slowly at first. It was aided by the national schools. In those schools it was the only medium of education for a people who were still Gaelic speaking. Side by side with this peaceful penetration the Irish language decayed, and when the people had adopted a new language and had come to look to England for government they learned to see in English customs and English culture the models on which to fashion their own.

"The 'gifts' wrung from England—Catholic emancipation, land acts, local government—while not actually destructive in themselves of the Gaelic social system, helped in the denationalisation process. These gifts undoubtedly brought ameliorative changes, but the people got into the habit of always looking to a foreign authority, and they inevitably came to lose their self-respect, their self-reliance, and their national strength. The system made them forget to look to themselves, and that taught them to turn their backs upon their own country. We became the beggars of the rich neighbour who had robbed us. We lost reverence for our own nation, and we came very near to losing our national identity.

" O'Connell was the product of the Ireland which arose out of this perversion, prompted by the Young Irelanders, and urged on by the zeal of the people, stirred for the moment to national consciousness by the teachings of Davis. He talked of national liberty, but he did nothing to win it. He was a follower and not a leader of the people. He feared any movement of a revolutionary nature. Himself a Gaelic speaker, he adopted the English language, so little did he understand the strength to the nation of its own native language. His aim was little more than to see the Irish people a free Catholic community. He would have had Ireland merely a prosperous province of Britain with no national distinctiveness. Generally speaking, he acquiesced in a situation which was bringing upon the Irish nation spiritual decay. This is the plain truth about O'Connell.

" The Young Irelanders, of whom Thomas Davis was the inspiration, were the real leaders. They saw and felt more deeply and aimed more truly. Davis spoke to the soul of the sleeping nation—the nation really drunk with the waters of forgetfulness. He sought to unite the whole people. He fought against sectarianism and all the other causes which divided them. He saw that unless we were Gaels we were not a nation. When he thought of the nation he thought of the men and women of the nation. He knew that, unless they were free, Ireland could not be free, and to fill them again with pride in their nation he sang to them of the old splendour of Ireland, of their heroes, of their language, of the strength of unity, of the glory of noble strife, of the beauties of the land, of the delights and richness of the Gaelic life.

" ' A nationality founded in the hearts and intelligence of the people,' he said, ' would bid defiance to the arms of the foe and guile of the traitor. The first step to nationality is the open and deliberate recognition of it by the people themselves. Once the Irish people declare the disconnection of themselves, their feelings and interests, from the men, feelings and interests of England, they are in march for freedom.'

"That was the true national gospel. 'Educate that you may be free,' he said. 'It is only by baptism at the fount of Gaelicism that we shall get the strength and ardour to fit us for freedom.' The spirit of Davis breathed again in those who succeeded to his teachings and who, directed by that inspiration, kept the footsteps of the nation on the right road for the march to freedom.

"Those who succeeded to these teachings saw that if we continued to turn to England, the nation would become extinct. We were tacitly accepting England's denial of our nationhood so useful for her propaganda purposes. We were selling our birthright for a mess of pottage. We pleaded with England for measures of reform and political emancipation—pleading with the spoilers for a portion of the spoils they had robbed from us. We saw that the nation could be preserved and freedom won only by the Irish people themselves.

"The future Ireland had its birth in the last decade of the last century. In days to come Irish history will recognise in the formation of the Gaelic League in 1893 the most important event of the nineteenth century. I may go further and say that it was the most important event in the whole history of our nation. It probably checked an assimilation of Ireland by the predominant neighbour, and once and for all turned the minds of the Irish people back to their own country. It did more than any other movement to restore the national pride, honour, and self-respect. Through the medium of the language it linked the people with the past and led them to look to a future which would be a noble continuation of it. Within its folds were nurtured the men and women who were to win for Ireland the power to achieve national freedom.

"A good tree brings forth good fruit—a barren one

produces nothing. The policy advocated by O'Connell, Isaac Butt, and John Redmond ended, as it was bound to end, in impotence. The freedom which Ireland has achieved was dreamed of by Wolf Tone, was foreseen by Thomas Davis, and their efforts were broadened out until they took into their embrace all the true national movements by the 'grim resolve' of William Rooney, supported later by the strong arm of the Volunteers.

"And now we have no choice but to turn our eyes again to Ireland. The most completely anglicised person in Ireland will look henceforth to Britain in vain. Ireland is about to revolve once again on her own axis. But let us ever bear in mind that our real freedom can be won only when we are 'fit and willing' to win it.

"Can we claim that we are yet fit and willing? Is not our country still filled with men and women who are unfit and unwilling? Are we all yet educated to be free? Have not the greater number of us still the speech of the foreigner on our tongues? Are not even we who are proudly calling ourselves Gaels little more than imitation Englishmen? I am sad to have to believe that the day-by-day happenings prove that the answers to these questions are all in the affirmative.

"But we are free to remedy these things. Complete liberty—what it stands for in our Gaelic imaginations—cannot be got until we have impregnated the whole of our people with the Gaelic desire. Only then shall we be worthy of the fullest freedom. The bold outline of freedom has been drawn by the glorious efforts of the last five years. Will not those who co-operated in the conception and work of the masterpiece help with the finishing touches?

"Can we not see that the little we have not yet gained is the expression of the falling short of our own fitness for freedom? When we make ourselves fit we shall be free. If we could accept that truth we would be inspired again with the same fervour and devotion by our own grim resolve within the nation to complete the work which is so nearly done."

Here was the soul of Collins laid bare. Englishmen of my acquaintance frequently refer to the great Irishman as "a gunman," "a killer." The charge has foundation in fact. I saw Collins handle a service revolver—and he knew how! But the heart of him was the kindliest, gentlest, most peaceable any man ever had in his breast. It sickened him to have to stand and fight—his own. I know—because he confided in me—that had he lived to see the triumph of his Government over the Irregular forces led by De Valera, it would have been a sorry victory for him. The hurt that had been done him could never have been healed—FOR IN HIS FINE GAELIC IMAGINATION THE WICKED DESTRUCTION BEING DONE HIS COUNTRY BY IRISHMEN WAS ON A PAR WITH THE DESPOILING OF HIS SISTER BY ONE OF HIS BROTHERS!

"Mr. De Valera, in a speech he made in February," Collins went on, "warned the people of Ireland against a life of ease, against living 'practically the life of beasts,' which, he fears, they may be tempted to do under the Free State. The chance that materialism will take possession of the Irish people is no more likely in a free Ireland under the Free State than it would be in a free Ireland under a Republican or any other form of government. It is in the hands of the Irish people themselves.

"In the ancient days of Gaelic civilisation the people were prosperous and they were not materialists. They were one of the most spiritual and one of the most intellectual peoples in Europe. When Ireland was swept by destitution and famine the spirit of the Irish people came most nearly to extinction. It was with the improved economic conditions of the last twenty years or more that it has reawakened. The insistent needs of the body more adequately satisfied, the people regained desire once more to reach out to the higher things in which the spirit finds its satisfaction.

"What we hope for in the new Ireland is to have such material welfare as will give the Irish spirit that freedom. We want such widely-diffused prosperity that the Irish people will not be crushed by destitution into living 'practically the lives of beasts.' They were so crushed during the British occupation that they were described as being 'without the comforts of an English sow.' They must not be obliged—owing to unsound economic conditions—to spend all their powers of both mind and body in an effort to satisfy the bodily needs alone.

" The uses of wealth are to provide good health, comfort, moderate luxury, and to give the freedom which comes from the possession of these things. Our object in building up the country economically must not be lost sight of. That object is not to be able to boast of enormous wealth nor of a great volume of trade—for their own sake. It is not to see our country covered with smoking chimneys and factories. It is not to be able to show a great national balance-sheet, nor to point to a people 'producing wealth with the self-obliteration of a hive of bees.' The real riches of the Irish nation will be the men and women of the Irish nation—the extent to which they are rich in body and mind and character.

" What the future holds in store for Ireland is the opportunity for everyone to be able to produce sufficient wealth to ensure these advantages for themselves. That such wealth can be produced in Ireland there can be no doubt.

> " ' For the island is so endowed with so many dowries of nature, considering the fruitfulness of the soil, the ports, the rivers, the fishing, and especially the race and generation of men, valiant, hard and active, as it is not easy to find such a confluence of commodities.'

Such was the impression made upon a visitor who came long ago to Ireland.

" We have now the opportunity to make our land indeed fruitful, to work up our natural resources, to bring prosperity to all our people. If our national economy is to be on a sound footing from the beginning it will, in the new Ireland, be possible for our people to provide themselves with the ordinary requirements of decent living. It will be possible for each one to have sufficient food, a good home in which to live in fair contentment and comfort. We shall be able to give our children bodily and mental health, and we shall be able to secure them against the inevitable times of sickness and old age.

"That must be our object. What we must aim at is the building up of a sound economic life in which great discrepancies cannot occur. We must not have the destitution of poverty at one end, and at the other an excess of riches in the possession of a few individuals beyond what they can spend with satisfaction and justification. The growing wealth of Ireland will, we hope, be diffused for the benefit of all of our people, all sharing in the growing prosperity, each receiving in accordance with what each contributes in the making of that prosperity, so that the weal of all will be assured.

"How are we to increase the wealth of Ireland, and ensure that all producing it shall share in it? That is the question which will be engaging the minds of our people, and will engage the attention of the new Government. The keynote to the economic revival must be the development of Irish resources by Irish capital for the benefit of the Irish consumer. Thus the people will have steady work at just remuneration and their own share of control.

"How are we to develop Irish resources? The earth is our bountiful mother. Upon free access to it depends not only agriculture, but all other trades and industries. Land must be freely available. Agriculture, our main industry, must be improved and developed. Our existing industries must be given opportunities to expand. Conditions must be created which will make it possible for new ones to arise. Means of transit must be extended and cheapened. Our harbours must be developed. Our water-power must be utilised. Our mineral resources must be exploited. Foreign trade must be stimulated by making facilities for the transport and marketing of Irish goods abroad, and foreign goods in Ireland. Investors must be urged and encouraged to invest Irish capital in Irish concerns. Taxation, where it hinders, must be adjusted and must be imposed where the burden will fall lightest, and can best be borne, and where it will encourage rather than penalise industry.

" We have now in Ireland, owing to the restrictions put upon emigration during the European war, a larger population of young men and women than we have had for a great many years. For their own sake, and to maintain the strength of the nation, room must and can be found for them. If room is to be found for our growing population, land must be freely available. We have not free access to the land in Ireland. Thousands of acres of the best land lie idle, or are occupied as ranches, or form part of extensive private estates, or are given over to sport. Side by side with this condition there are thousands of labourers unable to get land on which to keep a cow or grow vegetables. While the fertile lands of Kildare and Westmeath lie idle, men and women have to labour from dawn to late at night to win a bare living out of the rocks of Donegal, and families in Connaught have to send their children to labour in the potato fields of Scotland.

" The ranches must be broken up. Pressure must be brought to bear on owners of land and upon those who are withholding land so that it may be suitably used for procuring wealth and giving employment. Thus opportunities will be presented to all of our population.

" For purposes of development Ireland has three great natural resources. Our coal deposits are by no means inconsiderable. The bogs of Ireland are estimated as having 500,000,000,000 tons of peat fuel. Water-power is concentrated in her 237 rivers and 180 lakes. The huge Lough Corrib system could be utilised, for instance, to work the granite in the neighbourhood of Galway. In the opinion of experts, reporting to the Committee on the Water-Power Resources of Ireland, a total of 500,000 horse-power can be developed from Irish lakes and rivers. The magnitude of these figures is appreciated when it is known that to raise this power in steam would require 7,500,000 tons of coal.

"Schemes have been worked out to utilise the water-power of the Shannon, the Erne, the Bann, and the Liffey. That the advantages of water-power are not lost on some of the keenest minds of the day is shown by the following extract from an interview given to an American journalist in London by Lord Northcliffe for publication on St. Patrick's Day, 1917 :

> "'The growth of the population of Great Britain has been largely due to manufactures based on the great asset, black coal. Ireland has none of the coal which has made England rich, but she possesses in her mighty rivers white coal of which millions of horse-power are being lost to Ireland every year. . . . I can see in the future very plainly prosperous cities, old and new, fed by the greatest river in the United Kingdom—the Shannon. I should like to read recent experts' reports on the Moy, the Suir, and the Lee.'

"The profits from all national enterprises will belong to the nation for the advantage of the nation. But Irish men and women as private individuals must do their share to increase the prosperity of the country. Business cannot succeed without capital. Millions of Irish money are lying idle in banks. The deposits in Irish Joint Stock banks increased in the aggregate by £7,318,000 during the half-year ended December 31, 1921. At that time the total amount of deposits and cash balances in Irish banks was £194,391,000, in addition to which there was a sum of almost £14,000,000 in the Post Office Savings Bank. The Irish people have also a large amount of capital invested abroad. With scope for our energies, with restoration of our confidence, the inevitable tendency will be towards return of this capital to Ireland. It will then flow in its proper channel. Ireland will provide splendid opportunities for the investment of Irish capital, and it is for the Irish people to take advantage of these opportunities. *If they do not, investors and exploiters from outside will come in to reap the rich profits which are to be made. And what is worse still, they will bring with them all the evils that we want to avoid in the new Ireland.*

"A prosperous Ireland will mean a united Ireland. With equitable taxation and flourishing trade our North-East countrymen will need no persuasion to come in and share in the healthy economic life of the country.

"Such are the *possibilities* of the future. Can we not see in them the great achievement that our efforts have won? Can we not think of what we have gained—and not for ever dwell upon the thought of what we might have gained? If we would only put away dreams, and face realities, we would realise that nearly all the things that count we now have for our country. Is not the test of the Government we want simply whether it conforms with Irish tradition and national character? Whether it will suit us and enable us to live happily and prosper? Whether under it we can achieve something which our old free Irish democratic life would have developed into?

"We have shaken off the foreign domination which prevented us from living our own life in our own way. We are now free to do this. It depends on *ourselves alone* whether we do it. And I have lasting faith in the Irish people."

CHAPTER XXI

WHAT THE TREATY MEANS—A SYMPOSIUM

In an endeavour to ascertain the considered opinions of representative Irish men and women—Treaty proponents and Treaty opponents equally—as to Ireland's chance of freedom under existing circumstances, I propounded to Irish leaders of outstanding importance the following question :

> " Under the terms of the Treaty, what does the future hold in store for Ireland ? "

In due course I received the following written answers :

From Sean McKeon

> [Major-General McKeon, T.D., immortalised as " the Blacksmith of Ballinalee," fought more successful battles against the Black and Tans than any other leader of the I.R.A., and, since the murder of Michael Collins, is to-day the most popular hero in Ireland.]

" Although I am on record as an advocate of accepting the Treaty, I want it thoroughly understood that, like every other member of my party, I am an Irish Republican. Anything less than full independence will never completely satisfy any Irishman. But with this much said, I am willing to discuss Ireland's future under the Treaty.

" There are possibilities under the terms of the Treaty of tremendous advantage to Ireland. It gives us far more than many of us ever dared hope could be won in our lifetime. It gives us far more than we ever could have won by force of arms alone—so long as our strength remained relatively negligible as compared with England's armed power. It does not give us all we want; all we are determined one day to have, all that is ours by right. But it does give us a far better chance than Ireland has ever known before to achieve our ultimate ideal.

"Not unnaturally, I am inclined to view the purely political phase of the present situation through the eyes of a soldier. Soldiering is my profession. Politics is not. Conferences appeal to me not at all. Explorations of avenues that may lead to agreement seem to me waste of time—when the explorers, metaphorically speaking, are more intent on conducting the expedition into a morass than to success.

"A general in the field realises that a war is not won in a single battle. Only a counsel of desperation risks disaster in one final offensive. Day by day minor gains are consolidated, minor losses accepted. The final goal—decisive victory—is none the less ever uppermost in mind. But the high command recognise it can be won only by patient acceptance of gains or reverses as mere incidents in the general scheme.

"The most strenuous of the opponents of the Treaty base their arguments on the assumption that all Ireland has to do is flout England and thus gain complete independence on the spot. They forget that Ireland's Declaration of Independence was published to the world in 1916—and now, after six years, has yet to be recognised by any government in the world. They forget that for most of this period British armed forces were in practical control of all Ireland. Repudiation of the Treaty by Dail Eireann now—accompanied by a reaffirmation of the Republic—would surely result in a return to the conditions under which Ireland lived during the Reign of Terror. Those of us whose duty it is to protect our people will not shirk that duty if it is imposed upon us—but it must be the people who impose it upon us—if that be their will. And I for one do not believe it is.

"The future of Ireland under the Treaty is a brighter future than any living or dead Irishman ever knew; the future of Ireland if the Treaty be turned down is hopeless. Hopeless, at least, in so far as existing generations are concerned. For who doubts that England, given what the world would consider ample justification, would once again, and more eagerly than ever, send her armed forces back amongst us—this time to make our subjugation more complete than ever?

(*Signed*) " SEAN McKEON."

FROM CATHAL BRUGHA

[Mr. Brugha, T.D., formerly Minister of Defence under De Valera's Presidency of Dail Eireann, killed during the July rebellion, was an uncompromising Republican whose public utterances proved him an ardent advocate of the use of force.]

"During the Dail debate on the Articles of Agreement President de Valera said he was against the pact because, amongst other reasons, he believed it would not bring peace. That same view was expressed by other deputies. The correctness of their judgment is being brought home to us every day.

"The most ominous proof of it was the I.R.A. Convention held Sunday, March 26. That Convention represented over 80 per cent. of the Republican army. One division alone, which stands solidly behind the Republic, has 38,000 men on its roll. The Convention elected an executive to control the army in future. These men had all taken an oath of allegiance to the Republic and to Dail Eireann as the Government of the Republic. Even when the majority of An Dail had approved of the alleged Treaty the army held fast.

"When the new Government formed by the Treaty party

was elected, the President gave an undertaking that the Republic would be maintained until the electorate got an opportunity of expressing its opinion on the Treaty. The new Minister for Defence promised the Dail that the army would continue as the army of the Republic until the people had spoken. Both those undertakings were basely broken. The Provisional Government was set up and allowed to supplant An Dail. Its chairman and two of his alleged ministers publicly repudiated the supremacy of An Dail at one of its sittings. They denied that they were in any way responsible to it. They did this in the presence of President Griffith without any remonstrance from him.

"In regard to the promise given by the new Minister for Defence, instead of adhering to it, he allowed the army to be made use of to build up an army for this usurping Provisional Government. The net result of this double-dealing was the calling together of the I.R.A. Convention and the election of an independent executive.

"The army is determined to maintain the existing Republic. Whoever else may have been play-acting when they took the oath of allegiance to the Republic, it is quite evident that those men were not. Upon them principally has been the burden of guarding the Republic against its enemies during the time of stress. How well they played their part the world already knows. The world may hear from them again when people who did nothing to establish the Republic or to maintain it attempt to give it away.

"It is almost incredible that any responsible person who has been in touch with things should be so misled as to believe that those men could be seduced from their allegiance so simply.

"What we are now asked to do is to surrender the sovereignty of the Irish people, to yield at last to our oppressors and admit ourselves their subjects. Why, the weakest day Ireland ever saw she never did that. There was always a body of opinion in Ireland that denied England's right to interfere in Irish affairs. They were with us in every generation. Whenever they considered themselves strong enough they went out in arms against the usurper. Though beaten in the field they never bent the knee. That tradition has been carried on, and no amount of dragooning could break it. The prison-cell, the hangman's rope and the firing-squad—all have failed.

"So tenacious is the fibre of which Irishmen are made that the greater the persecution, the stronger became the spirit of resistance. It is conceivable, though unlikely, that the threat of war might stampede the Irish people into voting in favour of the Treaty without realising what it involves. It is possible that the anti-Republicans, aided by the pro-British Press, could so confuse the issue that a majority of the present out-of-date register might accept the Free State.

"The signatories to the Treaty do not agree on what it means. One of them says it gives us freedom. Another says it gives us freedom to achieve freedom. We know it gives us neither. Between us all it would be no wonder if the electorate were befogged. But even if guile succeeded, sooner or later the struggle would begin again when the people found out that they were deceived. It is almost certain that this would occur in our own time.

"We are better organised now militarily than ever we were in modern times. We are also better armed. Above all, the traditional hope of finally expelling the invader that has always lived in the hearts of the Irish race is now stronger and more widespread than ever. That yearning for complete nationhood has now become an overmastering desire. People hitherto apathetic had become infused with this enthusiasm before the Treaty was signed. The past four years have not gone for nothing. Though we did not actually drive out the tyrant, we made him impotent. Those who have tasted the delicious wine of freedom will not be put off with a draught of inferior quality. The Free Stater who thinks otherwise is living in a fool's paradise.

(*Signed*) " CATHAL BRUGHA."

What the Treaty Means

FROM PROF. EOIN MACNEILL

[Professor MacNeill, T.D., formerly speaker of Dail Eireann and one of its most erudite members, was President and Chief-of-Staff of the Irish Volunteers at the time of the Easter Week rising in 1916; for his Sinn Fein activities he was sentenced to penal servitude for life.]

"The Anglo-Irish Treaty of December, 1921, is an agreement between two nation-states, Ireland and Britain, to enter into a free partnership. This partnership includes also Canada, South Africa, Australia, and New Zealand. For the present, the consent of the non-signatory states is presumed, but the presumption does not imply an admission that the British Government can bind any of these states without their express consent, and an express agreement between Ireland and the non-signatory states will doubtless follow in due course.

"The Treaty does not regulate the internal political status of Ireland. It regulates by agreement the form of the partnership between the nation-state Ireland and the other nation-states. The essence of the Treaty is that it guarantees no less freedom and sovereignty to Ireland within her natural territorial bounds than the freedom and sovereignty—not as recorded in any British statute, but as actually enjoyed and exercised—belonging to the other states, Canada being named as an example. This, of course, means the full freedom and sovereignty exercised by any of the states, since it is certain that Canada would not admit restrictions not imposed on a partner state.

"Any claim of British suzerainty now or hereafter set up as against Ireland would imply a similar claim as against Canada. Britain, on the other hand, claims certain facilities for defence as necessary to her safety, and Ireland, without adopting the reasons on which this claim is based, concedes certain facilities. Ireland, of course, remains entitled to guard against any use of these facilities to her detriment or danger.

"Under the Treaty, then, Ireland can and will insist on holding as partner the maximum status as it exists in practice, not in British law, of the other states. Her status must be maximum from the outset because, as Mr. Winston Churchill has acknowledged, she comes into the partnership not as a colonial offshoot but as 'a mother country.' It is necessary to be clear on this, for the British Press in general indulges in the notion that Britain is endowing Ireland with powers, and the attitude of the British Ministry since the signing of the Treaty can be interpreted in some respects as being afflicted with the same notion.

"So far as Ireland is concerned, the Treaty requires no statute or resolution of the British legislature to give it effect, nor can any statute or resolution of that legislature invalidate or modify the Treaty. Britain can break the agreement; she cannot change it, except as she made it, that is, jointly with Ireland. The only force of British legislation in regard to the Treaty is to legalise it from the purely British standpoint—not to legalise it for Ireland.

"It will soon be seen that the existence of future good relations between Britain and Ireland will have for its essential condition the absolute cessation of all manner of interference by the British Government or by British political agencies in the domestic affairs of Ireland. Ireland will not seek to interfere in British affairs. There is, however, a certain aristocratic and semi-aristocratic element which has family connections and property connections in both countries and plenty of leisure to be meddlesome, and this element constitutes a danger to be watched.

"Above all, there is the situation which the British Government and British political agencies have deliberately created in Ulster. There, simultaneously with the Black and Tan war against Ireland generally, a campaign of sectarian violence was let loose two years ago. In the same year a British statute divided Ireland into two separate administrative, legislative and judicial areas. There was no Irish demand, in or out of Ulster, for this division. It was a purely British governmental device directed against the peace and progress of Ireland. This policy cannot be maintained without violating the essence of the Treaty; yet certain British ministers seem to think that we do not understand it.

"Having barely mentioned certain points which as yet do not appear to have penetrated the public intelligence of our neighbours—many of whom still think they own us by divine right—let me say that I am confident that we, on our part, if we act with a single purpose for the good of Ireland, can surmount every surviving difficulty and make Ireland as free as any other nation. We are young, vigorous, resourceful, and, in spite of all the past, we are one of the few nations of Europe that are solvent. The Black and Tan war and its Ulster accompaniment have raised the temperature and produced some fever, but we are organically sound and, as a people, we mean to have a reign of justice.

(*Signed*) " EOIN MACNEILL."

FROM SEAN MACENTEE

[Mr. MacEntee is a native of Belfast and, until his defeat in the summer elections, one of the younger members of Dail Eireann, most active in support of De Valera.]

"Two things stand out in the Treaty: first, that Ireland, under threat of war, is compelled to forego her right to independence; of our natural right, the latter a violation of our territory.

"Liberty is 'the inalienable right' of the Irish as of all other peoples, and Ireland's territorial integrity is as truly essential to Ireland's national existence as was the preservation of the Federal Union to America under Lincoln. America waged wars to secure her liberties and to preserve that Union; Ireland in the same just cause will fight to the end. Under the Treaty, therefore, Ireland can never be at peace, but must be at war.

"The Treaty will not bring peace to Ireland; neither

will it bring prosperity. Ireland cannot be prosperous while Ireland is not free, for all that is best in the country of intellect and of character will address itself to the struggle for liberty. All that is material will be sacrificed to that great spiritual passion—the phenomenon of ages will be repeated—Irish youth growing to manhood will have but one thought, not to become rich, but to become free. All its energy, all its courage, all its capacity will be devoted to that ideal. And with all this we shall have the same political instability, the same civil turmoil; these are everywhere the invariable concomitants of injustice and oppression, and these are essentially destructive of material prosperity.

" Based upon partition, the Treaty will perpetuate disunion. Its real object is to establish and consolidate in North-Eastern Ireland an English settlement which England plans shall be the inveterate and relentless enemy of the Irish nation. England feels herself assured of the loyalty of that settlement as she is assured of the loyalty, say, of Scotland. There is no power, no authority she may concede to the Irish Free State that she will not give more unreservedly and more freely to Northern Ireland. By such a policy she hopes to make the breach which she has forced between North and South wider and deeper. She knows Northern Ireland as established under the Treaty will strive to become wholly English, while Southern Ireland strives to become wholly Irish. So that in a little time she calculates there will be in Ireland two peoples speaking different languages, holding different religions, following different political ideals.

" By her North-Eastern settlement and not by an oath of allegiance England hopes to hold Ireland for the British Empire. Northern Ireland, as established by the Treaty, is to be her new Gibraltar, a Gibraltar which, if the Treaty were to stand, would reduce Ireland for ever to political impotency and paralysis.

" The Treaty, in short, makes Ireland neither a free country nor a British Dominion, but a sort of hybrid among states, a mule among nations—impotent and abject, condemned to servitude and decay. It will not stand, however ; for those who made Ireland great, the men who fought and the women who suffered, stand against it. They still stand true to the Irish Republic. The authority, legitimacy and territorial integrity of that Republic will yet be vindicated by this living generation, so that its flag, floating over every inch of Irish soil, shall secure the loyalty and homage of all who claim Ireland for their home. But when this is done, it shall be done, not by means of, but in spite of, the Treaty.

(*Signed*) " SEAN MACENTEE."

FROM ERNEST BLYTHE

[Mr. Blythe, T.D., is Minister of Economics in Dail Eireann and one of its most brilliant members, who has always been a great admirer of Griffith's Sinn Fein policy—although an Ulster man and a Protestant.]

" I believe the people who think that national effort in future is likely to concentrate itself along the lines of Republican agitation and revolutionary action are entirely mistaken. The Treaty gives, for the present, ample scope for national growth and reconstruction. The mind of the country will be given chiefly to economic and cultural development.

" The left wing in the year after next will not be constituted of the Republican doctrinaires, but of the advanced workers for a revival of the Irish language and of the advocates of tariff and banking reform. In the new situation it will be recognised that the nation's ' soul ' is to be saved no longer by the maintenance of a political effervescence, but by preserving and spreading the use of the historic languages of the Gael. When Irish has again been made common speech throughout the country, all thought will be given a distinctively Irish tinge and objective ; Irish brains shall, at last, pay a toll of service to Ireland instead of going entirely to build up the culture and literature of other countries.

"On the material side we shall have attention turned not to the expulsion of British maintenance parties from the few coastal posts they will hold, but to the development of industries, to the utilisation of our peat and mineral deposits and water-power, and to the opening up of direct trade relations with the many countries with which our lines of communication at present run through Liverpool or London. There are abundant proofs that the fostering care of a national government will be able to transform the economic condition of Ireland. The country is at present very backward industrially. To bring it to the point at which it ought to be will be a big task. When the back of that task has been broken, when the future of the Irish language has been unmistakably assured, then only will doctrinaire Republicanism really come to the forefront again.

(*Signed*) "ERNEST BLYTHE."

FROM COUNTESS MARKIEVICZ

[Constance Georgina Markievicz, T.D., was sentenced to death by court-martial for having commanded the insurgents in the Royal College of Surgeons during the Easter Week rising in Dublin, but was later released in the general amnesty. Her hatred of England is the one dominating passion of her life.]

"Your question demands a prophecy, and at most times there is a risk in hazarding an opinion as to future events; but in this case I do not hesitate to stake any reputation that I may have by giving as my honest and thought-out opinion that under the Treaty the future holds little but trouble for Ireland.

"A friendship or agreement between two persons, parties or nations must be based on a mutual understanding.

The oath which it includes is translated as meaning one thing by Mr. Griffith, Mr. Collins and their followers when explaining it to the Irish people, while the meaning given to it by Mr. Lloyd George and his followers is the direct contradiction.

"Mr. Griffith said, speaking openly before the assembly of Dail Eireann:

"'It is an oath, I say, that any Irishman could take with honour, as he pledges his allegiance to the Free State and faithfulness, after, to the head of the British Commonwealth of Nations.'

"Mr. Collins said: '. . . And we have obtained . . . a compromise on allegiance not ideal, but which enables us to pledge our true faith and allegiance only to our own Saorstat, and declares fidelity to the Crown merely in its capacity as the link between the two nations.'

"Their followers are now declaring quite openly that this oath binds them to do nothing more than to try the Free State, and make use of it to obtain the Republic; and that they would be willing to take a fresh oath for every gun they could procure by so doing—and much more on the same lines.

"So much for the pro-Treaty-ites. Now turn to their English friends speaking in defence of the Treaty in the English House of Commons. The most definite statement among many of the same kind was made by Sir Worthington Evans, December 15, 1921:

"' . . . Part of the terms of the settlement will be that the members who go to serve in that Free State Parliament will have to swear true faith and allegiance to the Constitution as passed by the House of Commons. How is it possible to say that within the terms of that oath they set up a Republic and still maintain their oath?'

"He further stated: ' . . . Anson's description of the Oath of Allegiance is that it was a declaration of fidelity to the Throne, so that in this oath we have got this: we have got an oath of allegiance in the declaration of fidelity: "I will be faithful to His Majesty King George V., and his heirs and successors by law "—and we have got something in addition, a declaration of fidelity to the Constitution of the Irish Free State, and in further addition we have the declaration of fidelity to the Empire itself.'

"Whether our envoys were themselves tricked or whether they agreed to trick the Irish people is the obvious question that Irish people are asking to-day. Whichever way the question is answered, it will not help these men to keep the confidence of the Irish people, and unless they have the confidence and the support of the people they will be powerless to govern efficiently. Nor can this Treaty based on misunderstanding bring anything but dissension between the two nations.

"Then there is the question of the Northern Pale deliberately set up by the British Cabinet in anticipation of the South becoming unanimously separatist. The situation there becomes daily worse. Mr. Collins called off the Belfast boycott. If he did so to propitiate Sir James Craig it would appear from the Press that he failed. Then, too, Mr. Lloyd George seems to interpret this Treaty so as to secure power to himself to postpone the Boundary Commission. This gives the Irish people much cause for thought and reason for suspicion, both of the sincerity of Mr. Lloyd George and of the capacity of Mr. Collins and his advisers.

"Next comes the question of the formation of the Constitution. Mr. Griffith and Mr. Collins believe that looseness of the Treaty can be made use of by them. Mr. Collins makes the amazing announcement that 'we make our own decision, and it is we who decide how we are to deal with Mr. Lloyd George.' Mr. Griffith even went so far as to pledge himself openly to the Southern Unionists to give them their ' full share of representation in the First Chamber of the Irish Parliament, and as to the Upper Chamber, we will consult them on its constitution, and undertake that their interests will be duly represented.'

"Labour has already expressed itself on this pronouncement of Mr. Griffith's, and labour is a power in Ireland to-day. The people, too, are suspicious.

" These are only a few of the points that the people of Ireland are pondering over to-day, and these are the questions that are daily being asked with more and more insistence :

" Have the signatories been fooled again in the old way and by the old enemy, and will the result of all these negotiations be :

> " 1. The establishment of a new English Pale on the old lines, and
>
> " 2. The division of the rest of Ireland into two parties also on the old lines which in the past gave us the 'Queens,' O'Neills, O'Reillys, etc., *i.e.*, those who were guarding the English interests in Ireland and who derived their power from the English King and the forces behind him—and the Irish rebels who derived their powers from the will and love of the Irish people.

" These rebels will be there and stand for an independent Ireland till that day when nationality has ceased to be an inspiration ; when language is dead and our history forgotten ; when Irish idealism has been lost in British materialism, and we a smug British province.

" That day will never come. Therefore I see naught but trouble in front of us till our national aspirations are achieved by the establishment and recognition of the Irish Republic.
(*Signed*) " CONSTANCE MARKIEVICZ."

FROM WILLIAM ROACHE

[Liam de Roiste, T.D., successor in Dail Eireann of William O'Brien for Cork City, has worked for years for the revival of Irish industries ; it was he who induced Henry Ford to establish a factory in Cork, and put through a scheme whereby the Moore MacCormack Steamship Company's liners ply direct between Cork and New York.]

"Unless divinely inspired, prophecy is untrustworthy. No one can say dogmatically what the future holds in store for Ireland or for any other country. One can only express an opinion as to what it should hold, granted certain premises.

"Ireland, owing to the blighting influence of foreign rule, is a nation of arrested development, intellectually, nationally, socially, politically, economically. Now that the Irish people have secured power in their own hands what should be expected is almost immediate development in the spheres of activity indicated. For such development, however, order and at least comparative peace are essential.

"Intellectually the Irish nation can develop to perfection only on the basis of its ancient civilisation and culture which are enshrined, as it were, in the native language. Already, owing to the freedom secured under the Treaty and the taking over of the educational systems of the country by the Irish authorities, a gigantic fillip has been given to the study of the Irish language and its literature. Granted orderly development, so far as one can see, this intellectual progress, drawing inspiration from purely native ideals, is likely to be maintained. The world will, therefore, be presented with the spectacle of an ancient civilisation reanimated—a civilisation that has much in it from which the world may learn.

"The sense of national distinctiveness is very strong indeed in Ireland. It was fostered rather than checked by the repressive laws of the English. National feeling is often intolerant. That intolerance is based upon ignorance or is due to conditions where the national feeling must continually show itself in protest. With a development of education in Ireland and freedom from restrictions of all national feelings it may be anticipated that the expression of the national distinctiveness of the Irish nation will be in the sphere of culture rather than in the sphere of politics.

"Socially and politically it may be expected that the development in Ireland will be towards democratic control of all activities, that there will be few, if any, privileged classes, that there will be a more just distribution of wealth and power than is found in other countries, and that there will ultimately be great individual liberty.

"While not sternly Republican in the doctrinaire sense of a form of government, the Irish people of the present day are essentially a democratic people. So far as one can judge, there is no special regard for men of wealth as such, and none for men of title. There is regard for worth and for service to the community. The traditional struggle for Ireland has been simply to get power into the hands of the people of the country and out of the hands of select coteries and classes set up by the British. The political form in which that power may express itself has varied during the centuries in the minds of the people, and even now no one political form commands universal assent; except that the form conceived of must be democratic, one through which the will of the people can best express itself.

"The whole economic structure of Ireland needs remoulding, and under the Treaty terms this remoulding is at last possible. Ireland having full fiscal and economic freedom is at liberty to rebuild its industries, trade and commerce, to adjust agrarian grievances, to plant the people on the soil and to solve the problem of emigration. The outstanding economic factor in Ireland for the past 76 years has been the abnormal emigration of the young people of the country. No remedy has been possible during this period. The problem can now be solved in a manner that should ensure the increase of a healthy, industrious and virile people.

"As I view the position, the Treaty arrangement is a step, a big step, in the onward progress of the Irish nation. The Land Acts were steps; technical, agricultural and university education were steps; the establishment of local government was a step; the extension of the franchise was a step—all tending to greater and greater strength, to more and more liberty. The Irish language movement and the cultural Sinn Fein movement marked these steps, and the rising-out of 1916 roused the spirit of the people for the assertion of sovereign independence. With the increase of intellectual and material strength which is possible under the Treaty terms the progress of the Irish nation to fuller freedom and fuller development should be rapid.

"Unfortunately, however, the prospect is marred by the spectre of fratricidal strife. If fratricidal strife should eventuate, there is no prospect but defeat and disaster for the Irish nation in this generation.

(*Signed*) " LIAM DE ROISTE."

FROM PROF. W. F. P. STOCKLEY

[Professor Stockley, T.D., is one of the pacifist members of the Dail who, nevertheless, espouses the Republican cause.]

" Nothing is settled until it is settled right. The right settling of this world is not possible. But some right settling is.

"The English *Daily Mail*, publishing whole-sheet pictures of the Kaiser as our ally-to-be in the Boer War, declared that that holy war was ' a war to end war and make the world safe for decent men.' A later war was camouflaged by like aspirations. Countries, small and great, were now to live their own lives, resolve their own difficulties. The resulting peace without principle has plentifully praised past domestic resolvings of majority-minority strifes, as in the infant United States. But it has not been the instrument of a yet smaller minority being left in Ireland to understand itself and the world, and to calm down in that island geographically and historically one and indivisible. Any single passing from principles possible of application makes this a cry of peace where there is no peace and no right settling.

"The late Pope Benedict had principles for a peace-making. Ex-President Wilson embodied such in his abandoned claims. And the rising of heart, the will to act on the part of millions in their response to such higher practicality was proof of some possible doing. Indeed, never was there a better chance of peace between England and Ireland than when could have been applied between them this golden rule of do as done by. There never was a surer opportunity of getting rid of irritation by minding one's own business, not to say of mutual good-will, or even, as far as propriety and decency demanded, of forgive and forget.

" ' The right and the wise thing for England to do is to consent freely to the establishment of an Irish Republic unconditionally. I make that proposal because I want to see a true and final settlement of the differences between my country and England.' (Prof. Eoin MacNeill, *English Review*, Sept., 1917.)

" But England, powerful by arms, not less powerful by ruling when not pretending to rule—as over rajahs, maharajahs, and khedives—would not change. The whole world was filled with portraits of her as willing to let Ireland manage things Irish if only the Irish people would agree among themselves. Such was the portrait published in Washington's day also, of fond Mother England clasping to her breast her fractious colonial child to whom no soothing thing good for it was refused.

" What to-day has England done but refuse reality, keep up suspicions, and make the future unsure? In victims the hostile mind continues. Therefore out of world-unrealty and out of unrealiity towards Ireland there will come no lasting peace. From pretence will come resentment and also corruption, and all that makes for a revolt of the gallant and the wise

" Further, the circumstances of the signing of this so-called Treaty are circumstances shameful in unreality. As to Washington and Franklin and Adams, so to the Irish envoy—devastation of the resisting weak country was threatened—immediate and terrible war. A Treaty! And a Treaty freely made! And between equal nations! Can wilder falsehoods further go? Does any man, respecting common sense, think that on such pretence will be based a rock-built refuge for a nation, for two nations?

"(And now truly the English in the transaction, and most of the Irish in it, give up their pretences that they feared war or that war was intended. That was only a plea for a panic, as Washington dubbed the like—a working on nerves dreading responsibility for re-exposing Ireland to assassins rather than warriors. *John Bull*, in its issue of November 26, 1921, says, 'We do not want a war in Ireland, and we could not afford one if we did. . . . Better blot such a possibility out of the account. If Sinn Feiners will not come to terms they should be released from the Empire and left to find their own salvation.')

"Lastly, the unreality by this Treaty's own terms of pretending that Ireland is a Free State! Equal with England! England, therefore, 'free' when France has cut off Yorkshire and Lincoln, garrisoned them, and paid those English counties to serve France; when France is guaranteed rights to cover whole England with all machinery of war, if France's relations are anywhere 'strained'; when France holds in perpetuity the English ports of Hull, Liverpool, Portsmouth, Bristol! What need further? Is that a free England—an England having to swear, besides, fealty to France? Would the calling such an England 'free' settle anything—even if that English dog, with collar and chains, were fed fat with scraps from his French master's table? Who could have faith in a treaty calling unfree England free? Who could have faith in the future of a treaty that shuts men's eyes from the real Ireland, that Ireland that is and that will be, that is sure to be troubled, and sure in some measure to trouble both America and the world—until the reality of her national life is acknowledged and she contribute even in her comparative weakness to a more settled world, because, in this one matter, a world settled right.

(*Signed*) "W. F. P. STOCKLEY."

What the Treaty Means

From William Sears

[Mr. Sears, T.D., member of Dail Eireann for Sligo, is the most influential provincial newspaper proprietor in Ireland.]

" Seldom in history has a nation had such an opportunity as the Treaty gives to Ireland. It is, of course, not a new thing that a nation has suddenly burst its bonds and regained complete control of its affairs. But few people possess a land of such real and potential wealth as ours or occupy such a magnificent geographical position to make the most of that wealth.

" Imagine what possibilities there are for our existing industries, long discouraged and obstructed, when they can now count upon that driving force and fostering care that a native government can supply. Irish genius, that in the past was not permitted to direct Irish effort, can now bend itself unfettered to the task. And under the Treaty we have won the necessary fiscal freedom to make the most of our chance.

" Regarding foreign goods, we can open or close our ports to them just as we wish. The untapped resources of Ireland, long sealed up by the stranger, are in themselves a vast field for Irish enterprise and energy, even if our population were three times what it is at present.

" Then our country, fresh and vigorous, enters upon the international stage at a time when the rest of Europe bends under crushing debts and is disorganised and discouraged to the point of despair. In our people, although they have come through a terrible time, the industrial spirit and courage is equal to that of the youngest nation on the globe. It faces the future not merely with confidence, but with eagerness.

" There may be drawbacks to the Treaty from the idealist point of view ; there are none from the material. The obstacles to complete freedom that still remain can daunt only the faint-hearted The nation that frustrated the greatest military power in Europe, and won its way to the present position, cannot humanly be prevented from reaching the final stage save by some act of criminal folly on its own part.

"But perhaps it is not in the material field the Ireland of the future will make its greatest mark. The kindly neighbourliness of the Irish character, as is evidenced in the success of the co-operative movement, offered a better field for social reform than is elsewhere found. When the harsh reactions from the war have passed away, Ireland should furnish interesting headlines in social evolution, perhaps new departures the world may find of value. And from even higher fields she may garner a worthy crop, for the nation that has come through the fires of centuries of persecution must be handicapped with a little less of the world's dross than others.

"The purging, surely, was not all in vain, and perhaps that spiritual bent in the race that in the past earned for our island a glorious title may manifest itself again and add lustre once more to the 'Isle of Destiny.' We are encouraged to hope for the best when we recollect that the language that foreign tyranny set aside is now to be taken, as it were, from cold storage and to furnish to the nation a fresh and unfailing source of mental and spiritual energy and inspiration.

(*Signed*) "WILLIAM SEARS."

FROM H. J. BOLAND

[Mr. Boland, who died as the result of wounds received while resisting arrest by Free State troops, spent almost all of the time, from 1916 to the signing of the Treaty, in the United States, where he was the official representative of the Irish Republic, engaged in raising funds.]

"The future of Ireland under the Treaty is a very difficult subject to discuss. I prefer to deal with the

What the Treaty Means

immediate present. Ireland under the Treaty is now rent asunder and I cannot see any grounds for hope unless the Treaty-ites explicitly assert in the constitution of the Free State :

" 1. That the nation is one and indivisible.
" 2. That all authority in Ireland is derived from the people of Ireland, and
" 3. That the oath of allegiance and the Governor-General must be omitted from the Treaty.

" A constitution which will not debar those who would have Ireland free from giving constitutional expression in an Irish Parliament to the Republican ideal would, I think, be acceptable to the Republicans. But it must be understood that England forced the plenipotentiaries to sign under the threat of ' immediate and terrible war.' Of all England's abominable crimes against Ireland this latest is, to my mind, the most revolting.

" There are two shades of political thought represented in those who favour the Articles of Agreement signed in London. One, led by Mr. Arthur Griffith, asserts that the agreement gives Ireland essential liberty and is quite prepared to accept the arrangement in complete satisfaction of Ireland's claims or, in the words of Mr. Griffith, to ' march into the British Empire with our heads up '—and settle down, a contented Dominion of the Empire, with the hope that some day the ultra-Imperialists of the Six Counties called Ulster will come into the Imperial Free State.

" It is to be regretted that Mr. Griffith has taken this course, a course which is the very negation of all that for which he has given his life's work. Mr. Griffith, by his teachings of the past thirty years, is responsible to a great extent for the intense revival of Irish nationalism which found its expression in the Republic.

" The other group, led by Mr. Michael Collins, claims that the Treaty gives Ireland ' freedom to achieve freedom.' ' Get the British out of Ireland, build up the country, and in ten or twenty years Ireland will be in a better position to fight England and so establish the Republic.' This plea has secured many adherents to the Treaty—men who heretofore were considered implacable in their desire for the complete independence of Ireland. Indeed, were it not for the fact that Mr. Collins signed them, the Articles of Agreement would have received very short shrift in Dail Eireann.

"The Republican point of view expressed by De Valera and supported by the young men of the Irish Republican Army and by all those who would have Ireland as free as America, or as England, is a simple one, based on the fundamental right of the Irish nation to the undictated control of its own affairs, owing allegiance to no power on earth save the sovereign people of Ireland, prepared to stand on the fundamental rock of right, refusing to give a democratic title to the British King in Ireland, refusing to march into the Empire with heads up, as Mr. Griffith invites, or to march in with hands up for ten years or more, as Mr. Collins would have it. Of the two policies that of the ' heads up ' is the more honourable.

"Republicans argue that once the Irish nation sanctions this Treaty and ratifies it in the ballot-box, the honour of the nation is committed, and by so doing Ireland wills her own national death. The sanctity of treaties is invoked against Mr. Collins' arguments. It is pointed out that entering the Empire gives the lie to all that for which countless generations of Irishmen have contended. All the dead generations are fighting on the side of those who would maintain the independence of Ireland, and I am satisfied that this point of view will win in the coming election.

"Now that the army of the Republic has cut itself off from those who would accept the agreement, the future of Ireland under the Treaty is very doubtful. It remains to be seen whether Messrs. Collins and Griffith will persevere in their efforts to force the Free State against the Irish Republican Army opposition. If they so persist, then I look for serious trouble in Ireland. If, on the other hand, they tell the British that they cannot ' deliver the goods,' I feel sure that a just peace can be negotiated between

England and Ireland. Of one thing I am certain : this so-called Treaty will not bring peace to Ireland or to England, for Ireland unfree will never be at peace. The manhood of Ireland is in revolt against this agreement, signed, as it was, with a pistol at the heads of the delegates. In the words of Franklin, ' Those who would give up essential liberty to purchase a life-safety deserve neither safety nor liberty '—and history proves that Ireland will never submit to the status of a dismembered Dominion of an Empire with which she has been at war for centuries.

(*Signed*) " HARRY BOLAND."

FROM DAN MACCARTHY

[Mr. MacCarthy, T.D., is the whip of the Treaty party, and generally recognised in Irish political circles as the most efficient organiser in the country.]

" The Ireland of the future under the terms of the Treaty will be an Ireland governed by Irishmen for the common good of Irishmen. In this way we can develop our own civilisation without being subjected to, and hampered by, the interference of the foreign invader.

" Dublin Castle—the symbol of English authority in this country for seven hundred years—is in Irish hands for the first time in history. Irishmen the world over know what Dublin Castle stood for. From its inception it was meant for a government of corruptioners, and all the time its rulers aimed at the extermination of the Irish people.

" For centuries it has been the ideal and aim of Irishmen to loosen the chains by which Dublin Castle bound the people of Ireland, and this at last is achieved under the Treaty.

" By the Treaty we can develop Ireland in an Irish way. No longer fettered by English imperialistic aims, we can make our land fit for Irishmen to live in. England saw to it that education in Ireland was totally unsuitable to the people. We can change all that ; we can restore the

Irish language to be the language of our people; we can develop our agricultural districts; we can open up our mines, and find employment for our people, so that no longer will it be necessary for the sons and daughters of Erin to leave their native shores to earn a living in the land of the foreigner.

"Under English rule we have been subjected to over-taxation which crippled and ruined our industries; our shipping all disappeared and Ireland became the slave of her English master. The Treaty gives us power to levy our own taxation without outside interference.

"The future holds bright things for the Irish people. With an Irish Government replacing the rule of the foreigner by the rule of the plain people of Ireland, I can see in the near future a prosperous and well-contented country. Our work now is to build up the nation, and the vast majority of Irishmen are taking up that work with a pride and a zest unequalled.

"The Treaty gives us the means of attaining our complete freedom. Irish soldiers are replacing the Britisher in our streets and in the barracks throughout the country. The army of the Free State will be used to defend Ireland's rights; they will see that nothing that she has gained is taken from her. The soldiers which the Irish people will see in Ireland will be green-clad boys of Ireland—the token of her freedom—not the khaki-clad soldiers of Britain, the symbol of Ireland's subjection.

"Under the Free State the Irish people will work out their own salvation and their destiny as glorious as the people of America worked out their fate under the Federal Constitution.

(*Signed*) "DAN MACCARTHY."

FROM JOSEPH MACDONAGH

[Mr. MacDonagh, T.D., is a brother of Thomas MacDonagh, one of the leaders of the 1916 Rebellion, who was executed by the British after the Easter Week rising.]

" There are many arguments against the Treaty. The principal ones are :

" 1. The Irish Republican Army (not the ' Free State ' Army, with headquarters at Beggars Bush), which has renounced its allegiance to Dail Eireann since that body handed over its powers to the Provisional Government and ceased to function as the Government of the Irish Republic.

" 2. All the men and women killed or murdered by the British during the last six years gave their lives for an Irish Republic, and all the sophistries of the pro-Treaty party are unable to hide the fact that the proposed pact is a betrayal of the dead who died for Ireland.

" 3. If the Treaty is accepted by the people, Ireland will assume a share of the British war debt, and will require such an army to prevent the young men of Ireland from re-establishing the Republic that taxation will become intolerable and make a trade or industrial revival impossible.

" 4. The partition of Ireland is admitted for the first time by people claiming to be Irish Nationalists.

" The above four arguments show how impossible it is to expect a settlement on the lines of the Treaty. The first argument—the Irish Republican Army, which still remains faithful to its oath of allegiance to the Irish Republic—will not allow that Republic which was proclaimed by Pearse and his colleagues, less than 1,000 men, mostly unarmed, to be disestablished while it can count on upwards of 50,000 men mostly armed and well used to fighting. The establishment of the ' Free State ' means the disbandment of the Irish Republican Army by force, and that means civil war.

" The second argument will make it certain that even if the ' Free State ' be now established, the patriotic youth of every coming generation in Ireland will try by force of arms to re-establish the Republic for which the heroes from 1916 to 1922 died. That will mean civil war.

" The third argument shows that Ireland, which should be prosperous, must remain poor in order that it may be made safe for the British Empire. Those people who are now clamorous for peace, thinking it is the forerunner of prosperity, will soon realise that the Treaty means national decay.

"Lord Birkenhead may congratulate his colleague on having set the Irish fighting; Mr. Churchill on the great achievement of British statesmanship, and on the chance of making 'Irish civilisation a by-word throughout the world'; Mr. Griffith on having achieved freedom for Ireland and ended the fight of seven hundred and fifty years; and Mr. Collins on having obtained the freedom to achieve freedom. But the I.R.A. are, above all, realists. They realise that the seven hundred and fifty years' fight is not yet ended and that the Treaty does not give even freedom to achieve freedom. They are aware of the fact that they possess an instrument which, if used, renders the establishment of the 'Free State' and the disestablishment of the Irish Republic impossible. They mean to use that instrument!

(*Signed*) " JOSEPH MACDONAGH."

FROM P. J. HOGAN

[Mr. Hogan is Minister of Agriculture in Dail Eireann, and occupies the same Cabinet position in the Provisional Government.]

"The land is the outstanding problem in the new Ireland. The changed political order, which sets free the energies of the people for the task of reconstruction and nation-building, has definitely brought the question of the settlement of the broader aspects of the land problem into the first place. Land purchase on the established lines will have to be completed at once.

"The present position of land purchase is that about three-fourths of the tenanted land has been sold to the occupiers through the machinery of the British Land Acts. The benefits of land purchase need no arguing. The improvement in the material and mental outlook of those who have been made the owners of the land they till is admitted by all. It is there to see.

"The financing of a future scheme presents considerable difficulties. The finances of the existing Land Purchase Acts have broken down. Ireland cannot afford to finance future land purchase on the lines of the last Acts. Whatever way out is found, however, it is plain that the raising of the necessary money is a matter of national credit, and from this point of view the present insecurity is most unfortunate.

"Following the completion of the transfer of the occupied land to its tenants must come the acquisition, division, and establishment of homesteads on the untenanted ranches. Due largely to the plantations of the past—these ranches consist of wide areas of some of the most fertile land in the country, hungered after by the owners of tiny or barren holdings adjoining and by other classes of deserving claimants. The acquisition of these untenanted areas and their conversion into suitable holdings is a problem of immediate urgency in view of the necessity of providing for the needs even of our present population pending the development and exploitation of Ireland's industrial resources.

"But while land settlement must be regarded as the first step towards an efficient and economical use of the land which is our greatest national asset, supplementary assistance must be given by way of a loan chargeable on the property with a view to providing the proprietor with the equipment and housing necessary to a progressive agriculture. In the case of new settlements such provision will, of course, be absolutely essential. There is little use of educating the farmer as to the necessity of proper housing for stock and implements or of the desirability of initiating different lines of development if through lack of capital or credit he is unable to effect the necessary changes.

"Equally important to the country is an efficient system of agricultural education. It is one of the anomalies with which unfortunately we have been too familiar that in this agricultural country the schemes of education have been directed to fit the youth of the country for anything rather than agriculture. Only within the last year or so has there even been a beginning made towards the establishment of faculties of agriculture in the university centres. It is a primary condition of success in developing our knowledge of the potentialities of the land, and disseminating that knowledge so as to be of practical value to our farmers, that attention to this, the fundamental industry of the country, should be firmly established as a most important function of the universities. Quite apart from agricultural research in its ordinary meaning, it would seem desirable that in these centres new possibilities of farm practice might be tested on a commercial scale. In Ireland we have too few farmers, whatever may be their enlightenment, who are so fortunately circumstanced as to be able to take the risks inherent in pioneering.

" The problems referred to are those which seem to call most for immediate attention from the State authority. But there still remains almost untouched a wide field of possible agricultural developments.

" The questions of new agricultural industries, organisation of markets, transit facilities or improvements, reclamation of waste lands, might be mentioned as typical. There is also awaiting attention the question of congestion in the West. So far only the fringe of this difficult problem has been touched. A population is there eking out a precarious existence on holdings which are either too small or too unproductive to support them. This situation has to be remedied.

" We can see, therefore, that agriculture in Ireland is at a trying period, and in grievous need of reconstruction and development. By virtue of the Treaty we have complete control of the industry. If we have difficulties and problems, we have, likewise, for the first time, power to deal with them. If we fail to bring agriculture to the level of efficiency and productiveness it has reached in such countries as Denmark, then we shall have nobody to blame for failure but ourselves.

(*Signed*) " P. J. HOGAN."

De Valera promised to contribute to the symposium, but failed to do so. However, I did obtain from him an exclusive interview during the session of Dail Eireann in December 1921, and it may be of interest to include here parts of his statement to me at that time.

" Our opponents in the Dail," De Valera began—" and, really, I think it is only fair to explain they are not our opponents in fact—however, politically speaking, our opponents have been playing politics in this matter of Document No. 2. They have succeeded in inducing a large section of the Press to make much of the seeming similarity between the oath contained in the Treaty and the oath which I suggested verbally at the secret session. As a result of their success in this attempt to mislead the people with regard to the true facts, almost all of the Irish newspapers are displaying this sort of thing . . ."

Here De Valera spread out an evening newspaper on the table and pointed with his forefinger to a box containing under the caption, " The Two Oaths," an italicised statement which read as follows :

> " Mr. Sean Milroy on Tuesday revealed Mr. De Valera's alternative oath. It is for the Irish nation to say if they agree with Mr. Griffith that this is a quibble."

The two oaths followed in parallel columns, and the statement concluded with a further italicised line, which read :

> " Mr. Milroy declared that the whole issue at stake was the difference between these two oaths."

De Valera's " explanation " of the difference, as he stated it to me, was as follows :

" The trouble with the oath contained in the Treaty," he said, " is not at all with regard to swearing to be ' faithful ' to the King of England ; the trouble is swearing allegiance to the Constitution of the Irish Free State ' as by law established,' which amounts to swearing allegiance to the King—the King under the Treaty terms actually being the titular head of the Constitution—the very Constitution itself.

"Now, since it is impossible to win the status of an isolated Republic, but because it is possible to arrange an external association with the British Commonwealth of Nations, I can see no harm in recognising the King as the head of that Commonwealth. It seems to me there is a very real difference between these two viewpoints, as there is between the two oaths.

"I suppose that the world appreciates Ireland's true ambition. The Irish people have always wanted an isolated status like that of Switzerland or Denmark, with guarantees of neutrality. But England, rightly or wrongly, never has been able to see her way clear to consenting to this—perhaps fearing in the case of war with another Power that she might have to violate such Irish neutrality and thus earn the same stigma as Germany in regard to Belgium.

"Knowing that it is impossible to win this much, and having already agreed to endeavour to find the way to effect a real peace between the Irish and English people, it does not strike me as being repugnant to recognise the King of England. I go even further, and say the objectionable feature of the Treaty oath is not in agreeing to be ' faithful ' to the King, because I disagree that there is any analogy between such a term and the fealty of a slave to his master. On the contrary, I take it to mean that it is the faithfulness of two equals who prove it in keeping a bargain made.

"The point is that the oath contained in the Treaty actually and unequivocally binds the taker to ' allegiance ' to the English King, for under the terms of the Treaty the Constitution of the Irish Free State ' as by law established ' is the King of England and nobody else.

"As a matter of fact, those in favour of the ratification of the Treaty are taking an unfair advantage in making it appear that the difference between the two oaths is the

What the Treaty Means

only actual difference between us. My verbally-proposed oath was the least of what I offered by way of counter-proposals. It is not even correctly expressed, as a study of it immediately makes apparent. I never put it on paper. Had I done so, it would have been properly expressed. I did not expect it to be written down and used against me in a public session of the Dail.

"I have repeatedly said in the public sessions that the Treaty is objectionable because it does not mean peace. The reason for this is obvious. The Irish people never mean to become part of the British Empire, but they are eagerly willing to be faithful to any agreement they enter into, even an agreement designating the king as titular head of the negotiating party. We earnestly, honestly and faithfully want to establish and maintain peaceful relations with England, but this can be "—and here De Valera paused as if choosing his words with the greatest care—" only when 'we' means the Irish nation, and not British subjects within the Empire.

"My plan of peace is much more acceptable to Mr. Lloyd George than this Treaty, unbelievable as that may sound. It is more acceptable to him, if he only knew it, because it spells real peace, whereas the inclusion of Ireland within the Empire will never spell peace. If peace were to come on the lines I have proposed the greatest difficulty that might well eventuate would be to prevent too much fraternisation between the two countries!

"Whether the Dail will ratify the Treaty or reject the Treaty I do not know, nor can any man know. But one thing I do know, and I am sure that every man and woman in the Dail knows it too—ratification will not mean peace. It will mean sooner or later that the English Government will have to face the centuries'-old question of Ireland for the Irish people. This I am so convinced Mr. Lloyd George fully comprehends as to leave me little moved by the arguments of our opponents that rejection would be immediately followed by war.

"When Mr. Lloyd George knows, as I am positive he

knows, that he can have a permanent and faithful peace with Ireland, including the association of Ireland with the Commonwealth of Nations of the British Empire—so long as we remain ourselves and have not to become British subjects—I think there can still be arranged such a peace —not only can, but will be."

FROM SIR MAURICE DOCKRELL, M.P.

[Sir Maurice is the only Unionist member elected from the South of Ireland to the Imperial Parliament, who, after his experience in the House of Commons, became an ardent Home Ruler. He is one of the principal business men of Ireland.]

"One would need to be a super-optimist to predict a future for the Treaty amid all the happenings of the moment. The flash of light which heralded its arrival may either have revealed an unsuspected precipice or may have temporarily blinded us to its full meaning. We may resemble birds who, after being released from captivity, circle round and round in apparent perplexity as to which is the true course to their objective. All Irishmen who are lovers of their country will hope that we may soon find and pursue with unerring aim the road that leads to a happy and prosperous Ireland.

(*Signed*) " DOCKRELL."

FROM HIS GRACE MOST REV. DR. T. P. GILMARTIN

[Dr. Gilmartin is the Archbishop of Tuam.]

"If educated men with a sense of citizenship are returned to Parliament, if judges and police are worthy of their rôles, if, in a word, all the organs of the new State function normally, a great future awaits us. The country is fresh and undeveloped ; the population is healthy ; the people love their homes and their families ; the vices of civilisation are to a great extent unknown, and all the fixed factors of progress are, I think, realisable. But there are many unknown quantities in the problem, and there are many ' ifs ' in the political prophecy.

(Signed) " GILMARTIN."

FROM RICHARD CROKER

[The late Richard Croker dictated and signed the following statement while lying on his sick-bed a few weeks before his death in his home, Glencairn, in Stillorgan, a suburb of Dublin.]

" In my opinion there are four countries in the world to-day which can be properly called progressive. They are America, Japan, Germany and the Argentine Republic. In my opinion the Irish Free State will rank among the best of these if it is given a chance. But . . .

" The way the leaders of this Irish Free State are handicapped reminds me of last year's Grand National. Out of 27 starters two finished, and the second of these had fallen at the water-jump—all due to the impossible difficulties of the course. Just this applies to the men who are now trying to establish the Free State.

" These men are looking forward, instead of backward ; they are trying to bring prosperity to their country. Their faces are set to the future, and their minds are not dwelling on the wrongs and misrule of 750 years. But will their opponents take down the hurdles and lighten the weights and give the Free State a chance ? Until we have an answer to that question nobody can say what the future holds in store for Ireland.

" Progressive Irishmen have left Ireland for many years back, and have gone out into the world and taken commanding positions, filling important governmental posts in countries all over the world. They have done so chiefly because they had no opportunity in their own country to better their condition. Now the opportunity has come they should not let it escape.

"Men like Michael Collins and Arthur Griffith would rise to the highest positions in the Government if they were American born and had done one half of what they have done for Ireland. In 15 years from to-day, if the wreckers of the Treaty do not succeed in preventing it, Michael Collins will prove himself to be one of the great figures of the world. At least, this is my opinion.

"If the Free State leaders are sustained, the prosperity that will come to Ireland in the wake of returning sons and daughters, and the consequent opening up of industries, will provide work for every man that is now idle and will bring comfort and plenty to all the people. And yet nothing in the existing situation justifies anybody's predicting that they will be sustained.

"And this is none the less true for all that as between the opposing factions the only important difference is over a name. As to the patriotism and love of country and sincerity of all the men and women on both sides, there is no question whatever. But I cannot believe that the Treaty opponents will plunge the country into misery. If they do, it will be the sorriest day in all Ireland's sorry history.

(*Signed*) " RICHARD CROKER."

FROM ERSKINE CHILDERS

[Mr. Childers, who, until the summer elections, was the only member of the Dail born in England, and—because there is as yet no naturalisation machinery in Ireland—remained an Englishman, was generally considered the brains behind the Republican movement.]

"I approach the question as one who is deeply and vehemently opposed to the Treaty, but I will try to assume that the Irish people gives its sanction to the Treaty and that the Free State is set up. A most extraordinary position would result from the first. The election would have been decided on an obsolete register giving no fair reflection of the electorate as it exists to-day, and excluding from the franchise most of the young men who fought in the war of independence and are resolutely opposed to accepting the Treaty and entering the British Empire. The young women would also be excluded, although adult suffrage is, or should be, now universal in up-to-date democracies, and although these young women took a most important share in the winning of the war. You would, therefore, have from the first some of the most virile elements of the population smarting under the grievance of not having been able to give a vote in an election deciding the destiny of their country.

"But there is a wider question still. The election would be fought under the threat of renewed war by the British. Mr. Griffith has declared that the issue will be 'to honour the Treaty or revert to war.' To honour the Treaty means to surrender the existing Irish Republic and the independence of Ireland and agree to her entry into the British Empire as a conquered people. To ask that a national democracy choose with a bayonet at its throat between freedom and extermination is a thing never done before in history, and an iniquitous thing.

"The verdict at such an election, if it were for the Treaty, would be null and void, and would be considered so in their hearts even by those who voted for the Treaty.

"Apart from this, you would have the whole of the present Republican party, which, though it might be beaten at the polls, would, at any rate, be a large minority, violently opposed to the surrender of independence which would have been thrust upon them, and determined to use their utmost efforts to regain it.

"I am not saying anything about civil war. That does not enter into the question I am discussing. What I mean is that, talk as people will about the people of Ireland settling this question at an election, the question will not be settled unless it is settled by the defeat of the Treaty and by the return of the Irish people to that unity which can only be based on independent nationality. Otherwise you would have the nation divided against itself, some of its citizens prepared to live a lie and to send to Parliament members ready to swear an allegiance they do not feel to a foreign king, others disowning that Parliament, refusing to go into it and working to restore independence.

"This is how human nature will act inevitably, as it would in any other country in the world, and I, therefore, feel it impossible to estimate the gain to fine national development which might result from the use of the powers which the Free State has received, important as they undoubtedly are. A nation divided fundamentally on the question of its very existence as an independent nation cannot function and develop freely. I myself anticipate that the struggle could not last long and that it must end in the recognition of Irish independence. Then, and then only, can our nation find its true place in the world and express fully its own culture and civilisation.

(*Signed*) " ERSKINE CHILDERS."

FROM SEAN MILROY

[Mr. Milroy, T.D., one of the few members of Dail Eireann representing two constituencies—one of which is in Ulster—has proved himself repeatedly during the course of the Dail debates one of the most brilliant thinkers in that assemblage.]

" I am asked to express my opinion upon the question, ' Under the terms of the Treaty, what does the future hold in store for Ireland ? '

" That question might be dealt with by the reply that under the terms of the Treaty Ireland's future will be whatever the Irish people wish to make it. In the Proclamation of 1916 appeared the following passage :

" ' We declare the right of the people of Ireland to the ownership of Ireland and to the unfettered control of Irish destinies to be sovereign and indefeasible.'

What the Treaty Means 239

"That right has been vindicated by the Treaty, and through it the control of Irish destinies passes into the hands of the Irish people. A fair and legitimate test of the powers it brings to the Irish nation is the examination of how far the constructive programme embodied in the constitution of the Sinn Fein organisation is made possible as a result of the Treaty. Briefly that programme was as follows :

" 1. The protection of Irish industries and commerce.

" 2. The establishment and maintenance of an Irish consular service.

" 3. The re-establishment of an Irish mercantile marine.

" 4. The industrial survey of Ireland and the development of its mineral resources.

" 5. The establishment of a national stock exchange.

" 6. The creation of a national civil service.

" 7. The establishment of courts of arbitration.

" 8. The development of transit by road, rail, and water, and of waste lands.

" 9. The development of Irish sea fisheries.

" 10. The reform of education to render its basis national and industrial.

" 11. The abolition of the Poor Law system.

"The greater portion of that programme has been impossible hitherto ; only in four of the various aspects of it, *viz.*, 1, 4, 7, and 11, was it feasible to make any effort. In only one, *viz.*, the establishment of courts of arbitration, were comprehensive, practical results achieved.

"Under the Treaty the whole programme becomes a matter of practical work. It requires no great imagination to understand what a transformed Ireland we shall have when that is done.

"Another test of the value of the Treaty to Ireland :

"In 1919 an announcement was issued over the names of President De Valera and Michael Collins, Minister of Finance, advertising the loan of that year. The following is part of the wording of that announcement stating what might be achieved for Ireland if the loan was subscribed:

" ' You can recover Ireland for the Irish.
" ' You can re-people the land.
" ' You can harness the rivers.
" ' You can put her flag on every sea.
" ' You can plant the hillsides and the wastes.
" ' You can set the looms spinning.
" ' You can set the hammer ringing on the anvil.
" ' You can abolish the slums.
" ' You can send her ships to every port.
" ' You can garner the harvest of the seas.
" ' You can drain the bogs.
" ' You can save the boys and girls for Ireland.
" ' You can restore Ireland's health, her strength, her beauty, and her wealth.'

" That was a magnificent outline of what could be done for Ireland.

" The Treaty gives to Ireland the chance to secure that every one of these objects for which the loan was subscribed can become an accomplished fact within our own day.

" It is not likely that the Irish people will thoughtlessly throw away the fairest chance that Ireland has known for centuries of becoming free and progressive.

(*Signed*) " SEAN MILROY."

FROM MARY MACSWINEY

[Miss MacSwiney, T.D, is sister of the late Lord Mayor of Cork, who died in Brixton Prison after a hunger-strike that lasted for more than two months; in a speech at a session of Dail Eireann she vowed she would be an uncompromising rebel against the Free State as she always has been against British rule in Ireland.]

What the Treaty Means 241

"As I write, the peace committee of An Dail is still striving to find a basis of negotiations between the Republican party and those who favour the Treaty. They will have finished their deliberations long before this article reaches the public. If they succeeded in finding such a basis it will be such that Republicans can be certain it will not involve now, or at any future time, acceptance of the Articles of Agreement which put Ireland inside the British Empire.

"The future of Ireland is certain. Independence will bring prosperity, and, side by side with increasing prosperity, will spread Gaelic culture, which will make our people great as in the olden days when Ireland was the university of Europe. That Ireland—free and Gaelic—will have much to give humanity and will be generous in the giving. But all that development is contingent on real independence; not the loosening or lengthening of the tyrant's chain, but the breaking of it.

"The proposed Treaty could never bring peace to Ireland, because it would not bring real freedom, and 'Ireland unfree will never be at peace.' A certain material prosperity it might bring—for a time. But as soon as the natural development of Cork and Galway roused the jealousy of Southampton and Liverpool, we would have a repetition of the old economic coercion.

"England did not ask for a truce and negotiations because her conscience smote her for her frightfulness in Ireland, but because she hoped that the Welsh wizard would accomplish at the conference-table by his wiles what her Huns and her Black and Tans could not do by their terror; and because the Treaty is of English manufacture and in English interests it cannot bring peace to Ireland. Should it be forced on our people by the threat of 'immediate and terrible war,' which frightened our delegates into signing that disgraceful document on the 6th of last December, the result will not help England any more than it will bring peace to Ireland.

"The Treaty to Ireland will mean civil war and chaos

for a time, and an added spirit of hatred and revenge toward England. As long as there is a trace or a symbol of English domination in Ireland so long will the enmity between the nations last ; so long will there be Irishmen who will look upon every difficulty in which England finds herself as an opportunity for them to strike a blow again at our one and only enemy. Through the Treaty, therefore, there can be no peace ; the fight must be carried on until England withdraws her preposterous demand that Ireland become a Dominion of the British Empire ; that Irishmen take an oath of fidelity to a foreign monarch, and allow a Governor-General, no matter how camouflaged, in our country.

"Much effort is expended by our enemies in vilifying the Republican attitude. That vilification ought not to receive any support from any American who knows his history. That our country is passing through a terrible crisis at present is true ; that much lawlessness exists and dire poverty is equally true ; much of the poverty is part of the economic conditions which obtain all over Europe as a result of the world war. In so far as our difficulties are political, the blame lies on England chiefly for trying to force us to accept her Empire under threat of 'immediate and terrible war,' and, secondly, on those who gave way to that threat and so divided the country. Let England remove the threat of war and agree to abide by the free decision of the Irish people and we have no doubt—nor has England—what that decision will be.

"Meantime, a little more patience, renewed courage, and the victory is ours. Remember Washington's bitter cry at the condition of the States of the Union after the War of Independence had been won. And yet his country surmounted her difficulties. So will Ireland.

"And Ireland free will make Ireland great and noble. Men and women will bend themselves to the task of making this land of ours a real home for all its children ; where justice will abound ; where every child born to the noble heritage of Irish citizenship will be assured of its rights and will grow up to enjoy the blessings of freedom won by the heroic struggles of Ireland's martyrs, and to increase, in happier times and circumstances, the magnificence of that heritage for posterity.

(*Signed*) " MARY MACSWINEY."

FROM J. J. WALSH

[Mr. Walsh, T.D., Postmaster-General of the Provisional Government, fought in the Easter week rebellion, and thereafter spent long periods in gaol.]

" Ireland under the Treaty will have a Parliament elected by, and responsible to, the Irish people, an Executive Government responsible to that Parliament, power to legislate for every department of national life, a democratic constitution, an Irish judiciary, an army for the protection, instead of the repression, of Ireland, a police force or civic guard for the maintenance of Irish law and order (and not British), and a recognised place as a separate state amongst the nations. Notwithstanding certain imperfections in the Treaty, she can deal in her own way with everything that touches the lives of the people. She has government of the people, for the people, by the people, for the first time practically in eight hundred years.

" Ireland having complete control of education, it goes without saying that this means the scrapping of existing methods—from A B C to university—and the substitution of a system ensuring the complete re-Gaelicisation of the race. The present national education system (called ' national ' because it was intended to denationalise, and ' education ' because it was intended to delude) has, even in the short space of time since Irish ideas have begun to count, received its death-blow.

" For many years the Gaelic League has been doing its utmost to revive the native language and culture, but voluntary effort in such matters obtains little success. Now, however, the schools can do their natural part, and in the future bi-lingual education, in accordance with national sentiment, is assured, an incalculable advantage in the remodelling of the nation.

"So many avenues for strenuous effort exist that it is impossible to do more than touch on them here. The improvement of the physique of the race will be of prime importance. Forced emigration during the last half century has depleted Ireland of much of its young manhood. The ill-wind of the world-war, however, has blown good in this respect, as it kept scores of thousands of young people from emigrating, and no effort will now be spared to make it worth their while to remain at home. Good houses, land, and fruitful work will be provided; healthy sport will be encouraged; the Aonach Tailltean or Tailltean Games are being revived, though not by the Provisional Government, after the lapse of centuries, men and women of the Irish race throughout the world being eligible to compete.

"Vast areas require to be drained, mineral resources developed, and reafforestation on a large scale attempted, for under English rule effort in these respects was either stifled altogether or merely tinkered with. Development and misrule do not thrive together. And as the development of Irish industries proceeds it is hoped to link up Ireland for purposes of direct trading with all the great countries of the world.

"It is intended to make the country as attractive as possible for tourists. Roads will be improved for motorists and the country generally opened up. Already the question of instituting aerial services between Ireland, England and beyond for mails and passengers is under consideration. Further, it is hoped by studying the various systems of the world, and especially the American, to ensure an internal telephone system second to none.

"It will, of course, take some time to make the Irish landscape fruitful and smiling, but it is not too much to prophesy that after a few years Ireland will be as different from what she is at present as cheese is from chalk. Irish-speaking and Irish, she will take the distinct and worthy place amongst the nations which her history entitles her to.

"Many people look dismal at the prospect of further strife. They forget that there is an aftermath to every revolution. It will pass.

(*Signed*) " J. J. WALSH."

FROM SEAN ETCHINGHAM

[Mr. Etchingham, although a great friend and admirer of Arthur Griffith, is one of the Treaty's bitterest opponents. In spite of his advanced years, he took an active part in organising the rebellion in Wexford in 1916. He was beaten for re-election to the Dail in the summer elections.]

"The present situation in Ireland is the inevitable result of signing the Articles of Agreement in London and attempting to force acceptance of them on the people. If some members of the delegation had been preparing their minds for many months to the final act of December 6, 1921, the young men in the army had not such schooling of thought. Rather were they preparing for a renewal of the struggle, and this is what they were exhorted to.

"Out in the West—the real Ireland—the present Minister of Defence, General Richard Mulcahy, made a 'no surrender' address to the army at Galway, December 4, 1921. Away down to the South of Ireland the self-same intense feeling fills the minds and actions of Ireland's soldiers. President Griffith's action in asking the young fighting men to march into the British Empire with their 'heads up' displays an astounding lack of appreciation of the patriotism and self-sacrifice of the youth of Ireland. The Irish Republic is, with them, a firm faith.

"They say that it is the intention of those advocating acceptance of the Treaty to use it as a stepping-stone toward the Republic. Hell in the same way is paved with good intentions. To kill the Republic and resurrect it again may be a soothing balm to a troubled conscience, but it is beyond my grip. It is like putting it on the long finger.

"There was a newspaper in America which one morning announced the death of a prominent citizen. When this gentleman entered the editorial office a little later he demanded an explanation. 'I'm not dead,' he said. 'You can see that for yourself. Contradict it!' But the editor wasn't willing to admit the error. 'We never make a mistake,' he declared. 'But I'll tell you what I will do for you: I'll put you in the Birth Notices to-morrow.' You cannot solve the death and birth of the Republic here in that way.

"For instance, here in Dublin there are too many Republican plots, and the graves therein are memories not soon forgotten. If Ireland wants to avoid the horror of civil war she must consult the army. The soldiers of the Irish Republic are patriots.

"No, the Treaty will not bring peace to Ireland. That should have been apparent to even 'peace-at-any-price' people. There was not a rushlight in Ireland to celebrate it. Ireland wants peace, and peace can be had if President Griffith and Mr. Collins will but meet the situation. Both of them, I feel, want to do the best they can for Ireland. Both have worked well for Ireland in the past. They can now do the greatest work it was ever given two Irishmen to do. They can make it possible to unite their people and bring peace to their country. It is better not to make known to the world at the moment how that can be done. Enough that it is in their power to do.

(Signed) "SEAN ETCHINGHAM."

FROM KEVIN O'HIGGINS

[Mr. O'Higgins, T.D., is Minister of Commerce in the Provisional Government and in Dail Eireann.]

"When some people in America cabled Mr. De Valera

remonstrating with him on the conditions of anarchy and fratricidal strife his policy is precipitating in Ireland, he replied, ' Oh, ye of little faith, hold up your heads ! ' To my mind the men ' of little faith ' are those who speak and think of their nation as if it were some dead thing that could be wrapped up for all time like a mummy in a bit of parchment called a Treaty.

" The Irish nation is a living, growing organism whose development cannot be stayed by a formula nor cease with the full stop of a document.

" You ask what the Treaty offers for Ireland in the future. One cannot answer apart from existing conditions. Mr. De Valera, at the head of a fraction of the population, cannot secure better terms for the nation, but he has great power for evil. He can sour the auspices, he can poison the wells, he can sap morale, kill enterprise, lock up capital, and foster anarchy. He can do what the British could not do —he can kill the Irish nation.

" And the Irish nation is the thing that matters, not the phrase or formula used to describe the mechanics of its Government. The Irish nation is something greater than Republic or Free State—the Irish nation thinking nationally —not thinking in terms of murder, brigandage or civil war, not thinking in terms of ' wading through Irish blood,' but thinking in terms of reconstruction and progress and national consciousness.

" All this could have been secured if Mr. De Valera had been big enough to take his stand with Collins and Griffith and advise his people to accept this Treaty, not as a recognition of their full rights, not as an ideal thing, not as a final thing, but as affording them an opportunity to grow strong, to attain internal unity, to rid themselves of the slave-mind born of vested interests in the British administration, to solve the North-eastern problem, and then to go forward proudly to the fulfilment of their destiny.

" For the metaphysical difference he professes to see between his Document No. 2 and the Treaty, he has preferred to throw the country into a welter in which national morale is giving place to party spirit or to despair and cynicism, and in which all the moral elevating effect of our six years' struggle is fast running out.

"In the existing conditions I cannot prophesy. We of the Provisional Government, we who stand for acceptance of the Treaty simply because we can give the country no reasonable assurance of securing better, are doing, and will continue to do, our best towards reconstruction and development that will enable Ireland to export something henceforth other than her sons and daughters But as I have said, Mr. De Valera and his friends have great power for evil —one cannot reconstruct while people are wading through one's blood.

"The opposition we are faced with is not constitutional, the democratic principle of the majority's will being the deciding factor in political affairs is waived aside, the exploded doctrine of 'the right divine of kings to govern wrong' is revived in altered form as the divine right of Document Two-ites to shove their patent medicine down the necks of the people at the point of the revolver. Well-meaning Irish-Americans who subscribe funds to the opponents of the Treaty are adding their weight and strength to hurl Ireland, in the very hour of her delivery, down to a hell of anarchy and despair. . . . No! I will not prophesy!

"So much depends on what Mr. De Valera may do, and my experience of Mr. De Valera leads me to the view that it is utterly impossible to base any opinion on a calculation of that kind. In any case, it is generally accepted that he has set factors at work that he will not be able to control when—and if—he recovers sufficient sanity to wish to do so

(*Signed*) "KEVIN O'HIGGINS."

CHAPTER XXII

ADDENDUM

FOLLOWING the publication in a London newspaper of some of the foregoing chapters, an official statement was issued by General Pierce Beasley, Chief of the Irish Censorship Bureau, charging that what had been published was "a deliberate forgery," and threatening to use "all the powers of international law" to prevent publication of this book. Immediately I learned of this repudiation I furnished the newspaper in question with irrefutable proof of the authenticity of what I had written—proof furnished by Michael Collins himself in a series of letters and telegrams covering a period of six months.

At that time I wrote as follows :

"After twenty years of newspaper work in almost every part of the world I have finally won the distinction of being called a liar, a forger, and a defamer—and the charges emanate from Irishmen.

"The fact that I have worked twenty years for one newspaper organisation would seem in itself sufficient proof that I am neither a liar nor a forger nor a defamer. Therefore what I am now about to say is less a refutation of these patently absurd charges than an attempt to arrive at the probable motives actuating those who have made them.

"First, Colonel Commandant Joe O'Reilly—a youngster with qualities as lovable as those of Collins himself—says that my account of Collins' escape from the Mansion House is 'pure fiction,' and adds that Collins never had 'a bodyguard.'"

(In my hastily-written notes, made while Collins was

telling me this narrative, I find that I have used the expression "bodyguard" referring to O'Reilly, and "Black and Tans" referring to the British forces engaged in hunting down Collins. In deference to O'Reilly's, extreme sensitiveness I have corrected these two inaccuracies in the narrative as published in this book.)

"If the story, as published, is fiction—it is fiction that was supplied to me not only by Collins, but also by O'Reilly himself!

"It was O'Reilly—who knew all about his chief's working with me on his memoirs—who suggested that I persuade 'the big fellow' to tell me about the Mansion House escape—and it was O'Reilly who contributed the amusing feature of his use of the germicide sprayer!

"Is it possible that O'Reilly was indulging in that delightful trait of romancing? Sure, if he was I'd not hold it against him—but in all fairness he ought not to label as a lie my recital of a tale which he himself was primarily responsible for my hearing!

"Come now, Joe, be a good lad and admit what you know is the truth—that your late Commander-in-Chief was closeted with me many, many hours in many, many different places, at all times of the day and night—and almost always it was you who were close by; and if you were not acting as bodyguard to the big fellow, how did it happen you were carrying that service revolver that you playfully 'drew' on me one day because of the extra work I was causing you by these many conferences? Was it just to keep your hand in, Joe? Or was it because you were, in fact, Collins' bodyguard?

"One word more, Joe, and then we can get on to the next calumniator. What of the letter I have now before me which you sent by my private messenger, August 29, 1922? Does it begin 'Dear Hayden,' and does it include a final paragraph reading, 'I would like to see you as soon as possible?' Does it, Joe?

"And does it say that you cannot give me certain information because 'anything that has to be done must be done

Addendum

with the permission of the Government?' Is that right, Joe?

"And did you underscore the following sentence in that letter:

"'You are requested to write nothing and publish nothing about our late Commander-in-Chief for the present.'

"Is that right, Joe? If it is—how does it happen UNLESS YOU KNEW I HAD SOMETHING TO WRITE?

"As for General Pierce Beasley and his accusation that what I have written is 'a deliberate forgery'—let us see. Beasley I hardly know. During the sessions of Dail Eireann, early in the year, I met him once or twice. I know something about him, however. So do most of the London correspondents of American newspapers.

"For a year past Beasley has been trying to negotiate in these quarters—and with the Dublin newspaper correspondents as well—for the publication of 'inside stuff' about Michael Collins. So far as I know, he has failed to sell a single story.

"I do know—and I challenge him to deny it—that in the past nine months I have been alone with Michael Collins more days than he has been minutes. I don't need his permission to write Michael Collins' memoirs. I have Michael Collins' permission. And if the greatest, kindliest, squarest Irishman who ever lived had not been struck down by the other kind of Irishman I could safely leave General Pierce Beasley to him! Michael Collins had no patience with self-seekers!

"Finally, the *Irish Republic*—a venomous publication then edited by Erskine Childers—characterises my articles as 'A Defamation of Michael Collins.' Surely comment is superfluous.

"These are the charges. I offer a few facts of an affirmative kind in the belief that they may not lack interest.

"The last night I was with Collins—August 2, 1922—just twenty days before he was killed—there were two others who saw me with him. One of these was McGann, once upon a time De Valera's private secretary, and at this time serving Collins in the same capacity. I have seen a statement attributed to McGann quoting him as saying that Collins had not 'authorised' me to write his memoirs. Let me jog McGann's memory.

"As Collins' private secretary, it was McGann who notified me of most of the appointments his chief made with me. In the six months that McGann occupied the post he advised me at least thirty times of such appointments—and I purposely understate the number. He knows—because he heard the conversation—the whole story of my obtaining Collins' autographs on four big art photograph mounts on that occasion.

"McGann heard me ask Collins to do this, and he heard me explain that one of these autographed mounts was to be used as the frontispiece of the memoirs. It was McGann who, talking with me before Collins' arrival that night, bewailed the fact that there was not one photograph in existence that did Collins justice, and certainly not one good enough to be used as a frontispiece in his book ! It was McGann who had been trying for a month to persuade Collins to go to a photograph studio to pose for a portrait for this purpose!

"Finally, it was McGann who helped the private messenger I sent from London to Dublin immediately after the murder of Collins to recover these autographed mounts from the photographer with whom I had left them. McGann had planned to have this photographer make the frontispiece portrait—and affix it to the mount—but after the death of Collins the value of each mount alone had jumped to £100. It was McGann who knew that my ownership of these mounts was indisputable, and it was he who enabled my messenger to get them from the photographer.

"This last interview with Collins was arranged with a two-fold purpose. As I have earlier stated, Collins had been planning for a long time to have me meet Sean McGarry—'the man,' according to Collins, 'who was closer in the confidence of the Easter Week martyrs than any living Irishman.' In order that my story might be as comprehensive as possible, Collins insisted that I hear McGarry's account of the famous Howth gun-running exploit. The other object of this last interview was to get Collins' tale of his birth and boyhood—the only part of the whole narrative that remained to be told.

"McGarry arrived before Collins. He and McGann and I sat in an outer office in the Provisional Government headquarters and chatted. Eventually Collins came in—a magnificent figure of a soldier-statesman in his general's greatcoat. He bade McGarry and me to follow him into an inner room.

"There he told McGarry that I was writing the inside story of Ireland's fight for freedom—that he had furnished me with most of the facts—and that he wanted 'Sean,' as he called him, to supply the unpublished details of the Howth gun-running. And Sean McGarry thereupon did as Collins ordered.

"Now, General Pierce Beasley, you need look no further. Although I am not sure of McGarry's rank, I think he must be less than a general. As his superior officer, call him before you and let him tell you what I tell you—that you are not telling the truth!

"Michael Collins is dead, but Sean McGarry is alive, and from what I saw of him and from what Collins told me about him I am willing to leave the matter to McGarry. Collins could not have been so fond of him if he were not both courageous and honest, and he would now have to be both a coward and a liar if he contradicted one word of what I have written about that last interview at which he was present. Call Sean McGarry before you, General Pierce Beasley, and then write the apology you owe me!"

(Although this was published several months ago, the only response I have had from Beasley was indirect—contained in a letter sent to the proprietor of the newspaper which printed my statement, in which Beasley contented himself with merely denying my charge that he had ever attempted to negotiate with London correspondents of American newspapers. If it were worth while, I could prove this charge by the sworn statements of these correspondents, but after all, I have no interest in the matter beyond establishing my own integrity.)

"McGarry had not begun to tell us all that was on his mind when Collins interrupted sharply, saying it was late and he had little time left in which to tell his own story. To the best of my recollection McGarry then left—although of this I am not positive—and Collins began to answer my typewritten questions about his ancestry and boyhood. Fortunately I preserved my lead-pencil notes of this last interview. In themselves they prove conclusively the authenticity of these memoirs. For it was when I stumbled over the spelling of " Clonakilty "—misunderstanding Collins to have said " County Kilty "—that he took the pencil out of my hand, and wrote not only that word, but two additional lines citing the Irish pronunciation of his birthplace.

"So much for that.

" Now as to the motives actuating these various persons. I want to make it clear that I am very fond of Joe O'Reilly, and know him to be made of the right stuff. But he is suffering grief beyond the comprehension of any man not Irish born. In the hour that my messenger was with him —the day following Collins' funeral—he never spoke above a whisper, and never raised his eyes from the ground. He cannot understand the ruthless demands of journalism. To his mind it is profanation to utter the name of his late Commander-in-Chief in an ordinary tone. A single inaccuracy in a printed narrative concerning the man he loved finds him honestly, deeply resentful. And I should be a very young, inexperienced journalist if I insisted any fact-narrative of my writing could not contain inaccuracies. Those of us who have grown beyond the 'cub' stage in newspaperdom know better than to make any such claim.

"For inaccurately describing the uniform in which Collins made his escape from the Mansion House as that of a Black and Tan officer, and for denominating his pursuers on that occasion as Black and Tans (when, according to O'Reilly, there were no Black and Tans in Ireland at that time) I apologise, Joe. I should have said—as I have now done in the narrative as it appears within these covers—' British' instead of Black and Tans. And I quite appreciate what an important distinction this is in your mind, Joe.

"McGann's statement that Collins did not authorise me to publish his memoirs puzzles me. Although I never got so close to McGann as I did to O'Reilly I always found him to be gracious and helpful. I like to believe there was no ulterior motive behind his making this statement—if, indeed, he ever made it. I do believe that sober reflection will serve to make him realise the injustice he has done me —and in time he will either repudiate the statement attributed to him or admit its untruthfulness.

" As for the motives of Beasley and the renegade editor of the *Republic of Ireland*, Childers, it is possible they may be discovered in the story an Irishman of my acquaintance— just arrived in London from Dublin—has told me.

"'Sure, it's plain as the nose on your face,' said my friend. ' You can go to Dublin to-night and make yourself *persona grata* all over the place—IF YOU WILL SPLIT WITH SOME OF THE BOYS ! That's what the matter is. They don't like to think of all the money you're making out of these Collins articles—with never a penny of it spent in Ireland—and with many of them badly in need of a few pounds ! I don't know do you intend returning to Ireland —but there is how you can do it—and find yourself with as many friends as you could hope to have ! '

"I wonder !"

I loved Ireland. In all the world there can be no fairer scene than the gently curving crescent beach from Killiney to Bray—no more beauteous home site than on the luxuriantly wooded slopes of Killiney Mountain, almost as tropical as Southern California. For nine months I wandered afoot, and rode in jaunting-cars, through a countryside as gloriously rich as any I have ever seen. I dreamed of a home in Ireland. But that dream was shattered at 4 o'clock in the morning of August 22, 1922, when an editor of a London newspaper told me over the telephone of the murder of Michael Collins.

The assassination of my friend, Dr. Walter Rathenau, did not surprise me. It was understandable. It left me unchanged as regards my feelings towards Germany.

Not so with the murder of Michael Collins.

" Had he fallen at the hand of an external enemy, we could have borne it, but that such a rich and bounteous nature, such a triumphant and romantic battler for Ireland's cause, such a glory of our race and nation, such an idol of the people should be slain by a spiteful faction of our own countrymen is a chagrin, a bitterness and a shame too heavy to bear.

. . . . .

" Sooner or later, and the sooner the better, the people will get going in earnest, and when they do, they will make short work of the wreckers. Then will the heroic figure of Michael Collins tower high in glory, while they who contrived his death lie buried in shame."

I quote from a statement issued by Most Rev. Dr. Fogarty in Dublin the day of Collins' funeral.

Until the Irishmen I know " get going in earnest "—until they prove themselves fit to have been followers of their great leader—until they avenge his murder in the only way possible to avenge it—until they adequately punish a crime as unnatural and as hideous as incest—the Ireland that Michael Collins typified, the Ireland that Michael Collins would have recreated, the Ireland that Michael Collins gave his life for, will never be.

THE END

Messrs. Hutchinson & Co.

have pleasure in giving the following brief notices of many important new books of serious interest for the Autumn, 1923.

Messrs. Hutchinson's list of NEW NOVELS includes the most recent works of nearly all the leading authors of to-day and whose names are given below.

SIR PHILIP GIBBS	ETHEL M. DELL
GILBERT FRANKAU	E. F. BENSON
MAY SINCLAIR	RAFAEL SABATINI
H. DE VERE STACPOOLE	EDEN PHILLPOTTS
ROBERT HICHENS	FRANK SWINNERTON
KATHLYN RHODES	BOYD CABLE
DOLF WYLLARDE	ELINOR MORDAUNT
BARONESS VON HUTTEN	E. TEMPLE THURSTON
DOROTHEA CONYERS	MRS. BAILLIE-SAUNDERS
E. M. DELAFIELD	WINIFRED GRAHAM
"RITA"	MABEL BARNES-GRUNDY
ISABEL C. CLARKE	MRS. BELLOC-LOWNDES
MARIE BJELKE PETERSEN	C. A. NICHOLSON
M. E. FRANCIS	A. M. LUDOVICI
DIANA PATRICK	MRS. FRANCES EVERARD
NORMA LORIMER	ACHMED ABDULLAH
JOHN AYSCOUGH	UNA L. SILBERRAD
CURTIS YORKE	ESSEX SMITH
SELWYN JEPSON	TICKNER EDWARDES
HORACE HUTCHINSON	G. B. BURGIN
E. CHARLES VIVIAN	M. P. WILLCOCKS
ROBERT ELSON	ROBERT WELLES RITCHIE
ROY BRIDGES	FREDERICK SLEATH
KATHARINE NEWLIN BURT	STEPHEN McKENNA
MAUDE ANNESLEY	ONOTO WATANNA
CHARLES CANNELL	ANDREW SOUTAR
RONALD M. NEWMAN	EDWIN L. SABIN
JOHN CHANCELLOR	RANN DALY
NEVILLE LANGTON	F. A. M. WEBSTER
HARRY SINCLAIR DRAGO and JOSEPH NOEL	WILLIAM GARRETT
	TALBOT MUNDY & BRADLEY KING

London : HUTCHINSON & CO., Paternoster Row, E.C.

Hutchinson's Important New Books

The Royal Naval Division By DOUGLAS JERROLD
With an Introduction by
The Rt. Hon. WINSTON CHURCHILL, C.H.

In one large handsome volume, with 8 folding maps and 24 illustrations, 21s. net.

In his long and brilliantly written introduction Mr. Churchill pays tribute to "the extraordinary achievements and almost incomparable prowess which this small band of men continued to display in every theatre where they fought during the whole course of the war." This authoritative account of the Royal Naval Division will certainly be widely read with pride and a profound interest. The despatch of the Royal Naval Division to the trenches defending Antwerp in October, 1914; the full story of its achievements in the operations at Gallipoli; the less widely known but no less distinguished part which the Division played in the final campaigns in France are here described with much vivid detail. Problems of training and tactics, with their solution on progressive lines, will prove valuable to the expert. A record of almost continuous adventures, the book will equally appeal to the general reader.

"Mr. Winston Churchill stands sponsor, contributing a brilliant and characteristic introduction. This volume is worthy of the subject, and that in itself is high praise."—*Daily Telegraph.*

"Mr. Jerrold writes well. He has an analytical and critical mind; he speaks with the authority of knowledge . . . and he has a deep but properly controlled enthusiasm."—*Morning Post.*

'Every page bristles with the tale of heroic exploits . . . a very valuable addition to the literature of the war."—*Evening News.*

"An admirable account of the operations of that famous unit. . . . To it Mr. Winston Churchill contributes an introduction, passages from which are worthy of a place in any future anthology of English prose, from their eloquence and dignity."—*Daily Mail.*

Fields of Adventure By ERNEST SMITH

In one large handsome volume, with 16 illustrations, 18s. net.

The writer has been for twenty-five years a special correspondent of a leading London daily, and in the course of his wanderings has known the cities and ways of many men. Moreover, from the almost infinite variety of his experiences he possesses an enviable knack of selecting the most entertaining incidents. His reminiscences will thus be found of outstanding interest to the general reader. Royalty in stories of Queen Victoria, King Edward, the late King of Italy, the ex-Kaiser (both in his glory and in exile), the Shah of Persia; such eminent statesmen as Bismarck, Gladstone, Marshal von Biberstein; Pope Leo XIII.; literary giants of many nations; great soldiers, "queer" people and anarchists—all contribute to the vast interest of these pages. Very few descriptions of the outbreak of the War are surpassed by the author's reminiscences of Paris in the early days of August, 1914. A snowstorm in Jerusalem, sunset on the Volga, the siege of Ladysmith, the guillotining of a French criminal are but a few of the varied sights which Mr. Ernest Smith has witnessed in his time and describes so realistically and with all the assurance of a practised pen.

Hutchinson's Important New Books

"Just My Story" By STEPHEN DONOGHUE
Dedicated, by special permission, to
H.R.H. the PRINCE OF WALES, K.G.

In one large handsome volume, with 32 coloured and other illustrations, **21s.** *net.*
An Edition de Luxe, limited to 200 copies only, numbered and signed by the Author, will be issued at **2 guineas** *net.*

This autobiography of the most prominent horseman of to-day, who by his unique achievements holds and deserves a very high place in the history of the Turf, is of far more than passing interest. For the story of one who against heavy odds and entirely without influence attained, by sheer force of will and endeavour, a world-wide fame is illumined with romance, steadily growing until the author's most recent achievement, the winning of a third successive Derby. The book abounds in vivid descriptions of important races, including much information hitherto unpublished of great horses and their owners, as well as intimate reminiscences of other distinguished Turf personalities. Thrilling adventures in many countries are realistically depicted. With its numerous and well chosen illustrations, "Just My Story" will be found a valuable addition to every sportsman's library.

My Russian Life By PRINCESS ANATOLE MARIE BARIATINSKY

In one large handsome volume, with 16 illustrations, **21s.** *net.*

The writer's husband was a personal friend of the late Nicholas II., so that both Prince and Princess attended all important Court functions. The Czar's Coronation, the magnificent ball that followed, the Emperor's historic visit to Paris in 1901, life in Manchuria, regimental duties in Tashkent, "home" life on the vast Bariatinsky estate are vividly depicted in these reminiscences of an intelligent observer. The personalities of the Czar and Czarina, Grand Dukes and Russian Generals are intimately portrayed, while other acquaintances included the late Pierre Loti and Jerome K. Jerome. During the War the Princess superintended a hospital at Kieff, once invaded by Bolsheviks. As a writer, she possesses a distinct gift of graphic suggestive description, while a lively style adds to the attractiveness of her reminiscences.

The greatest Romance of real life ever told.
With Lawrence in Arabia By LOWELL THOMAS

In demy 8vo, with 16 illustrations on art paper, **10s. 6d.** *net.*

The profusely illustrated narrative of the greatest adventure of a century is now presented to the public in this popular form. The famous exploits of Colonel Lawrence, "the uncrowned King of Arabia"—whom Mr. Lloyd George described as "one of the most remarkable and romantic figures of modern times"—will be read with eager interest by all who appreciate the importance of his services to the Empire. This thrilling story of our men's gallant deeds in the East is not only a splendid record of critical years of the war, but also a permanent chronicle of British enterprise and courage which will be treasured throughout the Empire.

Hutchinson's Important New Books

Memories
By VISCOUNT LONG OF WRAXALL, F.R.S.
(Walter Long)
In one large handsome volume, with Frontispiece, **24s.** *net.*

This volume is a faithful record of over forty years' continuous devotion to public service and of personal experiences of country life of even longer duration. The writer has the rare distinction of having been a Cabinet Minister during two great wars, and his concise accounts of these most important and critical epochs of British history are of uncommon interest. Lord Long's record of his close association with the Dominions and Colonies and of personal relations with many of their most distinguished representatives makes excellent reading. Throughout his career he has followed with enthusiasm almost every form of country sports and pursuits, and his comments upon the changes which have characterised country life during the last half-century will be widely appreciated.

Second Large Edition at once called for.
The Life of Fred Archer By E. M. HUMPHRIS
Edited by LORD ARTHUR GROSVENOR,
with a Preface by ARTHUR F. B. PORTMAN
In one large handsome volume, with coloured Frontispiece and 24 other illustrations, **18s.** *net.*

This well-written biography of one of the world's greatest jockeys will strongly appeal to sportsmen and the wide public who appreciate a fine story of a man of true British pluck and a nerve of iron. Prominence is naturally given to descriptions of Archer's races and to Lord Falmouth, his principal patron, and other leading sportsmen of the day, and letters from some of these are included.

"A well-written and admirably compiled record of one of the greatest periods of Turf history."—*The Times.*
"A valuable contribution to the history of the turf."—*Westminster Gazette.*

The Story of Boxing By TREVOR C. WIGNALL
Author of "Jimmy Lambert," "Thus Gods are Made."

In one large handsome volume, with 32 original cartoons by Charles Grave, **21s.** *net.*

The writer has long been boxing expert to a leading paper, while his vigorous novels on the sport are no less widely appreciated than his well-informed Press contributions. This record of his judgments of past time contests and fighters and of his own experiences will doubtless be regarded as the standard work on the subject, while his easy vivid style renders the book invariably entertaining. Its scope extends from the days of James Figg, the first champion of England, in 1719, up to the far-famed successes of Dempsey and Carpentier. The personalities as well as the chief fights of eminent prize-fighters are intimately described, and on both subjects Mr. Wignall has gleaned much information as yet unrecorded. Reproductions of old prints enhance the wide interest of this noteworthy volume.

Hutchinson's Important New Books

Embassies of Other Days
By WALBURGA, LADY PAGET

In two large handsome volumes, with 16 illustrations on art paper, **42s.** *net.*

Lady Paget, herself one of its most prominent figures, now gives her first-hand impressions of most of the leading personalities of Victorian society for a period of half a century and describes a wide experience of Court life in England and in the defunct Empires of Austria and Germany. She gives a most interesting account of meetings with Queen Victoria, the Prince Consort, the ex-Emperors of Austria and Germany, Princess Metternich, Lord Salisbury, Lord Spencer, Lord Palmerston, Sir Edward Burne-Jones, and of many others famous in the worlds of Society, politics and art. The book contains many new and fascinating anecdotes, and also possesses a historic value as a first-hand authority on many of the central figures of the Victorian era.

Insanity and the Criminal
By JOHN C. GOODWIN
Author of " Sidelights on Criminal Matters."

In one large handsome volume, cloth gilt, **18s.** *net.*

Readers of Mr. Goodwin's stimulating volume, " Sidelights on Criminal Matters," will recollect its concluding chapter on the relationship between insanity and crime. It is this all-important phase of criminology that he develops, with force and lucidity, in the present book. The forms of insanity most likely to cause crime, the respective influences of heredity, environment, bodily health, drink or drugs, the mentality of revolutionaries and other " social misfits " are, in due order, discussed with a regard to detail characteristic of the writer. Of particular interest are his fearless comments on our prison system and his conjectures as to the practical employment of psycho-analysis in the realm of crime. " Good " stories abound in a book which, compiled with a wide and intimate knowledge of the subject treated, is throughout extremely interesting and of real value.

Wild Fowl of the World
By FRANK FINN, B.A., F.Z.S.
Author of "Birds of the Countryside," " Familiar London Birds," etc.

In crown 8vo, cloth, with many illustrations, **4s. 6d.** *net.*

A complete account of the wild fowl of all countries, their appearance, habits, and natural haunts. From his own unrivalled experience the author supplies, in practical form, much useful information both for the ornithologist and the sportsman, while the general reader will readily appreciate its educative value. The text is copiously illustrated by beautiful photographs, taken direct from life.

Hutchinson's Important New Books

An Englishwoman in Angora
By GRACE ELLISON

Author of " An Englishwoman in a Turkish Harem," etc.

In one large handsome volume, with 35 illustrations reproduced from the Author's own sketches and exclusive photographs, **18s.** *net.*

While British civilians were evacuating Smyrna and war between the Allies and Turkey seemed inevitable, Miss Ellison braved the lines of bayonets surrounding Angora and proceeded to examine the Nationalist Movement at its capital. Befriended by the Turks, she was able to frequent the National Assembly, to see and talk with many of the deputies, to visit and have many frank interviews with Kemal Pasha. She describes the life of Angora from within the Assembly, the Greeks, the story of the hard work and the devotion of the whole population to the National Cause Miss Ellison afterwards attended the Lausanne Conference. Her memoirs comprise a fascinating record, both of interest and of value, and related with much vivid detail. Many unique photographs are reproduced.

The Life of Anne Boleyn
By PHILIP W. SERGEANT, B.A.

Author of " The Empress Josephine," " Cleopatra," etc.

In one large handsome volume, with 8 illustrations, **18s.** *net.*

In our admiration of the amazing personality of Queen Elizabeth, few have probably paused to estimate how many of her great qualities may have been inherited from her unfortunate mother. Yet, as an impartial study of this well-written biography will serve to convince us, the beautiful daughter of Sir Thomas Boleyn, willing to sell both his daughters for the King's favour; a Maid of Honour to the Tudor Queen of Louis XII. at his vicious court; and, later, twice a betrothed but in neither case a bride, Anne is surely a pathetic figure, rather than an object of censure. In her time of trouble all her professed friends betrayed her—including her father, though her courage and constancy remained unshaken to the end. Of this attractive personality Mr. Sergeant writes with a clear insight and a profound sympathy, though without minimising the faults of one who " lived gaily." His book is thus a noteworthy addition to our knowledge of the Tudor period.

Pharaoh's Dream Book
Compiled by LADY THRELFALL

In crown 8vo, cloth, **3s. 6d.** *net.*

The origin of this fascinating volume is in itself romantic. Some years ago when in Australia the writer secured two old and very rare books on the interpretations of dreams. Having tested many of these interpretations, both in her own case and in those of many friends, and found them remarkably exact, Lady Threlfall has carefully compiled the contents of each volume, rendering the wording into modern phraseology and adding further explanations founded on actual experiences. All who have been puzzled over the meaning of a dream and its warning will find this authentic and complete treatise of distinct interest.

Hutchinson's Important New Books

Recollections of Imperial Russia
By MERIEL BUCHANAN
Author of " Petrograd," etc.
In demy 8vo, with illustrations, **12s. 6d.** *net.*

The daughter of the last British Ambassador to the Russian Imperial Court, Miss Buchanan had unrivalled opportunities of meeting and conversing with distinguished people at Petrograd and elsewhere. Her memoirs are thus of remarkable interest. She writes with sympathy and understanding, graphically recording the sinister stages which brought about the downfall of the Romanovs. Moreover, she has read and studied widely the history of the country in which she lived. Stories of Moscow, Kiev, and other capitals provide fitting themes for her descriptive powers. Few will dispute her contention that old traditions—the cruelty of foreign invaders, the injustice of Tartar rule, religious oppression—have implanted in the minds of Russian peasantry that fatal resignation to successive tyrannies which has largely brought about their bitter sufferings to-day.

The Sands of Time   By WALTER SICHEL, M.A.
Author of " Disraeli," " Emma, Lady Hamilton," etc.
In one large handsome volume, with illustrations, **18s.** *net.*

Statesmen, great ladies, men and women distinguished in every branch of the arts, all of whom Mr. Sichel has known personally, are represented in this volume. Most numerous are those eminent in literature—George Eliot, Matthew Arnold, Ruskin, Trollope, De Morgan, Mrs. Humphry Ward, all figuring in these pages. Among poets, his friends included Robert Browning and Swinburne ; he knew Henry Irving, Ellen Terry, John Toole, Arthur Cecil and other " stars " of the drama ; of artists, Millais, Leighton and Sir William Richmond ; such distinguished ecclesiastics as Cardinal Manning and Bishop Gore ; two Lord Chief Justices, Lords Cockburn and Russell ; and of scholars, Professor Jowett. Rich in memories of such friendships, Mr. Sichel writes in his easy and distinguished style, so that his account of the eminent people is as charming as it is interesting.

The Art of Badminton
By SIR GEORGE THOMAS, Bt.
In crown 8vo, cloth, with 16 illustrations from photographs, **4s. 6d.** *net.*

The writer, the present holder for the fourth year in succession of the Singles Championship as well as of other distinctions, has compiled his experiences of first-class Badminton during more than twenty years. Elementary principles of the game, details of stroke executions and other practical instructions are carefully described, while later chapters on singles, the back and front formation will prove of special interest to tournament players. Illustrations of the author and other champions while at play enhance the value and interest of a volume practically indispensable for all who wish to succeed in this increasingly popular sport.

Hutchinson's Important New Books

The Life and Memoirs of Count Molé (1781-1855)
Edited by the MARQUIS DE NOAILLES.
Volume I. (1804-1815)

A large handsome volume with numerous illustrations, **18s.** *net.*

From his earliest years Mathieu Louis, Count Molé, was in the habit of recording in his diary his impressions of the events which took place before his eyes and in which he was intimately concerned. He also left two manuscripts dealing with the years 1813-14. Such is the material from which the skilled and learned editor, the Marquis de Noailles, has composed this extremely fascinating book. The present volume is of absorbing interest. In 1807 Napoleon made young Molé a member of the Council of State. Of his almost daily conversations with the Emperor on the most diverse subjects—some of them of great interest to Englishmen—Molé gives a literal record, with the added piquancy of his own witty comments upon prominent persons and the Emperor's opinion of them. In short, these memoirs will prove a rich mine of information for the general reader as well as a most important addition to Napoleonic literature.

Volume II. (1816-1817) of these brilliantly written Memoirs is now in preparation.

A Modern Mystery Merchant : His Trials, Tricks and Travels
By CARL HERTZ

A large handsome volume, with 24 illustrations, **18s.** *net.*

This lively and entertaining life story opens with the writer's account of his early struggles and hardships, and of the skill and perseverance by which he ultimately attained his present eminence. Strange and varied, indeed, are his experiences in many countries. Mr. Hertz's tricks and illusions have amused King Edward, the ex-Kaiser, the late Tsar, and many distinguished personages—including the assembled House of Commons; his frank exposures of their respective methods have confounded pseudo-spiritualists, cardsharpers, and swindlers. On one of his travels he was nearly kidnapped by bushrangers, on another scarcely escaped marriage with a princess! Readers, young and old, will welcome the long list of attractions presented in this amusing volume.

Character as Revealed by Handwriting
By PRINCESS ANATOLE MARIE BARIATINSKY and IVAN FORBES

In crown 8vo, cloth, **3s. 6d.** *net.*

The author gives specimens of the handwriting of the nobility, eminent statesmen, soldiers living and deceased, and men and women distinguished in every branch of art and literature, both English and foreign. She describes the system from which she deduces their respective characters and distinctive qualities.

Hutchinson's Important New Books

Nell Gwyn — By LEWIS MELVILLE
Author of "The Thackeray Country," "First Gentleman of Europe," etc.

In one large handsome volume, cloth gilt, 21s. net.

With 12 coloured and 16 black-and-white illustrations by KITTY SHANNON (Mrs. Keigwin).

In an age richly distinguished for its wit, beauty, and talent, "pretty, witty Nell" was pre-eminently endowed with all these qualities; moreover, she added to them an unfailing kindliness, generosity, and constancy towards old friends. Succeeding generations have taken her to their hearts as scarcely less than a national heroine, while romance has claimed her for its own. In his latest biography Mr. Lewis Melville has carefully compiled all the information available. He traces Nell Gwyn's career from orange girl to King's Favourite, tells of her youthful troubles, her lovers, her stage successes, her struggles with rival favourites, vast popularity, and later years in her Pall Mall mansion. A living record of an intensely living personality, this volume will be found of remarkable interest and charm.

Dogs and I — By MAJOR HARDING COX
Author of "Chasing and Racing," "A Sportsman at Large," etc.

In demy 8vo, cloth gilt, with 16 illustrations, 16s. net.

No books of sporting reminiscences have so rapidly caught the fancy both of the Press and public as Major Harding Cox's lively yet authoritative volumes. In his latest venture he deals with his personal experiences of the canine race in all its breed and characteristics, bringing into action his long and intimate knowledge of the subject. The author is recognised throughout the world as one of the greatest of canine experts. He has been invited to judge various breeds of hounds and dogs at every important show in many parts of the world. "Dogs and I" is not a merely technical book; it is a light treatise, chattily and intimately written, with copious illustrations and anecdotes.

A Tale of Indian Heroes: Being the Stories of the Mahabharata and Ramayana — By FLORA ANNIE STEEL
Author of "The Potter's Thumb," "On the Face of the Waters," etc.

In demy 8vo, cloth gilt, 10s. 6d. net.

In her interesting and illuminating preface the writer introduces these two famous Indian epics as yet unfamiliar to English readers. She has skilfully simplified and condensed a powerful study of the profoundest problem of human existence. Deeds of heroism are told with a charm and simplicity that will appeal, especially to youthful readers. Beauty in expression, a high moral tone and a vein of pathos and irony will claim for "A Tale of Indian Heroes" a high place in literature.

Hutchinson's Important New Books

The Book of Wonders: First Series
By RUDOLF J. and AMELIE WILLARD BODMER

In one large handsome volume, copiously illustrated, **16s.** *net.*

In this volume the writers give the plain and simple answers which all should be able to, but so often cannot, give. Such practical information, concise in form and of almost endless variety, is certainly unobtainable from any other single volume. Hundreds of illustrations, many of quite unusual character, stimulate the vast interest of the work and add to its educative value. A Second Series will follow shortly.

Salmon and Trout Angling : Its Theory, and Practice on Southern Streams, by Torrent River and Mountain Loch
By JOSEPH ADAMS (" Corrigeen ")

Author of " Ten Thousand Miles through Canada," " The Gentle Art of Angling," etc.

With a Foreword by THE MARQUESS OF HARTINGTON

In demy 8vo, with 18 illustrations, **16s.** *net.*

A lifelong enthusiast of angling and a contributor of many years standing to the chief London sporting papers, Mr. Adams has compiled his experiences on all kinds of fisheries under varying climates throughout the British Isles, in Canada and British Columbia. He gives full and concise accounts of his methods in spate and low waters ; describes vividly his own luck, and includes some simple instructions in the art of rod-making and fly-tying. The illustrations are numerous and beautiful.

" An attractive mixture of descriptive reminiscence and practical advice."—*Times.*

" The author's graphic experiences must delight every angler, while the chapter on rod and tackle will be of great assistance to those young in the art of fly-fishing."—*Daily Mail.*

The Art Book of the Year.

The Work of P. A. De László
Edited with Notes by OAKLEY WILLIAMS
With an Introduction by COMTE ROBERT DE MONTESQUIOU.

In one large folio volume containing 64 photogravure plates, representing some of the choicest examples of the artist's work.

A limited edition of 300 only signed and numbered copies will be issued at 10 guineas net. An Edition de Luxe on large paper, 75 copies only (numbered and signed by the artist), will be issued at 18 guineas net, with five extra plates produced in colour-photogravure.

Hutchinson's Important New Books

A Second Volume of this Important and Fascinating Record
The Farington Diary Volume II. (1802-1805).
By JOSEPH FARINGTON, R.A.
Edited by JAMES GREIG

A large handsome volume, cloth gilt, with photogravure Frontispiece and 12 other illustrations, **21s.** *net.*

The volume opens with a striking account of a visit which Farington paid to France during the Peace of Amiens, a description of a review of his troops by Napoleon, interesting glimpses of France, and of the diarist's gratitude on his own safe return home. The imminence of war is vividly depicted, the opinions of Pitt, Fox, Windham, Admiral Gardner and other leading men on the subject being impartially revealed. Once more the affairs of the Royal Academy are prominent in the Diary. We are told of Benjamin West's election as its President, of Beechey, and the King's candid opinion of both these artists ; of Opie's plan for the National Gallery ; of Sir Thomas Lawrence, both as an actor and as the lover of Mrs. Siddons, and of George Morland's death in a sponging-house. There are interesting entries about Coleridge and Wordsworth, and we are introduced to the latter poet, Fanny Burney, and Boydell, the publisher. George III., full of everybody else's affairs, bustles among the statesmen, and the Prince of Wales offers himself for military service. There are intimate personal reminiscences of Sheridan's " Brandy " appearance, and of Garrick's vanity ; allusions to Dr. Johnson's love of tea, and to the friendship of Cowper and Mrs. Unwin. Both as a singularly captivating record and a valuable addition to the history of the period, this volume will be widely welcomed, and its successors eagerly awaited.

3rd Edition now ready.
The Farington Diary Volume I (1793-1802)
A large handsome volume, with photogravure Frontispiece, and 16 other illustrations on art paper, **21s.** *net.*
The 3rd Volume (1805-1806) is now in preparation.

The Sidelights of London : Further Experiences and Reflections of a Metropolitan Police Magistrate
By J. A. R. CAIRNS
Author of " The Loom of the Law."
In demy 8vo, cloth gilt, **16s.** *net.*

In this volume Mr. Cairns continues his experiences of those phases of life which he has such unrivalled opportunities to study. On the depths of humanity's greatness his ideals and methods are worthy of study, and he says much that is of interest to the general reader. In a happy vein of philosophy he contrasts the East and West both by day and by night, discusses " Women and Crime," " Life's Misfits," and " The Glory of the Lost." As before, his experiences and conclusions will be found as instructive as they are throughout entertaining.

Hutchinson's Important New Books

The Second Volume of these authoritative and brilliantly written Reminiscences

An Ambassador's Memoirs Volume II (June 3rd, 1915—August 18th, 1916)

By MAURICE PALÉOLOGUE (Last French Ambassador to the Russian Court).

A large handsome volume, cloth gilt, with many beautiful exclusive drawings and other illustrations, **18s.** *net.*

In this second volume of his remarkable and enthralling memoirs the last French Ambassador to the Russian Court carries his story down to the entry of Rumania into the war in August, 1916. Once more we have astonishing revelations, of the very highest interest, of the secret history of the time as Russia, slowly but surely, picked her tortuous and sinister way to the " Slough of Despond." The stages of the journey are described by the author with the most terrible fidelity, and we realise both his official and personal feelings as he comes to recognise, as he did on August 4, 1916 (after the ardent pro-ally Foreign Minister—Sazonov—had been dismissed), that " Russia's defection is possible : it is an eventuality which must henceforth enter into the political and strategic calculations of the French Government. Of course the Emperor will remain faithful to the end. But he is not immortal. *How many Russians, even now and among those around him, are secretly longing for his disappearance ?*" As before, there are delightful " asides " on aspects of Russian nature, art, and life, which must surely make this book rank with the work of Tolstoy and Turgeniev as the most informative and striking revelation of Russian psychology.

Reprints are now ready of Vol. I (July 3rd, 1914—June 2nd, 1915) Cloth gilt, with many beautiful exclusive drawings and other illustrations, **18s.** *net.*

" These memoirs are recognised to-day by historians as among the most important documents treating of the period, and they have no less interest for the general reader."—*Times.*

" A brilliant ' war book ' . . . as fascinating as any romance."—*Daily Mirror.*

" Intimate details of the late Tsar and Tsaritsa . . . and profound views on Russian life and characteristics are given."—*Daily News.*

Vol. III. (Aug. 19th, 1916—May 17th, 1917) is now in preparation.

Inland Birds : Northern Observations by a Sportsman By H. MORTIMER BATTEN, F.Z.S.
Author of " Romances of the Wild," etc.

With an Introduction by The RT. HON. SIR HERBERT MAXWELL, Bart., F.R.S.

In demy 8vo, with 32 illustrations on art paper, **12s. 6d.** *net.*

A delightful work of first-hand observation, containing much fascinating information that is not to be gleaned from the average book on birds. The method of treatment is concise and most attractive, and effectively dissipates any preconceived idea that ornithology is a dull subject.

Hutchinson's Important New Books

Myself and Others — By JESSIE MILLWARD
Edited by J. B. BOOTH.

In demy 8vo, cloth gilt, with 18 illustrations, **16s.** *net.*

Miss Millward's records of theatrical gossip and amusing stories of stage life during the last thirty years will provide ample entertainment for readers young and old alike. She possesses keen powers of observation, a lively sense of humour and an agreeable style. As a girl she played with Henry Irving, was leading lady to William Terriss, while her later successes in " Lord and Lady Algy," " Mrs. Dane's Defence," " The Hypocrites," and other plays will be readily recalled. The Bancrofts, George R. Sims, Beerbohm Tree, Marie Lloyd, Mrs. Kendal, George Grossmith—Miss Millward knew them all and relates many amusing stories about them. A section of the reminiscences deals with her experiences in America.

Adventures Among Bees — By HERBERT MACE
Author of " A Book about the Bee," etc.

In crown 8vo, cloth, with 24 illustrations on art paper, **4s. 6d.** *net.*

In this concise yet comprehensive volume the author recounts the results of a lifetime's observations and practical experiences of beekeeping. Of particular interest are his useful hints on the handling of bees under difficult conditions and his discussions on the little creatures' relationship to other animals, weather and plants. Lively times in bee life are graphically described, so that the book will prove as entertaining as it is instructive.

The Irish Free State : Its Evolution and Possibilities — By ALBERT C. WHITE
Author of " Ireland : A Study in Facts," etc.

In cloth, **3s. 6d.** *net.*

From the standpoint of a vigorous and independent mind Mr. White traces the history of the relations between Great Britain and Ireland from the Act of Union down to the Great War. The Home Rule struggle, the four Home Rule Bills, of 1886, 1893, 1914 and 1920, and the terms of the Treaty concluded with Sinn Fein are fully described

Bergholt's Modern Auction—Its Bidding and Principles — By ERNEST BERGHOLT
Author of " Royal Auction Bridge," etc.

In cloth, with numerous illustrations, **7s. 6d.** *net.*

The author is perhaps the greatest authority on Bridge to-day, and the value of his articles in the Press is widely appreciated. In concise and attractive form he has now compiled his experiences of the game. This volume will prove highly instructive to practical players, while beginners will rapidly acquire proficiency from its clear and comprehensive directions.

Hutchinson's New and Forthcoming Books

The Outlands of Heaven
By the REV. G. VALE OWEN,
formerly Vicar of Orford, Lancashire

Author of " Life Beyond the Veil," " Facts and the Future Life," etc.

In crown 8vo, cloth, **4s. 6d.** *net.*

This volume includes " The Children of Heaven," the two works forming one complete narrative. It is a continuation of the script published under the general title " Life Beyond the Veil," and was received by Mr. Vale Owen from a band of spirit communicators acting under the leadership of one who gives his name as " Arnel," an Englishman who lived in Florence during the early days of the Renaissance. The whole forms a stimulating narrative of intense interest, full of helpful suggestions for all who seek to know something of the conditions of life and work awaiting them after death.

Familiar London Birds
By FRANK FINN, B.A., F.Z.S.

Author of " Birds of the Countryside," " Bird Behaviour," etc.

In crown 8vo, cloth, with 34 *illustrations,* **4s. 6d.** *net.*

London birds, when, where, and how they may be found, is the subject of this fascinating volume. Their identification will become an easy matter to all who read the full descriptions and study its many beautiful photographs.

Buying a Car? 1923
Compiled by LEONARD HENSLOWE

Author of " Quite Well, Thanks," " Motoring for the Million," etc.

Crown 8vo, fully illustrated, **1s. 6d.** *net.*

A new annual, brought out in the interests of the vast army of motorists, new and old, by one of the most experienced writers in the motoring world.

45th Year of Issue

The Year's Art, 1924 Compiled by A. C. R. CARTER

Crown 8vo, cloth, **8s. 6d.** *net. Over* **600** pages, with illustrations.

A concise epitome of all matters relating to the Arts of Painting, Sculpture, Engraving and Architecture, and to Schools of Design, containing events which have occurred during the year 1923, together with information respecting those of 1924.

Ready early in 1924

The Life and Letters of George Wyndham
By COLONEL GUY PERCY WYNDHAM, C.B., and PROFESSOR JOHN W. MACKAIL, LL.D.

Hutchinson's Important New Books

Hutchinson's
Animals of All Countries
The Living Animals of the World in Word and Picture

Published in about 48 fortnightly parts, with over 2,000 illustrations and about 50 fine Coloured Plates printed throughout on the best British art paper
1s. 3d. *each part.*

This great work, which is being produced at a cost of £75,000, covers every branch of natural history. Edited throughout by eminent specialists, it gives a clear, concise, anecdotal description of beasts, birds, fishes, reptiles and insects.

The illustrations, selected from many thousands for their artistic and educational value, are a special feature of the book. Many pictures show the wonderful achievement of the camera, animals in their wild state taken by the telephoto lens, fish and other marine creatures taken through the water, birds in flight, etc. Never before has such a complete set of illustrations been seen together.

Complete in 4 handsome volumes. Volume I. now ready, cloth gilt. **21s.** *net.*

Hutchinson's
Story of the British Nation
The first connected pictorial and authoritative history of the British peoples, from the earliest times to the present day.
Written by the leading historians and edited by

WALTER HUTCHINSON, M.A., F.R.G.S., F.R.A.I.
(Barrister-at-Law, Editor of Hutchinson's "History of the Nations," etc.)

In 48 fortnightly parts, price **1s. 3d.** *each. Complete in 4 volumes.*

The first three volumes, which have achieved a record success, are now supplied in handsome cloth gilt, each **21s.** *net, and in various leather bindings. Beautiful coloured plates are a special feature of this great work.*

Birds of Our Country
By FRANK FINN, B.A., F.Z.S., and E. KAY ROBINSON

Complete in two large handsome volumes.
Both volumes, handsomely bound in cloth gilt, and containing nearly 1,000 unique photographs of the living bird, and 47 fine coloured plates, are now ready, each **21s.** net.

Hutchinson's
Popular Botany
By A. E. KNIGHT and EDWARD STEP, F.L.S.

Complete in two large handsome volumes.
Both volumes, with about 1,000 beautiful illustrations and 18 coloured plates are now ready, each **12s. 6d.** net.

Hutchinson's Important New Books

A Popular Astronomy

Hutchinson's
Splendour of the Heavens
Edited by T. E. R. PHILLIPS, M.A., F.R.A.S. (Secretary of the Royal Astronomical Society), assisted by Leading Astronomers.

Published in fortnightly parts, each containing a coloured plate and about 60 beautiful illustrations on art paper, at the popular price of **1s. 3d.** *each part.*

This standard work, whose vast interest and value have been quickly appreciated by young and old alike, contains the fullest and most complete account yet published of the various classes of heavenly bodies, expressed in popular language. The mass of material dealing with the latest discoveries now before the Editor and Publishers has enabled them to bring to our knowledge, in a form simple and easily understood, the fresh wonders of the Universe. The work describes the solar system, the sun, earth, moon, the planets, the comets, meteors, stars, nebulæ, and numerous other bodies. It also includes the story of time, motion, light, gravitation, the tides, evolution of worlds, origin of the moon and stars. The illustrations are very numerous and of great educative value.

To be completed in about 24 fortnightly parts. Parts 1 to 7 are now ready.

Hutchinson's
Library of Standard Lives
Each volume attractively bound with three-colour pictorial wrapper, beautifully printed on the best quality paper. The prices are: Cloth, **2s.** *net; Full Leather,* **3s.** *net.*

Each biography contains approximately 384 pages of clear type and a frontispiece portrait and title page on art paper, an Appendix, Chronology, Notes, and a full Index, and is capably and judiciously edited.

Already Issued

Napoleon (544 pages)   By F. de BOURRIENNE
Nelson   By ROBERT SOUTHEY
Queen Elizabeth   By AGNES STRICKLAND
Marie Antoinette   By MADAME CAMPAN
Cleopatra   By PHILIP W. SERGEANT
Oliver Cromwell   By THOMAS CARLYLE
The Empress Josephine By PHILIP W. SERGEANT

The following volumes will be published at fortnightly intervals:

Wellington	Madame du Barry	Lady Hamilton
John Wesley	Queen Victoria	Samuel Johnson
Madame de Staël	Nell Gwyn	George Washington
	Mary Queen of Scots	

Hutchinson's New Novels. 7/6 Net

Heirs Apparent   By SIR PHILIP GIBBS
Author of "The Street of Adventure," "The Middle of the Road" (*30th thousand*).

In reviewing the outstanding success attained by Sir Philip Gibbs' last published novel, *The Times* commended his "remarkable talent for presenting a point of view in dramatic form." In his present work, concerned entirely with English life during the present year, the author interprets the mind of the young people of to-day—the leaders of to-morrow. Infused with the true spirit of youth, distinguished by brilliant and convincing characterisation, this fine story is of immediate and absorbing interest.

The Sequel to "The Blue Lagoon"
The Garden of God   By H. de VERE STACPOOLE
Author of "The Blue Lagoon," "Men, Women and Beasts," "Vanderdecken," etc.

Mr. Stacpoole again gives proof of his ingenuity and resource, and in his latest novel has recaptured the ghostly yet extraordinarily vivid and brilliant atmosphere that made "The Blue Lagoon" a classic among romances of the sea. On the glowing beach of Karolin. the lofty island whose longest reflexion slashes the sky, we see Katafa, the maid whom none may touch and who may touch no one. The author has developed the love story of this picturesque and fascinating character with skill and fervour, and his romance should prove one of the most noteworthy of the season's novels.

The Water Diviner   By DOLF WYLLARDE
Author of "Mafoota," "The Lavender Lad," "Our Earth Here," etc.

The character which gives this vivid and emotional story its title is no enterprising explorer, but a captivating English girl. Landia, the adopted niece of the owner of Cassidy, a Caribbean estate, inherits the money of her patroness. But it is for herself that Mallory, to whom Cassidy has been bequeathed, loves her. Miss Wyllarde writes fascinatingly—because intimately—of the intrigues and emotions that stir the hearts of men and women dwelling in distant lands. The young lovers' romantic adventures are thus dramatic and effective, while in colour and atmosphere the author's descriptive passages maintain a high literary excellence.

Vindication   By STEPHEN McKENNA
Author of "The Secret Victory," "Soliloquy," "The Commandment of Moses," etc.

Mr. McKenna has an uncanny knowledge of feminine psychology. This novel shows him as much an adept as ever in this strange labyrinth; and, following him, we hold the clue as to why a woman yields her dearest treasure to a man she fears and hates, and denies it to him for whom her whole being longs. It is not an entirely pleasant world, that in which Mr. McKenna bids us accompany him willy-nilly, but it is a curiously absorbing one, and, moreover, the shifting, changing world of to-day. Here, ex-chorus girls, with the garish glow of the footlights hardly dimmed, rule stately houses, and impoverished blue blood clings desperately to lost ideals of honour and womanhood.

Hutchinson's New Novels. 7/6 Net

Tetherstones   By ETHEL M. DELL

Author of "The Bars of Iron" (312*th thousand*), "The Hundredth Chance," (270*th thousand*), etc.

If Miss Dell is unsurpassed as a mistress of the art of story-telling the reason is surely because she has always a good story to tell and invariably tells it with a steadily maintained vigour of action that holds the reader's interest from start to finish. For the main scenes of her latest novel she has chosen the old farm of Tetherstones, hard by the Druidic circle in Devon, to the stones of which (according to tradition) victims were fastened prior to sacrifice. Into the tragic environment which not unnaturally clings to the farm itself comes the heroine, under strange circumstances. Mysterious happenings follow her arrival, which culminate, after many thrilling adventures, in the finding of a great treasure. With its practised craftsmanship, ingenious plot and admirable character-drawing, "Tetherstones" has been pronounced by prominent critics as Miss Dell's most finished work.

Visible and Invisible   By E. F. BENSON

Author of "Dodo Wonders," "Miss Mapp," "Colin," etc.

In this volume Mr. Benson, departing from his usual choice of subject, deals with the occult and supernatural, and these stories of engrossing interest are proofs of his versatility and considerable powers of imagination. Between our own and the other world lies a borderland of shadows, which eyes that can pierce the material plane may sometimes see and whose voices may be heard by listening ears. This unknown realm and its happenings are somewhat disquieting. The writer has subtly caught this vague uneasiness and made it the pervading influence upon his characters in these original and powerful stories.

The First Good Joy   By C. A. NICHOLSON

Author of "Martin, Son of John," "Their Chosen People," etc.

Racial antagonism is not the central theme of C. A. Nicholson's present novel. But the story is informed with such sympathetic insight into the life and character of the Jewish people and with the sincerity of one who knows profoundly their merits and shortcomings as to be in its way, a masterpiece. Justin Daris, seeing life in Brussels, meets his fate in Zosia, an "unfortunate" whom, out of pity, he marries. They part; hard work, success, and love for another woman absorb his life, though he yearns for Zosia and children of his own. For her Fate has a hard lot in store —yet husband and wife are destined to be reunited. The characters, some of whom appeared in "Their Chosen People," are strikingly well drawn. Justin, clever and sensitive; the beautiful Zosia, the victim of men's pleasure, with her constant appeal for her husband's affection; the widower who befriends her; Justin's shrewd father, and his mother so fearful for his spiritual welfare, become, one and all, extraordinarily living personages, in whose acts and opinions we are brought to feel personal interest

Hutchinson's New Novels. 7/6 Net

A Cure of Souls — By MAY SINCLAIR

Author of "Anne Severn and the Fieldings" (5th edition), "Uncanny Stories," etc.

In her latest novel this talented author has returned to her old style of writing. Her story is concerned with the life of a country rector and the trials and difficulties which he encounters in pursuit of a peace and comfort incompatible with the responsibilities of a cure of souls. Miss Sinclair is a past mistress in the technique of her art and in a profound understanding of human emotions that makes her characters intensely alive. Her plot is therefore intimate and refreshing, its interest further sustained by a subtle irony, while characters and incidents are presented with an unfailing skill.

The Last Time — By ROBERT HICHENS

Author of "The Garden of Allah," "The Spirit of the Time," etc.

These four stories are told with all the art of a practised story-teller. "The Last Time" deals with the tragedy of a woman, who makes a confession of the wreck of her life to a man in order that another woman's life may be made happy. "The Letter" is a love story in Mr. Hichens' most successful vein, with the picturesque countryside as its background. In "The Villa by the Sea" the author portrays in a brilliant psychological study some "lingering influences" and their effects on sensitive persons, while "The Façade" is a delightfully humorous tale of a beautiful "highbrow" actress. In each story the reader will find enough vivid and arresting incidents and realistic character studies as almost to compose a complete novel.

Reputation — By ELINOR MORDAUNT

Author of "The Park Wall," "Laura Creichton," "Short Shipments," etc.

In this dramatic and engrossing novel Mrs. Mordaunt convincingly refutes the widely cherished notion of Victorian women's demureness. In 1882 Claudia Waring (then aged 18) elects to elope from the country rectory that has always been her home. Her half-hearted explanations on her return serve to invest her escapade with the savour of romance. Twenty years later her brilliant novels have earned her an established reputation in London, nor does she again visit the dull countryside, save once—to save a young niece from an utter folly at the cost of confessing the real truth of her own supposed romance. Throughout the book Claudia's activities are many and of continuous interest. Yet in an epilogue of 1922 we find a maiden of the third generation wondering at the drab existences endured by the unprotesting Victorians! The style and narration of Mrs. Mordaunt's story are easy and graceful, the personality of Claudia, with those of the lesser characters, being set in a background minutely appropriate to the varying periods.

Hutchinson's New Novels. 7/6 Net

John o' Chimes
By MARGARET BAILLIE-SAUNDERS
Author of "Becky & Co.," "Makeshifts," "Madge Hinton's Husbands," etc.

Dame Imogen Giles, the youthful Lady of the Manor House in the old Kentish village, is a delightful character, of a simplicity and old-world charm yet up-to-date in interests and outlook. The reader follows with ready sympathy the course of her love for John La Ferronays. Meantime, the legend of muffled ringing of church bells buried beneath the sea haunts her mother; indeed, a strange mystery threatens for a while the lovers' happiness. The romance of this legend forms an admirable setting for this picturesque and attractive story, whose interest never flags and in which scenes and characters alike are portrayed with truth, vivacity, and conviction.

The Red Redmaynes   By EDEN PHILLPOTTS
Author of "The Grey Room," "The Three Brothers," "Told at 'The Plume,'" etc.

In his new story Mr. Eden Phillpotts again displays the masterly handling of crime and mystery which rendered "The Grey Room" so notable a success. Three men, two of whom are brothers, are successively murdered, suspicion in each case falling on Robert Redmayne. Two of the greatest detectives, an Englishman and an American, set out to track down and arrest the criminal. Mystery, excitement, and intense human interest distinguish this thrilling Dartmoor narrative, the characters in which are skilfully and realistically depicted.

The Gazebo   By BARONESS VON HUTTEN
Author of "Pam," "The Lordship of Love," etc.

The particular gazebo which gives the name to this book is a windowed balcony overlooking the village street, in the country home of Peg Doria, a well-known novelist, who befriends Jenny Mayes, a clever, but half educated, middle-class London girl, and later her own rival in love. It is from the gazebo that Jenny overhears a conversation from which she gathers that her suitor and Mrs. Doria care for each other; and from the gazebo, too, Mrs. Doria looks down on her derelict husband, who vainly tries to create a scandal in the village.

Viola Hudson   By ISABEL C. CLARKE
Author of "Carina," "Average Cabins," etc.

In her latest and longest novel Miss Clarke is mainly concerned with the life-story of Viola Hudson from the time of her meeting at Venice her old playmate, Esme Craye. From their subsequent marriage come the struggle of Viola's life and her heroic self-sacrifice for the spiritual welfare of her child. The fortunes both of mother and daughter make an earnest and appealing narrative, enhanced by the fidelity of characterisation and high standard of descriptive powers that distinguish all this author's works.

Hutchinson's New Novels. 7/6 Net

Wild Heart of Youth By KATHLYN RHODES
Author of " Courage," " Desert Justice," etc.

For the setting of her latest novel the author, forsaking the East, has chosen the pine woods of Surrey and the Cornish coast. Its central theme is the development of Martin Ryott's character under the influence of two women. In the one, his wife, methodical, lethargic, and opposed to activity whether of mind or body, he finds merely a comforter in domesticity. Inspiration, if it is to be his, will come from Isobel Winn, eager for life's ambitions and enthusiasms. His friendship and, indeed, his affection are naturally attracted from the one to the other woman, and, skilfully developed by the writer's convincing touch, infuse the story with an interest dramatic yet intensely true to life.

French Beans By ANTHONY M. LUDOVICI
Author of " What Woman Wishes," " The Goddess that Grew Up," etc., etc.

The eternal clash of East with West is skilfully and convincingly portrayed in this story of a Frenchman of Arab extraction, who tries to accommodate himself to English society. Quite unconscious of the deep ancestral promptings that are directing his action, the hero's career throws him into the most emancipated set of advanced feminists, to one of whom he becomes engaged. The lady endures with great impatience his highhanded masculine attitude, and the manner in which, after many vicissitudes, he eventually gains the victory over the whole set provides the main incidents of a novel and sprightly story.

The Terriford Mystery
By MRS. BELLOC-LOWNDES
Author of " The Red Cross Barge," " What Timmy Did," etc.

Mrs. Belloc-Lowndes is an excellent tale-teller, and the mystery which inspires the incidents of her latest novel is both convincing and ably sustained. Moreover, into an original story she has happily infused a delightful love romance. An innocent man has been accused of murder. Despite suspicious circumstances, the girl whom he loves never loses her faith in him and is untiring in her efforts to prove him guiltless. The scenes are laid mainly in an English village, while characters and descriptive passages fully illustrate the writer's literary power and ingenuity.

The King's Red-Haired Girl By SELWYN JEPSON
Author of " The Qualified Adventurer," " That Fellow MacArthur," etc.

In his latest novel Mr. Jepson's fancy lightly turns to imaginative adventure, mainly set in the distant republic of Kavallia. Banished by its President, one Mareno has conceived the ambition of overthrowing that potentate and restoring in his place Petronyevitch, son of the last king, with his own daughter Elizabeth as his wife and queen. This twofold ambition is opposed both by Peter Ambleton and his brother. Their counterplots and escapades, related with all Mr. Jepson's richness of imagination and humorous touch, make up a spirited narrative, full of good descriptions, and which moves with vigour from start to finish.

Hutchinson's New Novels. 7/6 Net

The Mating of Marcus
By MABEL BARNES-GRUNDY
Author of "A Girl for Sale," "The Great Husband Hunt," etc.

"From this day my hand shall be against every woman." Thus proclaims the bitterly disillusioned hero at the opening of Mrs. Barnes-Grundy's latest novel. And forthwith he hides himself in a distant habitation of a remote Essex village. But alas for him—the "Eternal Feminine" abounds everywhere. How his seclusion was persistently disturbed and by what allurements his heart eventually stormed are the main incidents in an original story which runs with a pleasant swing and whose characters are drawn with uncommon liveliness and truth.

A New Novel by the "Thomas Hardy of Sussex"
Sunset Bride   By TICKNER EDWARDES
Author of "The Honey-Star," "Tansy," "The Seventh Wave," etc.

As in all this author's previous books, the scene of this powerful and romantic novel is laid in a remote village in the South Down country which he has made essentially his own. Into a captivating story is subtly woven a charming and original contribution to the solution of an ever-perplexing problem—whether, in respect of Holy Matrimony, the ancient adage, "Better late than never," holds good or otherwise. With its vivid characterisation, humour, pathos and intense dramatic interest—above all, in the lovable personality of its heroine—this novel will certainly rank as one of the most successful of Mr. Edwardes' creations.

Fields of Sleep   By E. CHARLES VIVIAN
Author of "Passion-Fruit," "City of Wonder," etc.

The search for Clement Delarey, which led the searchers to the "Fields of Sleep," has called forth, in the words of an established critic, "one of the greatest works of modern imagination." From the day when Victor Marshall and the "little old lady" made the compact which sent Marshall on his quest, up to the moment of his return, the story becomes a panorama of swiftly changing incident, novel in conception and convincing and dramatic in presentation. The weird, terrible trees of sleep, the mystery and wisdom that characterise their guardians, and the impish contrast afforded by Erasmus Whauple—a unique creation—make up a romance of uncommon breadth and power.

The Man Who Understood   By "RITA"
Author of "Peg the Rake," "Conjugal Rights," etc.

The man who understands the heart of a woman, the weakness of man, and the faith and trust of a little child, is indeed a great character, meriting complete and detailed delineation. "The Man Who Understood" has a singularly human and lovable personality, always believing in the best and forgiving the worst; adapting the healing powers of Nature to a man's skill and patience, and never ceasing to preach the axiom that to love much is to forgive much.

Hutchinson's New Novels. 7/6 Net

A Fight to Windward   By BOYD CABLE

Author of " Grapes of Wrath," " The Old Contemptibles," " The Rolling Road," etc.

    Mr. Boyd Cable's very numerous readers will find " A Fight to Windward " as subtle in its humour, breezy in writing, and as packed with exciting incidents as any of this author's previous successes. It relates the strange adventures that befell Chick Summers, employed to write up " copy " for his paper from the latest startling events of the day. Such a sensation is provided for him by the mysterious disappearance of one William Goodenough, together with all the available funds of the important firm which employed him. In the search for the culprit Mary Griffiths becomes concerned. With her Chick proceeds as far as Australia, following clues valuable or false in a manner that often baffles and always diverts the reader. After a series of highly ingenious and amusing escapades he gets his big story—and with it a prize of even more permanent value.

Uncanny Stories   By MAY SINCLAIR

Author of " The Three Brontës," " Anne Severn and the Fieldings " (5th Edition), " A Cure of Souls," etc.

With many illustrations by the CHEVALIER JEAN DE BOSSCHÈRE

    Miss Sinclair is perhaps the most competent of modern novelists, and the brilliant writing and analysis which rendered " Anne Severn and the Fieldings " one of the literary events of the past season are no less conspicuous in her present volume. Its seven stories are original and arresting studies of supernatural happenings in this and the " other " world and in the borderland between them. In the first, " When Their Fire is not Quenched," Hell is presented, with a consummate art, as the eternal monotonous repetition of a sin. " The Flaw in the Crystal " deals with the gruesome possibilities of psychic healing, while " The Finding of the Absolute " is a masterly metaphysical phantasy. The remaining stories are ghost stories with a strong psychological interest. One and all are fine examples of the writer's high imaginative qualities. Striking designs by the Chevalier Jean de Bosschère suitably illustrate the book throughout.

The Runaway   By M. E. FRANCIS

Author of " Many Waters," " Renewal," " Beck of Beckford," etc.

    Mrs. Francis is one of the rare novelists who by long experience has acquired a facility in writing that always maintains a high literary standard and yet whose versatility, freshness and power to charm never fail her. The present story is mainly concerned with the love affairs of young Keith MacDonald, who, provoked by her taunts of the benefits which her wealth has conferred upon him, deserts his wife and seeks peace and employment among simple village folk. There he meets his true soul's mate, and his struggles to keep his honour unsullied, the intrigues of an ill-wisher and the claim of his wife are the main emotions by which his soul is swayed. The author's portrayal of the life and characters of the Welsh villagers makes a highly effective background to an admirably told story.

Hutchinson's New Novels. 7/6 Net

The Shadow of Egypt   By NORMA LORIMER
Author of " A Mender of Images," " The False Dawn," etc.

Eastern both in subject and setting, Miss Lorimer's romantic story appropriately reflects the passions, intrigues and dangers of Egypt of to-day. During an anti-British rising both the heroine and her husband are captured, while the all-powerful Haddad fulfils his evil designs. He succeeds in keeping the hapless wife a prisoner in his harem, and there and elsewhere thrilling adventures befall her. Incidentally there is an exciting search for treasure in the Theban hills, which, though actually written previous to the late Lord Carnarvon's discoveries, realistically depicts the difficulties of such an enterprise.

Sally's Sweetheart   By G. B. BURGIN
Author of " Many Memories," " Manetta's Marriage," " The Man Behind," etc.

In a brief " Foreword " to his seventieth and latest novel, Mr. Burgin confesses that, in the natural sequence, he ought to have written this story some twenty years ago, but that it has now insisted on writing itself! For this solution the reader will be grateful, since in returning to his favourite haunts at " Four Corners "—that charming little riverine Ottawa village which he has made his own—the author tells a fresh and ever delightful idyll. A lovers' quarrel between Ikey Marston and Miss Sally Plunket, Ikey's departure with " Old Man " Evans to old haunts among the Reservation Indians, and Miss Plunket's amusing escapades after following her affronted lover are its central interests, vividly described with Mr. Burgin's customary charm and literary skill.

All to Seek   By DIANA PATRICK
Author of " Islands of Desire," " The Manuscript of Youth," etc.

With the competent craftsmanship which we expect from her, the writer gives us in this novel a clever, realistic study of a girl's experiences of life and love. Melody is the daughter of a music teacher in a small Yorkshire town. Her younger sister marries, and chafing at the restriction of her own small world Melody goes to study in London. Her sister's experiences and her own misadventures in love convince her that no woman should sacrifice her liberty for a man's love. Melody's disillusionment on this idea and consequent happiness are the concluding episodes of a story that is throughout essentially true to life and which gains considerably from the sharp individualisation of its characters.

Whispering Sage By HARRY SINCLAIR DRAGO and JOSEPH NOEL

With its main theme a fierce struggle for water rights between Basque sheepmen and cowboys, and its emotional setting of personal hate, combat, struggles and revenge, these authors have evolved a powerful story forcibly told. The love of Mercedes, who after the murder of her father is only saved from an evil fate by her lover, the brave Kildare, handled with sympathy and understanding, adds romance to a novel of almost breathless interest.

Hutchinson's New Novels. 7/6 Net

Young Felix   By FRANK SWINNERTON
Author of " The Happy Family," " September," " Coquette," etc.

    Mr. Swinnerton's latest novel, the longest and in some respects the most ambitious book which he has written, describes a young man's life from childhood until about his thirtieth year. The analysis of young Felix's character is searching and detailed, but never overstressed, since with his life-story are involved the doings and sayings of his own family and those of others. The lad's evolution from childhood to an ambitious artist of quite uncommon type is, throughout, of engrossing interest as a close and vigorous study of real life. Moreover, the novel's characters and often humorous incidents are marked by shrewd observation and uncommon descriptive powers.

The Adventures of Gerry
By DOROTHEA CONYERS
Author of " The Strayings of Sandy," " Rooted Out," etc.

    The adventures of Gerald Dallas, the hero of this cleverly written and well meditated novel, arose from his discovery, on his wedding day, of an irreparable bar to his married happiness. He leaves his wife and seeks an undisturbed seclusion in Ballyoram, in dread of a seemingly inevitable fate. What actually befalls him, strange and unexpected, is told with all the writer's accomplished ease in a delightful and effective story. Incidents and characters (mainly Irish) throughout are depicted with knowledge and discrimination, while the hunting scenes are particularly enjoyable.

A First Novel of Eastern Magic and Adventure
Woven in a Prayer Rug   By NEVILLE LANGTON

    This new author has devised a romance of quite original interest; he writes lucidly and with a convincing earnestness, and depicts both his characters and scenes alike with much skill and charm. Absorbed in the mysterious history of carpets, Dennis Hastings, who works in his uncle's carpet store, spends his last shilling on a tattered old Eastern prayer rug. When the war breaks out, he leaves England and the girl of his love and is sent to Gallipoli. Capture by the Turks, thrilling adventures in the East, and a romantic association with an Arab maiden befall him. Through all these scenes the influence of the prayer rug is prominent. Eventually its mystery solved, it brings wealth and happiness to its possessor.

Brogmersfield   By JOHN AYSCOUGH
Author of " Dromina," " Monksbridge," etc.

    Brogmersfield is the country estate of his ancestors, to which a young Artillery officer, wounded in the Great War, succeeds. But he is not long in realising that there is something uncanny about this lonely house; that the occupants of it, dependents of the former owners, are remarkably queer. Is he on the track of a crime ? Is some diabolical influence threatening him ? Are the sins of old generations being visited on the new ? The surprising solution of these grim mysteries proves of enthralling interest in a story conceived and developed with the author's wonted ingenuity.

Hutchinson's New Novels. 7/6 Net

A Reversion to Type By E. M. DELAFIELD
Author of " The Heel of Achilles," " The Optimist," etc.

Cecil Aviolet is the only child of a marriage between Rose Smith, daughter of a bankrupt London tradesman, and Jim Aviolet, the scapegrace younger son of an old and noble English family. A hereditary taint appears in the boy when he is a very young child, and shows himself to be a congenital liar. The problem of his education leads to friction between Rose and the Aviolet family ; an unsatisfactory solution produces tragedy when Cecil grows up. Throughout Rose's courage never fails, although she is made to believe that the taint in Cecil is owing to his father's *mésalliance* with herself. This story of conflicting personalities and a mother's high devotion is of remarkable cleverness. As a psychological study it will rank as one of Miss Delafield's finest conceptions.

The Gold of the Sunset
By FREDERICK SLEATH
Author of " A Breaker of Ships," " The Red Vulture," etc.

Mr. Sleath is a writer of varying moods, whose admirable skill is equally successful in suggesting the atmosphere of horror proper to such tales as " A Breaker of Ships," or in symbolising the eternal urge of the human soul, as in this delightful tale of present-day Scottish life and character. It is ex-Captain Andrew Watson who tells it. From him we learn of the love of two men for one girl ; of the mysterious end of one of these suitors, and of the coming of the Captain's own " fair lady." Both incidents and characters will keep the reader's interest alert throughout.

Cattle By ONOTO WATANNA
Author of " A Japanese Nightingale," " Sunny-San," etc.

A powerful Canadian story set in the vast cattle ranches of Alberta, where the drama of sex has full play among rough men and primitive women. " Bull " Langdon, owner of much wealth and master of men and of the famous " Bar Q " cattle, wearies of his invalid wife. He casts lustful eyes on Nettie, whose beauty and goodness are unsullied by the evil around her. How his evil designs are thwarted and Nettie's happiness, after many harrowing dangers, at length attained are the main incidents of this thrilling, swiftly-moving story. The author describes stirring deeds with sustained, suspended interest and his descriptive passages throughout are vivid and full of colour.

If Ye Break Faith By ESSEX SMITH
Author of " Shepherdless Sheep," " The Revolving Fates," etc.

An absorbing, earnest story of high ideals upheld amid the degrading ugliness that mars so many phases of life to-day—a strong and heartfelt protest against its waste of strength, virtue and manhood. Howard Chance, owner of a fine old estate, returns from the war, to find a London utterly demoralised and, caught up in its whirl of gaieties, the girl whom he has long loved. She, too, has changed, for " we war girls are hard," she tells him. It is only after dire tragedies have intervened that Pauline learns to appreciate her lover's devotion, and a story, in which incidents and characters, though never sordid, are intensely realistic, ends in their happiness.

Hutchinson's New Novels. 7/6 Net

Jewelled Nights By MARIE BJELKE PETERSEN
Author of " The Captive Singer," " The Immortal Flame," " Dusk," etc.

The scenes of " Jewelled Nights " are laid in Tasmania, whose dizzy heights, dense jungles and treacherous rivers the author has seen and knows as does no other living writer—amid the weird fascination of the Osmiridium mining fields. Hither comes Dick Fleetwood, young and handsome, to seek his fortune. His adventures among the rough miners, their efforts to oust him from the field, and his friendship with a big stalwart digger are related in a series of thrilling episodes and original and often humorous incidents, while the brillant descriptive passages disclose that fine, deep vein of romance which has established so wide a popularity for all Miss Petersen's writings.

The Letters of Jean Armiter
By UNA L. SILBERRAD
Author of " Green Pastures," " The Honest Man," etc.

Jean Armiter, a spinster of thirty-five, becomes possessed of a small income and with it, she imagines, the liberty to lead her own life in her own way. In this ambition, however, she finds herself effectually thwarted by relatives, friends, and other ties. A charming love story runs through the book, which ends happily, for Jean is a sound, cheery Englishwoman very typical of her class to-day. Her letters, indeed, are so full of human interest that the reader comes quickly to regard them as real letters from a living person.

Fortune's Fool By RAFAEL SABATINI
Author of " Historical Nights' Entertainment," " Scaramouche," etc.

This romantic adventure-story tells of the hopes, struggles, and disillusionment of Colonel Randal Holles, who left service in Holland to offer his sword and experience to his own king. Throughout his career Fortune had mocked this old Parliamentarian, and she was to fool him yet again at the court of the Merry Monarch. Against the terrible background of the Great Plague flit such great figures as George Monk, Duke of Albemarle, the Duke of Buckingham, Sir George Etheredge. Mr. Sabatini possesses a happy gift of reanimating the dead past and imbues the scenes and personages whom he depicts with pungency and life, nor are his fictitious characters less convincing.

Broken Couplings By CHARLES CANNELL
Author of " The Guarded Woman "

From the moment when Tolway, gentleman adventurer, sees Ellen Woollaston, " the woman of the stairway," in company with his friend Newton, up to the final paragraph which tells how Ellen solved the problem life set before her, the changing drama of this book grips the reader's attention. It is a daringly intimate study of a woman's temperament, as displayed in the working out of a situation which, at first sight, admits of no satisfactory development. Though by no means lacking in humour the story is one of fine dramatic intensity, depicting real people confronted with real problems.

Hutchinson's New Novels. 7/6 Net

Battling Barker By ANDREW SOUTAR
Author of " The Road to Romance," " Corinthian Days," etc.

In a spirited and realistic story of the prize ring of to-day the central figures are Jerry Barker and his padre friend, both fired by the fine ambition of " cleaning up " British sport by the suppression of gambling, faked matches and similar evils, and Reuben Braddock, a powerful and wealthy sporting crook. As the mysterious " Masked Man," each friend by turns competes for the heavy-weight championship of England. These and other fights are depicted with all the writer's intimate knowledge of the ring and power of thrilling narrative. This story, in which there is also a pleasing love interest, will appeal especially to male readers.

Under Eastern Stars
By MRS. FRANCES EVERARD
Author of " A Daughter of the Sand," " A White Man," etc.

In her latest novel, Mrs. Everard takes her readers once more to the Africa which she knows so well. But apart from the fascinating pictures of Eastern life, she presents in this new and arresting story a brilliant penetrating study of a dangerous year of married life, a vivid portrayal of the hearts and minds of men and women in their social and domestic relations. Trevor Weyburn brings into his home and that of his invalid wife the young and beautiful girl whom he had loved in earlier years. As may be imagined, the consequences threaten to be disastrous, especially when the action is played out under the glamour of Eastern stars. The author develops this dramatic situation with an attractive and moving sympathy.

A First Novel of Adventure and Love
The Enchanted Island By RANN DALY

A stirring adventure story, swift in action and well thought out, of the South Seas, whose life, colour, and enchantment are evidently familiar to the author. From Sydney, Nina Brayne sets out to join her father on his copra plantation at Dulacca. There, too, she meets Delaunoy, his villainous partner, and others of the gang, intent on the discovery of hidden treasure. In the search for this, Nina herself becomes involved, and many exciting adventures befall her before a story of singular attraction and power ends in true lovers meeting and in their assured happiness.

Drums of Doom By ROBERT WELLES RITCHIE
Author of " Trails to Two Moons," " Dust of the Desert," etc.

In a vivid and picturesque story the author tells of Nathaniel Bullock, who lived alone in a strangely built house in San Francisco. At length Nancy Hannibal, with her father, comes to live next door. One day the girl enters the old recluse's house and takes away some papers. She is hotly pursued and dangers threaten her. But in young Peter Free she finds her true friend. And in the desert of old Mexico, full of mystery and haunting silence, where danger lurks in the shadows and written laws are meaningless, the two lovers find adventure—and more. " Drums of Doom " is a romance of stirring action, mystery and love.

Hutchinson's New Novels. 7/6 Net

Rat's Castle   By ROY BRIDGES
Author of " Dead Men's Gold," " Green Butterflies," etc.

The period of this adventurous romance is the reign of George III. after the Gordon Riots. Two boys, one of whom tells the story, are the chief characters and, seeking together a buried treasure, of which one of them is the rightful inheritor, meet with hazardous escapes and dangers on land and sea. The writer has a distinct flair for vivid descriptions and continues to give both his scenes and characters a genuine freshness, a circumstance which greatly enhances the interest of his virile and exciting story.

Morry   By ROBERT ELSON
Author of " Maxa," etc.

This original, cleverly conceived and well-written story describes the career of a great lawyer. The reader is admitted behind the scenes, participates in the legal struggles which are stepping-stones to honour and high position, and feels the thrill when success and failure hang in the balance. Interwoven with the dramatic episodes, in which figure men and women of all classes, from a society beauty to a poor labourer, is the story of the lawyer's inner life, a story of love and friendship, of misunderstandings and loneliness, and self-sacrifice rewarded at last.

Q.   By KATHARINE NEWLIN BURT
Author of " The Branding Iron," " Hidden Creek," etc.

In this exciting love story the writer has made an unusual departure from the typical Western romance. Instead of bringing the East to the West, she has brought the West to the East. The sleepy town of Sluypenkill, the home of the aristocratic Grinscoombe family, is invaded by a soft-spoken, clear-eyed, gently humorous stranger from the West. Q. T. Kinwydden has come to the East to gain an education and Heloise Grinscoombe, whom he has previously guided on a hunting trip. His gentleness and natural courtliness win him the hearts of the people. How he is blocked by an indolent rascally doctor ; how he unites two loving couples ; how he gains victory from seeming defeat, respect from contempt and distrust, make a fascinating story.

A First Novel of Thrilling Interest

The Man with the Million Pounds
By RONALD M. NEWMAN

The lucky individual of the title of this absorbing novel is a demobilised officer whose advertisement requesting this modest sum receives to his amazement an anonymous but favourable reply—on a certain condition. What this condition was and how it was fulfilled form the subject of Mr. Newman's entertaining and crisply-written novel, in which the reader will find enough thrills, humour and adventures to hold his interest firmly from start to finish.

Hutchinson's New Novels. 7/6 Net

Worlds Apart   By M. P. WILLCOCKS
Author of " The Sleeping Partner," " The Keystone," etc.

Two widely divergent characters, one a supreme but lovable egoist, the other an idealist, find in middle age the real challenge to their several ways of life from the younger generation, determined, active men from the war, whose fate is in the hands of circumstances, at work before they were born.

The story is one of heredity, hidden, transformed, but never eliminated. There are tragic moments, but the tone is one of humour, for the two forces inevitably opposed are depicted with a rare sympathy and a skill which holds the reader's interest throughout.

Alien Souls   By ACHMED ABDULLAH
Author of " Night Drums," " The Blue-Eyed Manchu," etc.

The writer is pre-eminently a man of world vision, and in this volume of stories has brought together what he has seen and learnt in many lands. The ideals, beliefs and characteristics of the Afghan, Persian, Turk, Russian, Arab—all are told with rare insight and an intimate and fascinating knowledge. Moreover, with the supreme skill of the story-teller, Achmed Abdullah has caught the magic atmosphere of the countries of which he writes. In each story the point of view is not that of a foreigner, but of the peoples themselves. Thus, apart from the sparkle and interest of these stories, they give a fine answer to the question as to how the other half of the world lives.

The Bubble Reputation
By TALBOT MUNDY and BRADLEY KING

Into the serious purpose of their novel, the revealing of the utter selfishness and cruelty of the American Press, these writers have woven a most romantic, appealing, and exciting tale. Jacqueline Lanier, on the day of her marriage to her guardian, is confronted by the profligate Calhoun, his rival for her love. A duel between the two men seriously compromises Jacqueline. In shame and despair she runs away to earn her own living —above all, to escape from the various reporters who pester her relentlessly as sensational " copy." The story of her subsequent life is full of colour and incident.

Friday to Monday   By WILLIAM GARRETT
Author of " The Secret of the Hills," etc.

The title of this engrossing story denotes the week-end visit which Sir Richard Montague, all unsuspecting, paid to the country house of an old friend. There he finds mystery, false impersonation, robbery and dangerous adventures depicted with a vigour and resourceful imagination which holds the reader's attention to an eminently satisfactory conclusion.

Hutchinson's New Novels. 7/6 Net

Her House of Dreams By CURTIS YORKE
Author of " The Unknown Road," " Briony," " Peter's People," etc.

This novel has won the distinction of a Jubilee celebration, being its talented author's fiftieth book. Yet the adventures of Margaret Ferrers, when her train to London broke down in the snow, the strange refuge which she found and its still more mysterious inmate make up a distinctly fresh and original story that shows the writer's fertility in imagination to be still unfailing. The subsequent happenings after " Peggy's " discoveries make very interesting telling, while the characters of this lively story and descriptive passages throughout are in the author's most successful manner.

A Powerful First Novel of Mystery and Romance
The Mystery of Norman's Court
By JOHN CHANCELLOR

The central incident in this new writer's thrilling story is the detection of a crime so astounding and baffling as to set the keenest and most sophisticated reader on his mettle to elucidate it. The circumstances under which Hugh Bowden is found murdered are, indeed, a remarkable conception, and the story of the detection of the criminal and of the final solution of the mystery moves briskly and with ever growing interest to its ingenious solution. Into this powerful narrative the writer has woven an element of romance and intrigue and, incidentally, a fascinating love episode, drawing his characters, virtuous and evil alike, with a skill and discernment that should rapidly secure him the favour of discriminating readers.

The Rose of Santa Fé By EDWIN L. SABIN
Author of " Desert Dust," etc.

A thrilling, swiftly-moving story of the days when caravans set out on the South-west Trail in the wilds of Western Missouri. On such a trail the Señorita Rosa journeys with her father. Dangers, swift, surprising and tense, threaten, for a while, on every side. Moreover, two young men who escort her are fierce rivals for her favour. It is all an enthralling drama of love, hatred, and adventure, whose romantic developments will prove entirely to the reader's taste.

The Hill of Riches By F. A. M. WEBSTER
Author of " The Curse of the Lion," " Black Shadows," " Old Ebbie," etc.

A beautiful Irish girl, the heroine in Captain Webster's eventful story, is left penniless, her parents and brother, with whom she had come to live in Nairobi, have died, and she accepts the post of governess in some local settlers' home. Pereira, an evil-minded " dago," offers marriage ; she accepts in despair—only to meet an even more intolerable fate. For she suffers with her husband the dire revenge of long-suffering natives. Her ultimate happiness is only attained after many exciting incidents and adventures. The mystery of the spirit message throughout the age is again subtly interwoven with the story. The writer possesses an extensive knowledge of life on the fringes of civilisation and develops strong emotional situations with much descriptive charm.

Hutchinson's New Novels. 7/6 Net

Where I Made One — By MAUDE ANNESLEY
Author of "The Sphinx in the Labyrinth," "Blind Understanding," etc.

The ideals and practical work of an Anti Capital-Punishment Association are the themes chosen by this clever writer for her latest novel, a subject which few authors could aspire successfully to handle. Her account of the feverish anxiety displayed by the Association in pleading for the murderer, James Porter, contains much good writing and much dramatic interest. Still more poignant is her description of a second murder, the result of which plays an important part in her story's development. Into this she has woven, with understanding and conviction, an aspect of the occult, enhancing the thought-provoking character of a story which is of quite uncommon interest.

The Fate of Osmund Brett — By HORACE HUTCHINSON
Author of "The Eight of Diamonds," etc.

An original and cleverly planned detective story, which at once arouses the reader's eager attention. Travelling home from the funeral of young Waring, his niece's husband, Mr. Brett disappears under most mysterious circumstances. The manner of Waring's decease is no less uncanny, and even more strange the discovery when his body is exhumed. A succession of exciting episodes, in which hypnotism plays a part, eventually leads to the unmasking of the culprit in a story wherein both detective and reader have more than a run for their money.

Gerald Cranston's Lady — By GILBERT FRANKAU
Author of "Peter Jackson, Cigar Merchant" (89th thousand), "Men, Maids and Mustard-Pot," etc.

[Ready in January.

Eve and the Elders — By WINIFRED GRAHAM
Author of "John Edgar's Angels," "The Daughter Terrible," "And It Was So," etc.

[Ready in January.

May Eve — By E. TEMPLE THURSTON
Author of "The City of Beautiful Nonsense," "David and Jonathan," "The Miracle," etc.

[Ready early in 1924.

New Books for Young People

Hutchinson's Popular Fairy Book Series.

Each volume in square 8vo, richly bound in cloth gilt. Price **5s.** *net.*

Two New Volumes this Year.

The Emerald Fairy Book
By JANE MULLEY

With 8 Coloured Plates by WINEFRED V. BARKER *and* 18 *Illustrations by* SYDNEY F. ALDRIDGE.

The Pearl Fairy Book
By KATHERINE PYLE

With 8 Coloured Plates by the Author and 4 others by WINEFRED V. BARKER.

---

483 *Editions already sold.*

MAYA : The Adventures of a Little Bee
By WALDEMAR BONSELS

With coloured Frontispiece and numerous illustrations by L. R. BRIGHTWELL, F.Z.S.
In handsome cloth gilt binding, **7s. 6d.** *net.*

The Rose-Coloured Wish
By FLORENCE BONE

With 5 coloured plates by KATE HOLMES.
In attractive cloth binding, **2s. 6d.** *net.*

Wee Men
By BRENDA GIRVIN and MONICA COSENS

With 4 coloured plates and numerous line drawings by CHARLES ROBINSON.
In crown 8vo, cloth, **2s. 6d.** *net.*

The Fairy Prince Next Door
By LILIAN TIMPSON

With 4 coloured plates and numerous line drawings by CHARLES ROBINSON.
In attractive cloth binding, **2s. 6d.** *net.*

OVER THREE MILLION ALREADY SOLD.

NEW VOLUMES OF

Hutchinson's Famous 3/6 Net Novels

Each in crown 8vo, cloth bound, with attractive coloured picture wrapper.

Charles Rex By ETHEL M. DELL
The Love Story of Aliette Brunton
By GILBERT FRANKAU
Mr. and Mrs. Neville Tyson By MAY SINCLAIR
Kitty Tailleur By MAY SINCLAIR
Two Sides of a Question By MAY SINCLAIR
The Thirteen Travellers By HUGH WALPOLE
Satan By H. De VERE STACPOOLE
Venetian Lovers By Sir PHILIP GIBBS
Oliver's Kind Women By Sir PHILIP GIBBS
Helen of Lancaster Gate By Sir PHILIP GIBBS
Back to Life By Sir PHILIP GIBBS
Courage By KATHLYN RHODES
The Post-War Girl By BERTA RUCK
The Young Diana By MARIE CORELLI

New Volumes of Notable 2/6 Net Novels

The Roll Call By ARNOLD BENNETT
Dusk By MARIE BJELKE PETERSEN
Queen Lucia By E. F. BENSON

Three Great Novels Just Published

Now in its Thirtieth Thousand
The Middle of the Road By SIR PHILIP GIBBS
Author of " The Street of Adventure," " Venetian Lovers," etc.

Sir Philip Gibbs takes the case of a young man who by family connections and friendly associations is between two opposing trends of thought in English life to-day, both of them extreme and passionate, and gives a very intimate picture of the great world-drama now being enacted in France, Germany and Russia.

" Sir Philip Gibbs has a remarkable talent for presenting a point of view in dramatic form."—*Times.*
" Sir Philip Gibbs has done nothing better than this novel."—*Sunday Times.*
" A fine novel. . . . It stands out above much contemporary fiction by reason of its force and idealism."—*Daily Mail.*
" A book of exceptional force and insight."—*English Review.*
" A complete success, for the book . . . is the most absorbing which he has yet written."—*Westminster Gazette.*

Already in its Twelfth Thousand
Men, Maids and Mustard-Pot
By GILBERT FRANKAU
Author of " Peter Jackson, Cigar Merchant " (*89th thousand*), etc.

Each of the tales in Mr. Gilbert Frankau's first published collection of short stories is a *tour-de-force*. From the heart of the English Shires to the heart of London's West End, from the palm-fringed beaches of Malaya to the tobacco-piled wharves of Havana harbour, his characters, men, maidens and that most amazing horse in fiction, Mustard-Pot, play out their parts in a series of thrilling incidents.

" Such an eager, full-blooded, hopeful view of human nature and human luck is mightily refreshing."—*Westminster Gazette*
" There are a wealth of incident, a width of interest, a diversity of scene, a variety of character, and a pervading dash of style in this collection of short stories . . . one of the best books Mr. Gilbert Frankau has yet given us."—*Sunday Times.*
" All the stories are full of energy and some have real power. . . ."—*Daily Mail.*
" He can tell a story. He carries you on by sheer narrative zest."—*Saturday Review.*

Four Large Editions Rapidly Exhausted
Time is Whispering By ELIZABETH ROBINS
Author of " The Magnetic North," etc.

The main theme of this most arresting story is the difficulty of a man and woman in middle life, faced on the one hand by the rigid dictates of convention, and on the other by the habits and prejudices of years. The author has chosen difficult types for her chief characters, but she has drawn them with a skill and consistency which will surprise even those readers who know her best.

" The book should be read. Judith Lathom is a delicious character, and there are passages of exceptional beauty and wisdom."—*Daily News.*
" Miss Robins is not only a mistress of her technique, but has that swift, sure insight into human nature with which those who possess it constantly amaze us with their seeming cognisance of our own private thoughts."—*Star.*
" She has skill, immense sympathy and understanding."—*Pall Mall and Globe.*

We'll Pay for Your Story NOW

A large illustrated monthly Magazine, profusely illustrated by well-known artists. For *the first time* the TRUE STORY MAGAZINE presents stories taken from the actual experiences of life. Its readers are invited to send their own life-stories. Those whose contributions are accepted must necessarily remain anonymous, though their names are scrupulously recorded as a guarantee of their truth. This entirely new enterprise has proved a record success, for no fiction possesses the lure of the true story, the inner secrets of a human heart.

16th of each Month, 1/- Net

THE BEST STORIES BY THE BEST WRITERS

Hutchinson's MONTHLY Magazine 1/- Net
Complete Stories by
Elinor Mordaunt, Dorothea Conyers, Agnes & Egerton Castle and others.
Cricket Article by Hon. Lionel Tennyson

HUTCHINSON'S MAGAZINE is now established as one of the most successful and popular of modern magazines. Its stories are selected from the contributions of to-day's leading writers. The best artists are engaged for its illustrations. Produced on the best super-calendered paper, HUTCHINSON'S MAGAZINE is now a fine art production.

12th of each Month, 1/- Net

For Men and Women

It's the story which counts in "HUTCHINSON'S ADVENTURE-STORY MAGAZINE." Each number is packed with gripping stories of adventure up and down the world. The "Adventure-Story Magazine" takes you to Thibet, to South America, to the South Seas, to all those parts of the world where danger is the spice of life.

The many stories which go to make this magazine the most popular among men and women are carefully chosen by the Editor for the gripping quality which carries the reader breathlessly from start to finish.

16th of each Month, 7d. Net

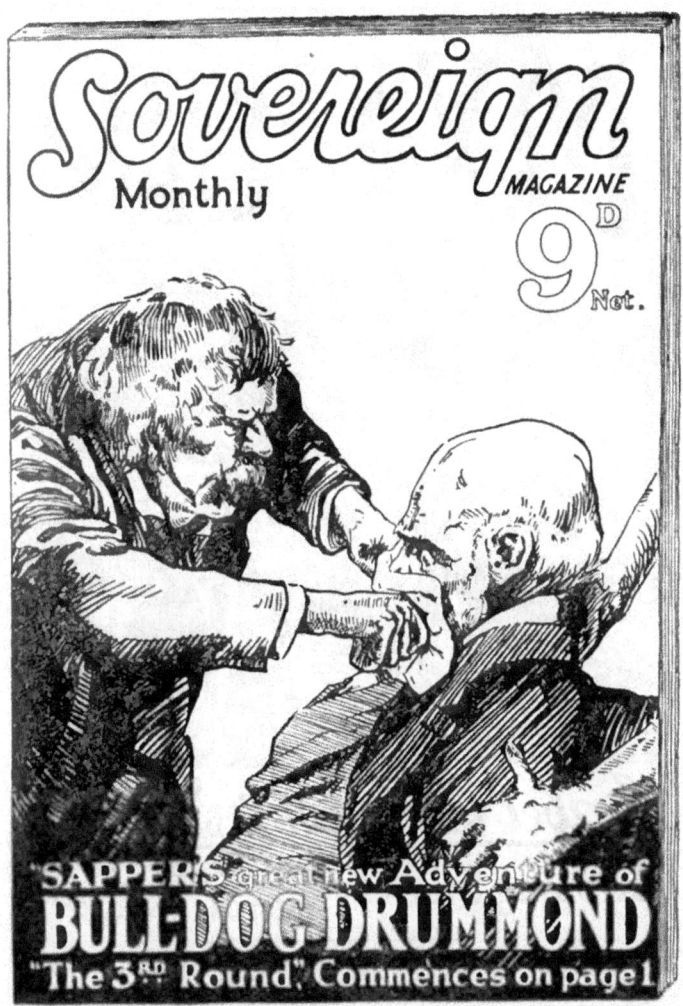

The **POPULAR MAGAZINE**, containing stories by the Leading Authors, including:

George Birmingham
William Le Queux
Alice Perrin
Kathlyn Rhodes
"Rita"
Mrs. Baillie Reynolds

Also the great new series of ADVENTURES OF BULLDOG DRUMMOND by "Sapper," entitled "The Third Round."

12th of each Month, 9d. Net

This novel and popular magazine was started to supply the needs of lovers of gripping mystery and detective stories. It is the finest miscellany of "thrills" obtainable to-day. Mystery is the keynote of *every* story in *every* issue.

Tales of murder and ingenious robbery, hair-raising ghost stories, detective yarns breathless with unexpected adventure.

16th of each Month, 7d. Net

www.ingramcontent.com/pod-product-compliance
Lightning Source LLC
Chambersburg PA
CBHW050549160426
43199CB00015B/2585